Every Book Is a Social Studies Book

Other Recently Published Teacher Ideas Press Titles

Shakespeare Kids: Performing his Plays, Speaking his Words
Carole Cox

Family Matters: Adoption and Foster Care in Children's Literature
Ruth Lyn Meese

Solving Word Problems for Life, Grades 6–8
Melony A. Brown

Abraham Lincoln and His Era: Using the American Memory Project to Teach with Primary Sources
Bobbi Ireland

Brushing Up on Grammar: An Acts of Teaching Approach
Joyce Armstrong Carroll, EdD, HLD, and Edward E. Wilson

The Comic Book Curriculum: Using Comics to Enhance Learning and Life
James Rourke

Hello Hi-Lo: Readers Theatre Math
Jeff Sanders and Nancy I. Sanders

War Stories for Readers Theatre: World War II
Suzanne I. Barchers

Think Green, Take Action: Books and Activities for Kids
Daniel A. Kriesberg

Storytelling and QAR Strategies
Phyllis Hostmeyer and Marilyn Adele Kinsella

Making Math Accessible for the At-Risk Student: Grades 7–12
Linda Ptacek

Wings and Tales: Learning About Birds Through Folklore, Facts and Fun Activities
Jennifer L. Kroll

Every Book Is a Social Studies Book

How to Meet Standards with Picture Books, K–6

Andrea S. Libresco, Jeannette Balantic, and Jonie C. Kipling

A Teacher Ideas Press Book

LIBRARIES UNLIMITED

AN IMPRINT OF ABC-CLIO, LLC
Santa Barbara, California • Denver, Colorado • Oxford, England

Library of Congress Cataloging-in-Publication Data

Libresco, Andrea S.
  Every book is a social studies book : how to meet standards with picture books, K–6 / Andrea S. Libresco, Jeannette Balantic, and Jonie C. Kipling.
    p. cm.
  "A Teacher Ideas Press book."
  Includes bibliographical references and index.
  ISBN 978-1-59884-520-4 (pbk.)—ISBN 978-1-59884-521-1 (ebook) 1. Social sciences—Study and teaching (Elementary)—Activity programs. 2. Picture books for children. I. Balantic, Jeannette. II. Kipling, Jonie C. III. Title.
  LB1584.L53 2011
  372.83'044—dc22   2010053649

ISBN: 978-1-59884-520-4
EISBN: 978-1-59884-521-1

15 14 13 12 11   1 2 3 4 5

This book is also available on the World Wide Web as an eBook.
Visit www.abc-clio.com for details.

Libraries Unlimited
An Imprint of ABC-CLIO, LLC

ABC-CLIO, LLC
130 Cremona Drive, P.O. Box 1911
Santa Barbara, California 93116-1911

This book is printed on acid-free paper ∞
Manufactured in the United States of America

Contents

Chapter 1

Introduction

Social Studies Is All Around Us

In Jon Sceiscka's *Math Curse,* Mrs. Fibonnaci proclaims to her class, "YOU KNOW, you can think of almost everything as a math problem." Students proceed to view their daily activities through the prism of mathematical equations. For example, the narrator wonders, practically, "How many quarts are in a gallon?" and, more absurdly, "If an M&M is about one centimeter long and the Mississippi River is about 4,000 kilometers long, how many M&Ms would it take to measure the length of this river?" By the end of the book, the student lands in science class, where Mr. Newton exclaims, "YOU KNOW you can think of almost everything as a science experiment."

Although many might not readily think of *Math Curse* as a perfect book for an elementary social studies lesson, we use it as a springboard to explore the ways in which students can think of everything as a social studies question. On the first day of elementary school, our students keep a record of the places they go, the people they see, and their interactions with others. The next day, we ask them to explain how their experiences from the last twenty-four hours connect to social studies. Students generate social studies–themed questions: "How will my friends and I decide what game to play at recess?" "What's the quickest way to get to the nurse's office?" "I wonder why the new student moved here from Colombia?" "Should I put my crayons in the class crayon box or keep them in my desk?" "Who 'owns' the building block area?" "How come they took the soda machines out of the school?" "How can we get the principal to let us eat lunch outside?" What they come to realize is that social studies is all around us.

This activity reflects a conscious decision to put social studies front and center in our classroom for the entire year. We have found ways to teach social studies concepts and skills despite our districts' mandated increases in the time devoted to math and language arts instruction.

Social studies is disappearing in American elementary schools. Within the first five years of the enactment of No Child Left Behind, the Center on Education Policy conducted a study that focused on a representative sample of 349 school districts and found that 36 percent of school districts cut elementary class time for social studies to give double and triple the time to tested subjects like math and language arts, respectively (McMurrer, 2007). In addition, North Carolina primary teachers report spending 15 to 30 minutes on social studies on the days that it is taught, which is only 2 or 3 days a week for half the year (O'Connor, et. al., 2007). In another study, Indiana elementary teachers averaged only 12 minutes per week teaching social studies (Van Fossen, 2005).

Putting social studies back in elementary schools is vital if we want to prepare students to think critically and participate in our multicultural democracy. In an effort to reclaim time for social studies, we emphasize the social studies themes and concepts in children's picture books so that the books serve dual purposes. This book is intended to serve as a resource for classroom teachers, school librarians, methods professors, staff developers, and curriculum writers as we all try to ensure that social studies is a robust part of the elementary curriculum.

The book provides strategies and activities that enable us to use picture books for both language arts *and* social studies; in essence, children's literature does double duty. We identify the social studies themes and concepts in books we already love and in lesser-known works. In addition, each chapter includes a diverse list of picture books, appropriate for the K–6 curriculum.

Just as the child in Jon Scieska's *Math Curse* discovers that everything in life can be a math problem, so, too, we discover that every book is a social studies book. And so will our students.

Integrating Social Studies and Literacy

Using picture books for the dual purposes of teaching social studies and language arts may be controversial because some fear that interdisciplinary instruction results in diminished attention to social studies concepts and content. However, research reveals that integration often results in language arts being the focal point of lessons, while less valuable, even trivial, aspects of social studies get addressed (Alleman and Brophy, 1993, 1994). Yet integration may be one of the only options, given the shrinking time allotted to social studies in many states.

On the other hand, integration may have certain advantages in teaching social studies. In a meta-analysis, McGowan et al. (1996) reported that advocates of literature-based teaching believe that literary works provide students with a more complete grasp of a wider range of topics than do more traditional social studies texts. Picture books offer young readers visual images that make social studies concepts more concrete. Literature-based accounts presented from multiple perspectives allow students to extend their understanding of the personalities and events that have shaped our world. McGowan et al. (1996) also found that kindergartners exposed to literacy instruction based on trade books could recall more information and showed increased understanding of concepts compared with young children receiving a more traditional teaching approach.

Integration can be a positive way to teach social studies, but only if it is done with social studies concepts at the center of curriculum and instruction. Literature can be used to promote civic competence, the underlying reason for teaching social studies. Alleman and Brophy (1991) suggest that when teachers plan social studies activities based on literature, they consider the following questions:

- Does the activity have a significant social [studies] education goal as its primary focus?

- Would this be a desirable activity for the social studies unit even if it did not feature across-subject integration?

- Would an outsider clearly recognize the activity as social studies?

- Does the activity allow students to develop meaningfully or apply authentically important social [studies] content?

- Does it involve authentic application of skills from other disciplines?

- If the activity is structured properly, will students understand and be able to explain its social [studies] purposes?

- If students engage in the activity with those purposes in mind, will they be likely to accomplish the purposes as a result?

These questions guided our selection of literature and the development of the activities that accompany them.

Even as we look for and emphasize the social studies in the books we love, we rely on the diverse repertoire of skills that are the hallmark of good literacy instruction. For students to have rich discussions about social studies concepts in the books, they must first be able to read and understand them. Some of our favorite strategies to promote student comprehension are the following:

- Read books more than once.

- Draw pictures to develop listening and note-taking skills.

- Create a sociogram of the characters in the book.

- Retell the story using as many details as possible.

- Make a timeline of the events in the story.

- Sketch a map of the story's setting.

- Act out parts of the book to seal memory.

- Generate a list of questions sparked by events or characters' choices in the book.

- Rewrite parts of the book from different characters' points of view.

- Craft different endings for the book to explore what is either possible or desirable.

- Discuss the author's motive for writing the book—what the author says about how we should behave, relate to one another, and make difficult choices.

Nurturing Citizens

The development of comprehension in students is not the end of instruction with picture books; comprehension helps students make sense of the world in which they live. Teaching social studies is critical to the development of a well-informed citizenry in a democracy. The National Council for the Social Studies (NCSS) identifies the attributes of effective citizens as follows (NCSS, Creating Effective Citizens). Effective citizens:

- Have knowledge of the people, history, documents, and traditions that have shaped our community, nation, and the world.

- Seek information from varied sources and perspectives to develop informed opinions and creative solutions to local, state, national, and global issues.

- Ask meaningful questions and are able to analyze and evaluate information and ideas.

- Use effective decision-making and problem-solving skills in public and private life.

- Have the ability to collaborate effectively as members of a group.

- Participate actively in school and community life.

The task of preparing students to play an active role in our multicultural democracy is a complex one; it is through social studies in the elementary grades that we begin to develop these attributes in students. Elementary teachers help students identify and develop the skills of active citizenship in the context of students' everyday interactions with their families, friends and classmates, as they make decisions about what to do in their free time, with whom to play, what books to read, and how to spend money (NCSS, Social Studies for Early Childhood and Elementary School Children Preparing for the 21st Century). As John Dewey noted, "A democracy is more than a form of government; it is primarily a mode of associated living, of conjoint communicated experience" (1916,

87). It is in our elementary classrooms where children begin to figure out what they also will need to understand as adults: how to participate effectively in their communities.

Seemingly simple picture books address complex issues such as perspective, and literature-based activities can help students understand and get along with the diverse members of their communities. The books and activities can be used at multiple grade levels. Margery Cuyler's *That's Good/That's Bad* details the wacky adventures of a little boy's day. Everything that happens to him (he is lifted in the air by a balloon, his balloon pops, he lands somewhere soft . . .) can be viewed as either good or bad, depending on one's perspective. On a more sophisticated level, *Motel of the Mysteries* by David Macauley turns readers into archeologists, in the year 4022, uncovering the remains of a civilization, circa 1985, that turns out to be our own. Before students recognize it as such, they have already made judgments about the "weird" rituals of the people of the civilization. This picture book becomes a springboard to a discussion of essential questions: How does our perspective affect our views of other cultures and peoples? Are certain cultural practices more valid than others? Are cultures more similar or more different from one another? Ultimately, both books, albeit on different levels, reinforce the value of putting oneself into others' shoes and the skill of reserving judgment until all of the data are in, vital for citizens in a multicultural democracy.

To promote further the skills of active citizenship, we are deliberate in the identification and development of social studies concepts and skills. It is not by accident that social studies happens in our classrooms. We are systematic in our planning and teaching of literature-based lessons to put social studies concepts and skills front and center. We craft lessons that promote critical thinking about social studies concepts (e.g., justice, equality, freedom, scarcity, culture, diversity, interdependence) and design activities that develop in students the skills necessary to make informed decisions. Students must be able to collect, organize, and interpret data from a variety of sources; think creatively about and draw inferences from the data; consider opposing points of view and develop well-supported positions; and communicate, orally and in writing, their positions to others.

As Thomas Jefferson noted, "If a nation expects to be ignorant and free, it expects what never was and never will be" (1816). Jefferson and other founders of the republic emphasized that the vitality of a democracy depends upon the education and participation of its citizens. This education begins in elementary social studies lessons, where students learn the skills necessary for active participation in our democratic society and are prepared to challenge injustice and promote the common good as competent, self-directed citizens.

Organization of Book

Ten Thematic Strands

The ten thematic strands identified by the NCSS provide the organizing framework for the book. Each chapter is devoted to helping students develop an understanding of the concepts related to one of the thematic strands (see NCSS, Curriculum Standard http://www.socialstudies.org/standards/strands).

Essential Questions

The seemingly straightforward strands are multifaceted and worthy of investigation. The essential questions (Wiggins and McTighe, 1998) included in each chapter frame class discussions related to each strand. For example, the first thematic strand is Culture; one of the essential questions related to this strand is: "Are people and societies more alike or different?" Thus, when teachers explore the books and activities, they have in the forefront of their minds the importance of making comparisons across and within cultures. It should also be noted that there are no right or wrong answers to the essential question, only answers supported or unsupported by data. Frankly, some days we think that cultures are more like other cultures, and other days, in the midst of war and strife, we are struck by the seemingly unbridgeable differences among peoples. This is what makes the questions worthy of discussion. The essential questions that guide each chapter are overarching and apply to multiple books. They also challenge the narrow conception that social studies is simply a chronological listing of people and dates or a list of vocabulary terms to commit to memory. The use of these essential questions encourages students to grapple with important issues.

The Books

Each chapter spotlights three picture books that illuminate the thematic strand and enable teachers to engage students in a discussion of the related essential questions. It was difficult selecting only three books per chapter, because there are so many beautifully written and provocative picture books. Some of the books we chose are well known but are not necessarily used to teach social studies. Others are lesser-known works that we have relied on for years. In addition to the social studies aspect, the commonality of all the books is that they are engaging and thoughtful, appropriate for elementary children (from primary through intermediate grades) and have literary merit. Surprisingly, not all people conceive of wonderful picture books as the basis for social studies lessons. In one of our graduate social studies methods classes, we required students to select a picture book to illustrate a social studies concept. Interestingly, when we questioned some students about their selection, one student acknowledged that she had brought in a boring book because she thought that social studies books had to be boring. Our goal is to shatter this negative impression of social studies. Now when we give the assignment, we tell students to bring in the most wonderful piece of literature that they can find and then identify the social studies issues and questions related to the book. They come to see, as we have, that every book is, indeed, a social studies book.

Social Studies Concepts and Discussion Questions

As we prepare to teach a new picture book, we identify the social studies concepts found in it; we then develop questions related to the concepts. To keep our instructional focus on social studies, we create a chart that pairs each social studies concept with text-based questions that help facilitate student discussion and understanding. The questions are not organized in the order in which the narrative unfolds. After all, we rarely ask questions in an exclusively chronological fashion. What actually happens in classrooms is that interesting questions beget interesting comments, and rich discussion ensues. (For a reproducible template you can use to identify the concepts and discussion questions in the books you select, see Appendix C. We have found that working with the template helps promote meaningful discussion with teachers on a grade level as we integrate new literature into our curriculum.)

Activities and Discussion Questions

To deepen students' understanding of the social studies concepts in the picture books, we design thoughtful, student-centered activities. The books and the activities that accompany them may be used on a variety of grade levels, sometimes with minor modifications to accommodate students' different reading levels. Each of the activities includes a description of the work we have done in our own classes; real-life student answers are included to give a sense of what kinds of responses teachers might expect from their own students. Also included are blank reproducible handouts for teachers to replicate the activities in their own classes. Discussion questions accompany the activities to move students from lower- to upper-level thinking about social studies concepts.

Applying the Concepts

It is critical to provide students with the opportunity to apply their new conceptual knowledge and skills. To this end, we include authentic learning experiences, in which students are able to demonstrate their level of understanding about what they have learned. The application activities are as varied as the picture books we have selected and include solving history mysteries, writing songs, interviewing family members, role-playing, designing monuments, making murals, creating dialogue poems, and so on.

The philosophy that underlies all of the activities in this book is that the active learning strategies of writing and delivering speeches, playing the role of a historical character, and creating and singing lyrics engage students and simultaneously challenge them to think deeply about social studies issues. Our work with colleagues over many years has led us to analyze critically and reevaluate some traditional activities. For example, when teaching about exploration, rather than selecting a book about Columbus' voyages that leads to students making models of the *Nina,* the *Pinta,* and the *Santa Maria,* we use Jane Yolen's *Encounter* to "explore" the effects of the clash of cultures when different civilizations met in the Americas. (Yolen's book and the activities related to it are detailed in Chapter 10.) All of the activities move children toward grappling with upper-level questions that emerge from the picture books and have application in real life.

Extending the Concepts in Your Class . . .

The activities included for each of the books are not the only ways to teach the social studies concepts. Teachers can follow multiple paths to deepen student understanding. For each book, we provide some ideas to continue the exploration of the social studies concepts in and beyond the classroom.

Recommended Books

Each chapter concludes with an annotated bibliography of picture books that further illuminate its social studies thematic strand. To facilitate navigation of the bibliography, the thematic strands are further subdivided by concept. Each entry includes an upper-level question that focuses on a key social studies issue in the book.

Of course, many books represent a variety of thematic strands and could have appropriately been included in several of our chapters. For example, some books on immigration fit equally well under the strands of *Culture* and *Individual Development and Identity.* Biographies of people who fought for rights could be included in *Individual Development and Identity; Individuals, Groups, and Institutions;* or *Power, Authority, and Governance.* Thus, in the Recommended Books listed at the end of each chapter, a note may be included to redirect you to booklists at the end of other chapters that share related concepts.

What Is Not Included

We respect that individual teachers have very different ideas about which books are appropriate at various ages. We also understand that teachers might use a book for one purpose in the primary grades and use the same book to develop a different concept in the intermediate grades. In addition, we know that some students in a particular grade may be ready to grapple with certain concepts in a book, whereas others may need another year or two before the book is appropriate for them. For all of these reasons, we do not prescribe a grade level for any of the books. We leave that up to teachers, who are best equipped to make these judgments each year, based on the needs of their students.

Similarly, we do not assign time frames for the activities. With all of the curriculum and assessment mandates on classroom teachers, the allotment of time for different subjects is not always completely in their control. Therefore, we leave the time frame of each activity up to teachers, who know best how to balance the various competing demands in their own classrooms.

From Our Classroom to Yours

We are excited about this book and had great fun writing it. The book reflects our commitment to the integration of literature and social studies and to engaging students in upper-level thinking about social studies issues. Collectively, we represent more than seventy years of teaching social studies and myriad experiences in social studies education, working with students from the primary to the doctoral level, as well as preservice and veteran elementary teachers. The ideas and activities in this book were developed in our own classrooms and through our work with colleagues. In its pages, we hope that you find picture books and ideas that you are eager to use in your own classrooms and that, like us, you decide that every book is a social studies book.

Recommended Books

Pedagogy

Barton, K., and Levstik, L. *Doing History: Investigating with Children in Elementary and Middle Schools.* Mahwah, NJ: Lawrence Erlbaum Associates, 2001. (The authors show children engaging in authentic historical investigations, often in the context of an integrated social studies curriculum. Barton et al. begin with the assumption that children can engage in valid forms of historical inquiry—collecting and analyzing data, examining the perspectives of people in the past, considering multiple interpretations, and creating evidence-based historical accounts.)

Cowey, M. *Black Ants and Buddhists: Thinking Critically and Teaching Differently in the Primary Grades.* Portland, ME: Stenhouse Publishers, 2006. (What would a classroom look like if understanding and respecting differences in race, culture, beliefs, and opinions were at its heart? Welcome to Mary Cowhey's Peace Class in Northampton, Massachusetts, where first and second graders view the entire curriculum through the framework of understanding the world and trying to do their part to make it a better place.)

Levy, S. *Starting from Scratch: One Classroom Builds Its Own Curriculum.* New York: Heinemann, 1996. (The inspiring projects and real-life learning that the author's fourth-grade students experienced in the process of exploring their world.)

Rogovin, P. *Classroom Interviews: A World of Learning.* New York: Heinemann, 1998. (An inspiring account of how a first-grade teacher uses interviews with family and community members.)

Rogovin, P. *The Research Workshop: Bringing the World into Your Classroom.* New York: Heinemann, 2001. (Demonstrating how children's interests and questions become the central focus of the curriculum, the author, a teacher in the New York City public schools for twenty-eight years, offers dozens of easy-to-use techniques for organizing the classroom and the school day to support student research.)

Wade, R. *Social Studies for Social Justice: Teaching Strategies for the Elementary Classroom.* New York: Teachers College Press, 2007. (Dedication to social justice teaching is important, yet putting one's ideals into practice in American schools is a challenging task. This book goes beyond theory and idealism to explore fully the value and impact of implementing social action and social justice activities in the elementary school classroom.)

Fiction

Cuyler, M. *That's Good/That's Bad.* New York: Henry Holt, 1991. *How can different perspectives change how we view events?*

Macauley, D. *Motel of the Mysteries.* New York: Houghton Mifflin, 1979. *What affects our assumptions about artifacts and civilizations?*

Rylant, C. *The Wonderful Happens.* New York: Simon & Schuster Books for Young Readers, 2000. (Describes some of the ordinary things that bring happiness and awe into our lives.) *How can being wide awake in the world bring us joy?*

Schotter, R. *Nothing Ever Happens on 90th Street.* New York: Orchard Books, 1997. (A would-be writer sits out on her New York City stoop, with her notebook, waiting for something to occur and eventually seeing the possibilities in the street life around her.) *How does being "wide awake" affect how we view our world?*

Sciescka, J. *Math Curse.* New York: Viking, 1995. (A boy's teacher suggests that everything can be seen as a math problem, and then he starts to see daily activities through the prism of mathematical equations.) *How might everything be seen as a social studies issue?*

References

Alleman, Janet, and Jere Brophy. "Activities as Instructional Tools: A Framework for Analysis and Evaluation." *Educational Researcher* 20, no. 4 (1991): 9–23.

Alleman, Janet, and Jere Brophy. "Is Curriculum Integration a Boon or a Threat to Social Studies?" *Social Education* 57 no. 6 (1993): 287–291.

Alleman, Janet, and Jere Brophy. "Trade-Offs Embedded in the Literary Approach to Early Elementary Social Studies." *Social Studies and the Young Learner* 6 no. 3 (1994): 6–8.

Dewey, John. *Democracy and education: An introduction to the philosophy of education.* New York: The Macmillan Co., 1916.

Jefferson, Thomas. "Letter to Colonel Charles Yancey (6 January 1816)," WikiQuote: Government. http://en.wikiquote.org/wiki/Government (cited March 10, 2010).

McGowan, Thomas M., Lynette Erickson, and Judith Neufeld. "With Reason and Rhetoric Building the Case for the Literature-Social Studies Connection." *Social Education,* 60 no. 4 (1996): 203–207.

McMurrer, Jennifer. "Choices, Changes, and Challenges: Curriculum and Instruction in the NCLB Era." Center on Education Policy, http://www.cep-dc.org/index.cfm?fuseaction=document.showDocument ByID&nodeID=1&DocumentID=212 (cited June 30, 2009).

National Council for the Social Studies. "Creating Effective Citizens." http://www.socialstudies.org/positions/effectivecitizens (cited January 20, 2009).

National Council for the Social Studies. "Curriculum Standards for Social Studies: II. Thematic Strands." http://www.socialstudies.org/standards/strands (cited January 20, 2009).

National Council for the Social Studies. "Social Studies for Early Childhood and Elementary School Children Preparing for the 21st Century." http://www.socialstudies.org/positions/elementary (cited January 20, 2009).

O'Connor, Katherine A., Tina Heafner, and Eric Groce. "Advocating for Social Studies: Documenting the Decline and Doing Something About It." *Social Education* 71 no. 5 (2007): 255–260.

VanFossen, Phillip J. " 'Reading and Math Take So Much of the Time . . .' An Overview of Social Studies Instruction in Elementary Classrooms in Indiana." *Theory and Research in Social Education* 33 no. 3 (2005): 376–403.

Wiggins, Grant, and Jay McTighe. *Understanding by Design.* Alexandria, VA: Association for Supervision and Curriculum Development, 1998.

Chapter 2

Culture

Students in the primary grades often bring some of their fears to class discussion—vampires, whether their family will move, strange-looking animals, monsters under the bed. *Jitterbug Jam* by Barbara Jean Hicks is an excellent book to help students deal with their fears. What links many of children's fears is the fear of the unknown. In *Jitterbug Jam*, a young monster is afraid to go to sleep at night because of the boy he finds under his bed. The boy lurking under his bed is strange, with pink skin and orange fur on his head where his horns should be.

We use this book to teach about the roots of prejudice—namely, that we often have apprehension about that which we do not know or understand. Once the monster sits down and talks with the weird-looking boy, he finds out his name and what he likes to do and discovers that they both share some interests. The monster concludes that the boy is not so weird after all. We use a common fear—strange-looking animals—to illustrate that knowledge and understanding can dispel fear. We post pictures of unusual animals around the room and ask children to react to the pictures. Students then read about the animals to discover that they are not as frightening as they first thought. They have mothers and fathers; they need nourishment; their actions can be predictable; they are often as afraid of humans as humans may be of them. This lesson lays the groundwork for understanding diversity and the prejudice that can accompany people from different cultures who do not yet know each other well enough.

Piggybook by Anthony Browne, *The Sneetches* by Dr. Seuss, and *Apple Pie 4th of July* by Janet P. Wong enable students to explore issues of culture and how we treat each other—within families, communities, and societies.

Essential Questions

Are people, families, and cultures more alike or more different?

How can family responsibilities be shared equitably? To what extent is it possible to extend this to the larger society?

To what extent can prejudice and discrimination be overcome in society?

Explore the impact of diversity on communities, nations, and the world.

To what extent should a community support the cultural pluralism of its residents?

What are the challenges and benefits of straddling two cultures?

Piggybook by Anthony Browne

Anthony Browne's *Piggybook* tells the whimsical but important story of a family in which the roles of its members are equal. Mrs. Piggottt finds herself doing all of the chores while her sons and husband sit back and enjoy themselves. One day, Mrs. Piggott decides that things must change, and she leaves. Left to their own devices, the men of the Piggott family literally turn into pigs (as the house around them turns into a pigsty).

While students revel in the humor in the illustrations (the floral design of the wallpaper turns into little pig faces; the fireplace tools develop pig heads; and the characters sprout hooves, tails, and snouts, etc.), it is important to direct students' attention to the issues of interdependence and fairness within families. Many teachers compare different aspects of families, reading books that examine different family structures and traditions. Although books and lessons examining family structures and traditions are important, it is equally important to examine other aspects of families in depth. This lesson delves into workload distribution in families and encourages students to research and compare the workload distribution in their own families with that of other students' families and make recommendations for an ideal sharing of jobs within families.

Social Studies Concepts and Discussion Questions

Social studies concepts	Questions to ask based on the text
Services	What are the different jobs that need to be done for this family to function?
	To what extent is work inside the home similar to/different from work that is paid outside the home?
Equity	In the beginning of the story, who does all of the chores in the Piggott household?
	What do other members of the household do while the chores are being done?
	What do you think of the distribution of chores in the Piggott household?
Identity	How are Mrs. Piggott's sense of self and identity lost in the family because of the work she, alone, does?
	How does she recover her identity at the end of the book?
Change	How does the household change with Mrs. Piggott away?
	How does it change when Mrs. Piggott returns?
Interdependence	In the beginning of the book, the members of the family are totally dependent on the mother. How are the members of the Piggott family's lives changed for the better when they embrace interdependence?

Activity

We build our analysis of the book around the issue of the equitable distribution of family jobs. To do so, we need to detail all of the jobs required to run a household. We elicit from our students a list of jobs done in and out of the home in the story and create a chart to document which family members perform these tasks, at both the beginning and the end of the book. We record these in different colors so that students can see the changes in workload distribution after Mrs. Piggott returns. When the story indicates that family members enjoy their jobs, we have students add in smiley faces. One or more rows can be left blank at the end of the chart for students to brainstorm chores that are not mentioned explicitly in the book but that they believe someone must be doing.

Name _____   Date _____

Student Handout:
Jobs and Workload Distribution in the Piggott Family

Jobs inside and outside the home	Mr. Piggott	Mrs. Piggott	Older son	Younger son
Make and serve breakfast				
Read the paper (job of an informed citizen)				
Wash breakfast dishes				
Make beds				
Vacuum				
Go to work (support the household)				
Go to school				
Cook dinner				
Wash dinner dishes				
Wash clothes				
Iron clothes				
Prepare future food				
Repair the car				

Key:

X = jobs before Mrs. Piggott leaves.

v = jobs after Mrs. Piggott returns.

☺ = enjoys her or his job.

From *Every Book Is a Social Studies Book: How to Meet Standards with Picture Books, K–6* by Andrea S. Libresco, Jeannette Balantic, and Jonie C. Kipling. Santa Barbara, CA: Libraries Unlimited. Copyright © 2011.

Jobs and Workload Distribution in the Piggott Family (Answer Sheet)

Jobs inside and outside the home	Mr. Piggott	Mrs. Piggott	Older son	Younger son
Make and serve breakfast	☺	Xv	☺	☺
Read the paper (job of an informed citizen)	X	?		
Wash breakfast dishes	v	X		
Make beds		X	v	v
Vacuum		X		
Go to work (support the household)	Xv	Xv		
Go to school			Xv	Xv
Cook dinner	v	Xv	v	v
Wash dinner dishes	v	X		
Wash clothes		X		
Iron clothes	v	X		
Prepare future food	☺	Xv	☺	☺
Repair the car		☺		

Key:

X = jobs before Mrs. Piggott leaves.

v = jobs after Mrs. Piggott returns.

☺ = enjoys her or his job.

Discussion Questions Based on the Job Chart Before Mrs. Piggott Leaves

- *What do you think of the distribution of chores in the Piggott household?*
- *How do you think each family member feels about the chores she or he does? How can you tell?*
- *What other jobs do you think are being done that aren't mentioned in the story? Who do you think is doing them?*
- *To what extent do you think this distribution of jobs reflects the distribution in your own household?*
- *What changes would you recommend for the Piggott family?*

Discussion Questions Based on the Job Chart After Mrs. Piggott Returns

- *How did the workload distribution change upon Mrs. Piggott's return?*
- *After the reallocation of chores, how do you think each family member feels about the chores she or he does? How can you tell?*
- *Is this an equitable distribution of jobs?*
- *Do you think there may be jobs that no one likes to do? How should those be distributed?*
- *To what extent do you think this new distribution of jobs reflects the distribution in your own household?*
- *Are there further changes you would recommend for the Piggott family?*

Applying the Concepts

During the activity, students comment on the extent to which the distribution of jobs in the Piggott household (before and after) represents the distribution in their own families. In this activity, students research to determine the accuracy of their earlier comments. Using the Piggott chore chart as a model, students create a jobs and workload distribution chart to describe their own families. Ever mindful of the fact that all families are structured differently, the chart allows students to fill in their own family members and adjust the number of columns, depending on the number of members in their immediate family. In some communities, it may be that students include a housekeeper or nanny on their charts. Our students thought of many other jobs not reflected in *Piggybook,* including jobs that revolve around seasonal needs, pet care, homework help, and so on. Students share their lists of chores with the class so that everyone's final chart reflects as many jobs as possible that might be done in their households. Although the charts have lots of similarities in the listing of chores, everyone's chart need not look the same, because different families do not all value and perform the same jobs.

As part of the data collection process, students need to interview different family members to determine who does which jobs. In the course of the interview process, students may discover other jobs that they should add to their list of chores. In addition to discovering which jobs each family member performs, students should find out how each member feels about the jobs for which she or he is responsible. Students can record this information by adding smiley or frowny faces to the appropriate boxes in their charts.

Name _____   Date _____

Student Handout: Jobs and Workload Distribution in My Family

Directions: List the chores done in your house in the first column of the chart. In the first row of the chart, identify the people who live in your house. Identify who does each chore – add a smiley or frowny face to indicate if the person who does that job enjoys or dislikes doing that chore.

Jobs inside and outside of my home	Family member: _____	Family member: _____	Family member: _____	Family member: _____

Discussion Questions

- *What other jobs are being done that weren't originally listed on chart?*

- *What did you find out about the distribution of chores in your own family? Does any one family member do more than any others?*

- *Do some jobs take more time than others?*

- *What did you find out about how each family member feels about the chores she or he does?*

- *Did you find that there are jobs that no one likes to do? How do you think those should be distributed?*

- *How does the distribution of jobs in your own family compare to the distribution in the Piggott household?*

- *How does the distribution of jobs in your own family compare to the distribution in some of your classmates' households?*

- *Are there any changes in job distribution that you would recommend for your own family?*

- *In what ways does your family depend on you? In what ways do you depend on your family?*

- *Now that you are aware of all of the different jobs required to keep a family running, are there any jobs that you think that you could be doing to help?*

- *What does it mean to be a responsible family member?*

Finally, students return to their chart, "Jobs and Workload Distribution in My Family," and use a new color to indicate the changes they would recommend now that they have analyzed the data about who does what in their households. After they adjust their charts, we encourage our students to talk with their families about the changes they recommend. Our final class discussion revolves around the extent to which the families make any of the proposed changes.

Extending the concepts in your class . . .

Interview grandparents about what chore distribution they had when they were children. Compare this to the one your family currently has.

Tally the class results and make a statement about the distribution of roles by gender and by age.

Examine other picture books and assess the distribution of roles in the families portrayed in them.

The Sneetches by Dr. Seuss

The Sneetches is the story of star-bellied sneetches who exclude plain-bellied sneetches from all of their activities. Sylvester McMonkey McBean exploits the prejudice of the sneetches by offering stars to the plain-bellied sneetches . . . for a price, of course. Ultimately, all of the sneetches come to the realization that "no kind of sneetch is the best kind of sneetch on the beaches," and they decide to play together.

Dr. Seuss' playful books are often used with young children to help their language acquisition. The whimsical illustrations draw children in, while the rhyme schemes and word repetition allow them to hone their literacy skills. The book affords teachers the opportunity to discuss the difficult, but important, issue of prejudice with their students.

Social Studies Concepts and Discussion Questions

Social studies concepts	Questions to ask based on the text
Cultural traditions	What are some of the cultural traditions of the star-bellied sneetches? (What are some of your cultural traditions?)
Cultural diversity and unity	How are the sneetches the same? How are the sneetches different? How do the sneetches become unified?
Prejudice and stereotypes	How do the sneetches feel about each other? How do you know? Are their feelings based on logical thinking? What is a stereotype? Where do stereotypes come from? Why are stereotypes harmful (even if they say something good about the whole group)?
Social class	What is social class? What is the evidence of social class in relations between the sneetches?
Capitalism	How does Sylvester McMonkey McBean capitalize on the sneetches' prejudice? Why do the sneetches "buy in" to McBean's scheme?
Citizenship	Why did none of the star-bellied sneetches speak up for the plain-bellied sneetches? If some of the star-bellied sneetches had spoken up earlier, do you think McBean would have made so much money?

Activity

The "lemon activity" that follows (from the Anti-Defamation League) allows children to confront their belief that all "lemons" are the same and that a member of a group has no separate identity beyond its group identity.

We begin this activity by showing our students a basket of lemons and asking them to describe what the basket contains. We then give one lemon to each group of four students and instruct them to get to know their lemons. The students examine their lemons, smelling them, touching them, throwing them in the air, rolling them around, and recording on paper any distinguishing characteristics. After a few minutes, we take the lemons back and display them in a row on the front desk. (We have the students turn their backs while the lemons are being displayed, so that we know which group had each lemon but our students do not.) We then ask students to find their lemons from among the "lineup." Most recognize their lemons at once, because they have gotten to know their lemon as a unique individual. We ask students:

- *Why was it so easy to identify your lemon?*

- *Have you ever had certain ideas about someone that changed once you got to know the person?*

- *Has someone ever had certain ideas about you that changed once they got to know you?*

- *How are the lemons like the groups of sneetches?*

- *Have you ever felt like a plain-bellied sneetch in a star-bellied world?*

- *Why can stereotypes be harmful?*

- *What happens when we allow stereotypes to go unchecked?*

- *How can we avoid stereotyping others?*

- *What evidence would you marshal to combat specific stereotypes?*

Applying the Concepts

After discussing stereotypes and their consequences, we engage students in an activity in which they combat stereotypes. We use "teachers" as our group in the scenario that we develop because we do not want any of our students to feel uncomfortable as the target of a stereotype in the activity. Groups of students are given the following scenario to which they are asked to respond.

End-of-Summer Scenario

A week or two before school, when kids are about to find out what teachers they will have in the coming year, you come upon a group of kids talking about teachers, saying things like: "Teachers are mean." "Teachers give too much homework." "Teachers are boring."

What would be your response? How would you combat these stereotypes? Would you give specific examples of your own past teachers? (For example, if someone said that older people are afraid to try something new," you could counter with, "But my grandfather is old, and he taught me how to use a digital camera!"

1. Role-play this scenario and your response.

2. Depict the scenario and your response in poem form à la Dr. Seuss or in cartoon format with word bubbles.

It is worth mentioning that the final story in *The Sneetches and Other Stories*, "What was I afraid of?," also addresses the issue of prejudging. The main character is afraid of a pair of "pale green pants with nobody inside them" because he doesn't know anything about the pants and is prejudging them. From this story, the students can discover the importance of acquiring reliable information before forming opinions, which is an important attribute of both unbiased people and good citizens.

<hr>

Extending the concepts in your class . . .

Examine the Jim Crow or Nuremberg laws to see the consequences of the institutionalization of prejudice.

Read the lyrics and listen to the song from *South Pacific*, "You've Got to Be Carefully Taught," and discuss its connection to stereotyping.

Share times in which students have seen another person challenge a stereotype, in real life, or in the media.

<hr>

Apple Pie 4th of July by Janet S. Wong

In *Apple Pie 4th of July,* Janet Wong delves into a young Chinese American girl's fears about being different and not fitting into American society. She is afraid that their customers, who are busy celebrating The 4th of July, won't buy the food her parents are preparing in their restaurant. Much to her surprise, the restaurant is crowded with customers, who love to eat Chinese food, even on this very American holiday.

Many teachers enjoy teaching about immigration, because it is a topic that allows students to share ethnic foods, pose questions to relatives, and perhaps take a real or virtual tour of Ellis Island. Students have fun doing these activities. However, it is important to bear in mind that these activities are not an end in themselves; rather, they can provide us with an excellent opportunity to have students grapple with essential questions at the very heart of the immigrant and the American experience: What does it mean to be *American*? Do people have to change to become American? *Should* they have to? Are immigrants' experiences more similar or more different? Is there such a thing as a *typical* immigration experience?

Social Studies Concepts and Discussion Questions

Social studies concepts	Questions to ask based on the text
Cultural traditions	What are some 4th of July traditions? What do they signify?
Cultural diversity and unity	How does the young girl feel on the 4th of July? Why does she feel this way? Can Chinese food and the 4th of July go together? Is there such a thing as "American" food? To what extent are the little girl and her family both Chinese and American?
Economics	Describe the hardships of owning your own restaurant.
Conflict	Why does the little girl doubt that her parents "understand all American things?"

Activity

There are myriad topics to explore in immigration: the factors that push people to leave their countries and pull them to America; the special circumstances of refugees and their special needs upon arrival; the difficulties of the journey; the processing at Ellis and Angel Islands and other entry locations; life in and out of the ghettoes; the ways in which the work of immigrants has built America; and the discrimination immigrants have faced from community members, employers, and the government at different times in history. Every one of these topics is addressed in the plethora of picture books that explore immigration. Although these picture books can be supplemented with other sources, it is also the case that many of those sources—photographs, oral histories, recipes, quotes, cartoons, and timelines—are an integral part of many of the picture books annotated at the end of this chapter.

We have used literature circles with picture books as the vehicle for students to explore some of the key themes and essential questions related to immigration. Literature circles are a mainstay in our classes; however, a gallery walk is a new activity to many of them. A gallery walk requires students to record information on large chart paper hung around the room—gallery-style. As students move from paper to paper, they recall and write key elements of the topic at hand. For the gallery walk on immigration, the chart papers include the following headings:

Reasons for coming to the U.S.	Experiences on the journey and upon arrival	Experiences in the first few years (in school, at work) *24/7 job in early years in America*	Family relationships *Children have conflicts with parents over how to behave in America*	Positive/negative aspects

To familiarize students with the activity, we model what we expect from our reading of *Apple Pie 4th of July*. Once we have read the book, students are asked to identify key details from the story that fit into each of the categories, which we record on the chart paper. This book illustrates the conflict between children and their immigrant parents over what it means to be American, which provides information for the "Family relationships" category. Other books may address other categories more effectively; thus, reading a variety of works on immigration paints a fuller picture of the immigrant experience.

In groups of four, students select an immigrant-themed picture book to read in their literature circles. Once students have read the book, they discuss the themes and then do the gallery walk, moving from paper to paper recording the details from their books that illustrate each theme. (Each group of students uses a different color marker to write its responses so that each book is represented by a different color.)

After the gallery walk is complete, we engage students in a discussion that includes the following questions:

• *Are immigrants' experiences more similar or more different? Is there such a thing as a typical immigration experience?*

• *What struggles did characters face as they adapted to their new home (e.g., name changes, eating customs, dress, role of elders, expectations for boys and girls, homesickness, getting along with other immigrant groups, fitting in both old and new cultures, etc.)*

• *What does it mean to be American? Do people have to change to become American? Should they have to?*

Students draw on the information from the charts, from their books and those of their classmates, to grapple with these questions.

Applying the Concepts

Literature circles with the fiction and nonfiction picture books about immigration serve as a vehicle for our students to generate questions they will use when they conduct immigration oral histories. Conducting and analyzing oral histories are worthwhile activities that help our students develop the literacy skills of listening, speaking, reading, and writing, as well as the social studies skills of inquiry and historical investigation. We engage students in the development of the interview questions that will help uncover immigration stories. Developing interview questions is difficult; students need guided support in this work. After engaging in the gallery walk and the rich discussion that follows, our students know a lot more about the immigrant experience. They now work backward to figure out which questions elicited those stories.

Students return to their literature circles to generate a list of questions inspired by their particular book. They record the questions on a handout that reflects the gallery walk headings. For example, one group of students read about Mei Mei's experience in school in *I Hate English* by Ellen Levine.

Aspects of the immigrant experience	Questions based on *I Hate English* by Ellen Levine
Reasons for coming to the United States	
Experiences on the journey and upon arrival	
Experiences in the first few years (in school, at work)	How did children treat you? What's your best memory of being in a new school? What's your worst memory of being in a new school? What would have made school life easier for you?
Family relationships	
Positive/negative aspects	

Name _____ Date _____

Student Handout: Immigration Oral History Question Ideas

Directions: Identify the book you read. Work with students who read the same book to write a list of questions inspired by your book. These questions will guide your oral history interview.

Aspects of the immigrant experience	Questions based on _____
Reasons for coming to the United States	
Experiences on the journey and upon arrival	
Experiences in the first few years (in school, at work)	
Family relationships	
Positive/negative aspects	

After all of the groups have generated questions, we add them to our gallery walk categories and ask students to prioritize the top ten to fifteen questions that are ultimately included in an oral history interview guide.

We then model and practice conducting oral history interviews. To demonstrate interview skills, we conduct mock interviews during which our students give input and feedback. Our mock interviewee has been prepped to, at times, give too-brief answers or go off on tangents. Students brainstorm ways to handle those situations.

We set aside a special day when we invite immigrants (or children of immigrants) into our classroom to tell their stories. Each literature group interviews a different immigrant. Picture books and other reference books on immigration are at each table where the interviews are conducted to spark conversation. Students then add the information they have acquired from their interviewee to the gallery chart papers around the room. We invite our guests to stay for the ensuing discussion so that they can add any relevant information for the whole class to hear. This additional information from real-life immigrants allows students to deepen their understanding of issues that immigrants faced and continue to face as they journey to America and become "American." We derive our inspiration for these interviews from the work of Paula Rogovin (1998), who has shown that students as young as first graders can conduct successful interviews and process the information they have acquired from them.

Extending the concepts in your class . . .

Compile your students' stories of the immigrants and their children into a class book, complete with photos.

When immigrants come for their oral history interviews, extend an invitation to them to prepare a small dish that reflects their heritage (or you can purchase or have your class make an appropriate dish).

Create an online museum of the stories and experiences as well as photos of the immigrants your students interviewed.

Recommended Books

For a list of books related to the concept of *Diversity*, please see *Where We Live Influences How We Live* on the Recommended Books list at the end of Chapter 4: "People, Places and Environments."

Immigration

Aliki. *Marianthe's Story: Painted Words and Spoken Memories*. New York: Greenwillow, 1998. (Two stories in one book show the difficulties a child faces when coming to a new land.) *What are the challenges a child faces when immigrating to a new country?*

Bartone, E. *Peppe the Lamplighter*. St. Petersburg, FL: Spoken Arts, 1994. (Despite his father's disapproval, Peppe becomes a lamplighter to help support his immigrant family in turn-of-the-century New York City.) *What challenges do families face when they immigrate to a new country?*

Beti, R. *Without Words*. Fort Lee, NJ: Sem Fronteiras Press, 2004. (A young immigrant boy misses his home in Brazil and learns to adapt to his new home through art.) *How difficult is it to move from one culture to another?*

Bierman, C. *Journey to Ellis Island: How My Father Came to America*. New York: Hyperion Books for Children, 1998. (A real-life account of a Russian Jewish family's journey to a new land.) *What was it like to immigrate to the United States?*

Broyles, A. *Shy Mama's Halloween*. Gardiner, ME: Tilbury House, 2002. (A girl and her mother, recent immigrants, become acclimated to American customs on Halloween.) *How do recent immigrants balance their home and adopted cultures?*

Bunting, E. *Going Home*. New York: HarperCollins, 1998. (Carlos and his family visit the family village in Mexico.) *How do immigrant families connect two worlds?*

Bunting, E. *How Many Days to America?: A Thanksgiving Story*. New York: Clarion Books, 1988. (A family from a Latin American country flees its village when the soldiers come. After a harrowing boat trip, the refugees land and are welcomed to America on Thanksgiving.) *What are the different experiences that people have when they immigrate to America?*

Bunting, E. *One Green Apple*. New York: Clarion Books, 2006. (A Muslim girl's headscarf sets her apart in school with varied reactions from classmates.) *How do immigrants feel when they come to a new land?*

Choi, Y. *The Name Jar*. New York: Alfred A. Knopf, 2001. (A Korean girl is teased about her name.) *What is it like for a child to immigrate to a new land?*

Cohen, B. *Molly's Pilgrim*. New York: Bantam, 1990. (A Russian immigrant girl finds parallels between her immigration experience and that of the Pilgrims.) *How are immigrant experiences similar and different?*

Currier, K. S. *Kai's Journey to Gold Mountain*. Tiburon, CA: Angel Island Association, 2005. (A 12-year-old Chinese boy is detained on Angel Island while trying to come to America.) *What are the different experiences that people have when they immigrate to America?*

Figueredo, D. H. *When This World Was New*. New York: Lee & Low Books, 2003. (A young boy's first-person account about his arrival in the United States from an unnamed Caribbean Spanish-speaking country and how he turns his greatest fears about his new home into enticing wonders.) *How difficult is it to move from one culture to another?*

Freedman, R. *Immigrant Kids*. New York: Puffin Books, 1995. (Captures the experience of being a young urban immigrant around the turn of the century; excellent photos.) *What are the different experiences that people have when they immigrate to America?*

Friedman, I. *How My Parents Learned to Eat*. Boston: Houghton Mifflin, 1984. (An American sailor courts a Japanese woman, and each tries to learn the other's way of eating.) *How difficult is it to move from one culture to another?*

Garland, S. *The Lotus Seed*. San Diego: Harcourt Brace Jovanovich, 1993. (A Vietnamese immigrant woman plants a lotus seed to bring her traditions to her new home.) *In what ways are immigrants connected to two cultures?*

Greenwood, B. *Factory Girl*. Toronto: Kids Can Press, 2007. (Re-creation of daily life of a poor, urban twelve-year-old girl, one hundred years ago.) *What are the different experiences that people have when they immigrate to America?*

Hall, B. *Henry and the Kite Dragon*. New York: Philomel Books, 2004. (Chinese and Italian immigrant children learn they share more than just the sky.) *How can children from different backgrounds find common ground?*

Hest, A. *When Jesse Came Across the Sea*. Cambridge: Candlewick, 2003. (A narrative of a thirteen-year-old boy's turn-of-the-century immigration from a small Eastern European country to New York City.) *How difficult is it to move from one culture to another?*

Hoffman, M. *The Color of Home.* New York: Phyllis Fogelman Books, 2002. (A recent immigrant from Somalia is homesick on his first day of school in America.) *How does it feel to immigrate to a new land?*

Hopkinson, D. *Shutting Out the Sky: Life in the Tenements of New York 1880–1924.* New York: Orchard Books, 2003. (Recounts the lives of five immigrants to New York's Lower East Side through oral histories and engaging narratives.) *What are the different experiences that people have when they immigrate to America?*

Kim, J. U. *Sumi's First Day of School.* New York: Viking, 2003. (A Korean American child is afraid when she starts school; a kind teacher and classmate reach out to her.) *How does it feel for a child to immigrate to a new land?*

Knight, M. B. *Who Belongs Here? An American Story.* Gardner, ME: Tilbury House, 1993. (A ten-year-old Cambodian boy tells of leaving his homeland and settling in this country.) *What are the different experiences that people have when they immigrate to America?*

Kuklin, S. *How My Family Lives in America.* New York: Aladdin, 1992. (Photo essay of children whose parents immigrated from Puerto Rico, Taiwan, and Senegal.) *Are different immigrants' and their children's experiences more alike or more different from one another?*

Lawlor, V. *I Was Dreaming to Come to America.* New York: Viking, 1995. (In fifteen excerpts, varied immigrants recount their reasons for and experiences in making the trip to America.) *What are the different experiences that people have when they immigrate to America?*

Lee, M. *Landed.* New York: Frances Foster Books/Farrar, Straus & Giroux, 2006. (A turn-of-the-century immigrant is detained at Angel Island in the years following the Chinese Exclusion Act.) *Are people's immigration experiences more similar or more different?*

Leighton, M. R. *An Ellis Island Christmas.* New York: Puffin, 2005. (A young Polish girl immigrates to America during the peak of the immigration era with her remaining family members and hopes to join her father in New York.) *How difficult are the challenges for immigrants to America?*

Levine, E. *I Hate English.* New York: Scholastic, 1989. (When her family moves to New York from Hong Kong, Mei Mei finds it difficult to adjust to school and learn the alien sounds of English.) *What difficulties do children face when they immigrate?*

Levine, E. *If Your Name Was Changed at Ellis Island.* New York: Scholastic Inc, 1993. (A comprehensive discussion of the immigration procedures followed at Ellis Island between 1892 and 1914.) *What was it like for immigrants coming through Ellis Island?*

Lofthouse, L. *Ziba Came on a Boat.* San Diego: Kane/Miller Book Publishing, 2007. (Young Ziba remembers everything she has left behind in her old country as she makes the journey to America in the crowded hull of a ship.) *What special challenges do refugees face?*

Maestro, B. *Coming to America: The Story of Immigration.* New York: Scholastic, 1996. (An overview of immigrant experiences in early America.) *What are the different experiences that people have when they immigrate to America?*

Nolan, J. *The St. Patrick's Day Shillelagh.* Morton Grove, IL: Albert Whitman, 2004. (After discovering a family heirloom in a closet, which was a piece of a tree his grandfather cut before leaving Ireland for America during the potato famine, a young boy learns about his family history and their passage to America.) *How do immigrant families retain their cultures?*

Nunes, S. M. *The Last Dragon.* New York: Clarion Books, 1995. (In Chinatown, a boy feels alienated until he discovers a worn-out dragon and gets various people in the neighborhood to repair different parts of it.) *In what ways can immigrants find new community connections?*

Partridge, E. *Oranges on Golden Mountain*. New York: Puffin, 2003. (A young boy adjusts to his new life in nineteenth-century California after being sent there by his widowed mother from their drought stricken village in China to live with his uncle.) *How difficult is it to move from one culture to another?*

Perez, A. I. *My Diary from Here to There/Mi diario de aqui hasta alla*. San Francisco: Children's Book Press, 2002. (In her first diary entry, Amada is anxious about her family's move from Mexico to Los Angeles.) *What special challenges do children face when they immigrate to a new land?*

Perry, M. F. *A Gift for Sadia*. Northfield, MN: Buttonweed Press, 2005. (Drawn together by her experience working with ESL students, the author tells the tale of a sad, young Somali immigrant's struggle to learn English in her new home in Minnesota.) *What special challenges do refugees face?*

Polacco, P. *The Keeping Quilt*. New York: Aladdin, 2001. (The author's first-person account of her Russian-Jewish family's immigration to America in the early 1900s and how her grandmother made a quilt from their clothing.) *How do immigrant families retain their cultures?*

Rael, E. O. *What Zeesie Saw on Delancey Street*. New York: Aladdin, 2000. (Set in a Jewish American community on Manhattan's Lower East Side in the early 1900s, this is the story of a community coming together to raise money to help other families from the same town they emigrated from pay for their passage to America.) *How do immigrants balance their old and new cultures?*

Recorvits, H. *My Name Is Yoon*. New York: Frances Foster Books, 2003. (A Korean girl's adjustment to life in America.) *What special challenges do children face when they immigrate to a new land?*

Robinson, A. *Gervelie's Journey: A Refugee Diary*. London: Frances Lincoln Children's Books, 2010. (A young girl and her family are forced to flee from war-torn Congo because of her father's political connections, which takes them first to the Ivory Coast, then to Ghana, across Europe, and finally to England.) *How difficult are the adjustments that refugees have to make when they go to a new land?*

Robinson, A. *Hamzat's Journey: A Refugee*. London: Frances Lincoln Children's Books, 2010. (A young Chechnyan boy and his family seek political asylum in the United Kingdom after the young boy steps on a land mine on his way to school and has to have his leg amputated.) *What special challenges do refugees face?*

Sandler, M. W. *Immigrants: A Library of Congress Book*. New York: HarperCollins, 1995. (More than one hundred photographs, posters, and paintings reveal what becoming an American meant to millions of people.) *What are the different experiences that people have when they immigrate to America?*

Say, A. *Grandfather's Journey*. Boston: Houghton Mifflin, 1993. (A Japanese American man recounts his grandfather's journey to America and the feelings of being torn between two countries.) *What are the different experiences that people have when they immigrate to America?*

Say, A. *Tea with Milk*. Boston: Houghton Mifflin, 1999. (A young Japanese American woman feels out of place when her family returns to Japan.) *What does it feel like to immigrate to a new land?*

Shea, P. D. *Tangled Threads: A Hmong Girl's Story*. New York: Clarion Books, 2003. (Mai becomes comfortable with American ways, in contrast to her grandmother, who fears assimilation.) *In what ways is it easier for children than adults to immigrate?*

Tan, S. *The Arrival*. New York: Arthur A. Levine Books, 2006. (Outstanding graphic novel/picture book of a man's journey to build a better future for his family.) *What are the different experiences that people have when they immigrate to America?*

Tarbescu, E. *Annushka's Voyage*. New York: Clarion Books, 1998. (At the turn of the century, two sisters travel from Russia with hopes of a better life.) *What are the different experiences that people have when they immigrate to America?*

Watson, M. *The Butterfly Seeds*. New York: HarperCollins, 1995. (A young boy prepares to leave his home to immigrate to America and is despondent over having to leave his grandfather behind. He is given hope when his grandfather gives him butterfly seeds, which he plants in the window box garden at his new third-floor tenement with the help of an Italian fruit vendor, an Irish blacksmith, and a Chinese fish peddler.) *How do immigrant families retain their cultures?*

Williams, K. L., and Mohammed, K. *My Name Is Sangoel*. Grand Rapids, MI: Eerdmans Books for Young Readers, 2009. (A refugee from Sudan to the United States, eight-year-old Sangoel is frustrated that no one can pronounce his name until he finds a clever way to solve the problem.) *What special problems do children face when they immigrate to a new land?*

Williams, M. *Brothers in Hope: The Story of the Lost Boys of Sudan*. New York: Lee & Low Books, 2005. (An eight-year-old boy, orphaned by the civil war in Sudan, finds the strength to lead other boys hundreds of miles to Ethiopia and then to the United States.) *What are the different experiences that people have when they immigrate to America?*

Wong, J. *Apple Pie Fourth of July*. San Diego: Harcourt, 2002. (A Chinese American girl worries that no one will want her parents' Chinese food on the 4th of July.) *To what extent should a community support the cultural pluralism of its residents?*

Woodruff, E. *The Memory Coat*. New York: Scholastic Press, 1998. (Cousins leave their Russian shtetl for America, hoping that they will pass the dreaded Ellis Island inspection.) *What was it like for immigrants to pass through Ellis Island?*

Yang, B. *Hannah Is My Name: A Young Immigrant's Story*. Cambridge, MA: Candlewick Press, 2004. (Hannah takes a new name and adjusts to a new life, as the family awaits green cards that mean they can stay.) *What are the different challenges immigrants face in a new land?*

Yin. *Brothers*. New York: Philomel Books, 2006. (Follow up to *Coolies*; Chinese immigrants' road to the American dream.) *What unique issues did Chinese immigrants face when they came to America?*

Yin. *Coolies*. New York: Philomel Books, 2001. (This book describes the harsh lives early Chinese immigrants faced in the 1800s.) *What are the different experiences immigrants face when they come to a new land?*

Yolen, J. *Naming Liberty*. New York: Philomel Books, 2008. (Using parallel narratives, the story tells the tale of the members of a Russian-Jewish family as they prepare to emigrate to America and also tells the story of French artist Frederic Auguste Bartholdi's creation of the Statue of Liberty.) *How difficult are the challenges for immigrants to America?*

Families

Browne. A. *Piggybook*. New York: Alfred A. Knopf, 1990. (When Mom leaves, Dad and sons realize how much she did for them; they resolve to pull their weight and share jobs.) *How can you be a good citizen in your own family?*

Bunting, E. *A Day's Work*. New York: Clarion Books, 1994. (When a young Mexican American boy tries to help his grandfather find work, he discovers that even though the old man cannot speak English, he has something even more valuable to teach his grandson.) *What can family members learn from each other?*

Bunting, E. *Sunshine Home*. New York: Clarion Books, 1994. (When he and his parents visit his grandmother in the nursing home where she is recovering from a broken hip, everyone pretends to be happy until Tim helps them express their true feelings.) *How can family members help each other?*

Cooper, H. *Pumpkin Soup*. New York: Farrar, Straus & Giroux, 1999. (Three animals live happily together and all have specific roles in the household until one day they decide they want to trade jobs. This book explores the challenges that are faced when there is a close-knit living arrangement.) *What is a family?*

Cruise, R. *Little Mamá Forgets.* New York: Farrar, Straus & Giroux, 2006. (Loving relationship between a little Mexican American girl and her grandmother, who has periods of forgetfulness.) *How can we help older members of our families?*

DePaola, T. *Nana Upstairs & Nana Downstairs.* New York: Puffin, 2000. (Four-year-old boy enjoys his relationship with both his grandmother and great-grandmother but eventually learns to face their inevitable death.) *How do different families cope with loss?*

DeRolf, S. *The Crayon Box That Talked.* New York: Random House, 1997. (The book conveys a message of appreciation for people's differences and shows that the differences help to create a whole.) *To what extent should a family support the individuality of its members?*

English, K. *The Baby on the Way.* New York: Farrar, Straus & Giroux Books for Young Readers, 2005. (Grandmother tells the story of how even she was once "the baby on the way.") *How important are our family histories?*

Garden, N. *Molly's Family.* New York: Farrar, Straus & Giroux Books for Young Readers, 2004. (When Molly draws a picture of her family for Open School Night, one of her classmates makes her feel bad because he says she cannot have a mommy and a mama.) *What is a family?*

Garza, C. L. *In My Family/En Mi Familia.* San Francisco: Children's Book Press, 1996. (The author describes, in bilingual text, growing up in an Hispanic community in Texas.) *Are families more similar or more different?*

Gerdner, L., and Langford, S. *Grandfather's Story Cloth.* Walnut Creek, CA: Shen's Books, 2008. (A ten-year-old Hmong boy helps his beloved grandfather with his failing memory, brought on by Alzheimer's disease, by showing him the story quilt Grandfather made after fleeing his homeland of Laos during wartime.) *How is culture an essential part of family?*

Gray, L. M. *My Mama Had a Dancing Heart.* New York: Orchard Books, 1995. (A young woman remembers how she and her mother danced to celebrate each season.) *How do families celebrate life?*

Howard, E. F. *Aunt Flossie's Hat and (Crab Cakes Later).* New York: Clarion Books, 2001. (A portrait of an African American family and of the ways in which shared memories can connect the generations.) *How important are our family histories?*

Isadora, R. *What a Family!: A Fresh Look at Family Trees.* New York: G.P. Putnam's Sons/Penguin Young Reader's Group, 2000. (Similarities and differences within families are celebrated.) *Are families more similar or more different?*

Johnston, T. *Yonder.* Layton, UT: Gibbs Smith, 2002. (A celebration of the life in one community.) *Are families' cycles of life more similar or different?*

Kerley, B. *You and Me Together: Moms, Dads, and Kids Around the World.* Des Moines: National Geographic Children's Books, 2005. (Photographs show the loving relationships of parents and children around the world.) *Are families more alike or different?*

Lainez, C. *Waiting for Papa/Esperando a Papa.* Houston, TX: Arte Publico Press, 2004. (It's been three years since a young boy and members of his family moved from El Salvador to America after their house burned down, and he still waits for his father, who could not obtain a visa for the trip.) *What challenges does immigration pose for families who cannot all come to America at the same time?*

L'Engle, M. *The Other Dog.* San Francisco: Chronicle Books, 2006. (Sibling rivalry as a new baby arrives, as told by the family dog.) *How do families resolve conflicts?*

Look, L. *Uncle Peter's Amazing Chinese Wedding.* New York: Atheneum Books for Young Readers/Simon & Schuster Children's Publishing, 2006. (A girl has difficulty with the idea of sharing her favorite uncle with a new aunt. The story also depicts Chinese wedding traditions.) *Are our family celebrations more similar or different?*

Maclachlan, P. *All the Places to Love.* New York: HarperCollins, 1994. (Told in the voice of a young boy who lives on a farm with his family, the story depicts the importance of the simple things in life to enjoy and appreciate.) *What things are important in a family?*

Morris, A. *Families.* New York: HarperCollins, 2000. (All children are a part of families that come in all shapes, sizes, nationalities, and configurations.) *Are families more alike or more different?*

Parnell, P., & Richardson, J. *And Tango Makes Three.* New York: Simon & Schuster Books for Young Readers, 2005. (Based on a true story of two male penguins living at Central Park Zoo, the penguins are "a bit different." They nestle together as other penguins do and have a natural desire to want to be parents, too. The zoo keepers give them the opportunity to care for an egg and nurture the penguin chick.) *What is a family?*

Parr, T. *The Family Book.* New York: Little, Brown and Company, 2003. (Celebrating all types of families, this book includes adopted families, stepfamilies, single-parent families, families with two parents of the same sex, as well as traditional nuclear families.) *Are families more alike or different?*

Pellegrini, N. *Families Are Different.* New York: Holiday House, 1991. (Told in the voice of the youngest child, the story is about two young Korean girls who were adopted by their Caucasian parents and the common concerns and experiences that adopted families encounter.) *What different struggles do families have?*

Polacco, P. *My Rotten Red-Headed Older Brother.* New York: Simon & Schuster Books for Young Readers, 1994. (A story of sibling rivalry told by the younger sister of a bratty older brother, she tries to do anything better than he can.) *What conflicts exist within a family?*

Polacco, P. *Thunder Cake.* New York: Philomel Books, 1990. (A grandmother helps alleviate the fear her granddaughter has of a thunderstorm by reassuring her that the sounds are the perfect ingredients for a "Thunder Cake.") *How are family members special to each other?*

Rosen, M. J. *Home: A Collaboration of Thirty Distinguished Authors and Illustrators of Children's Books to Aid the Homeless.* New York: HarperCollins, 1992. (Thirteen authors and seventeen illustrators celebrate the things that make up the home.) *How important is it for a family to have a home?*

Rotner, S., and Kelly, S. *Lots of Grandparents.* Minneapolis: Millbrook Press, 2001. (Photographs explore similarities and differences among grandparents.) *Are we more similar or different?*

Rotner, S., and Kelly, S. M. *Many Ways: How Families Practice Their Beliefs and Religions.* Minneapolis: Millbrook Press/Lerner, 2003. (Photos depict families from all parts of the world playing, working, and praying together.) *Are we more similar or more different?*

Rylant, C. *The Old Woman Who Named Things.* Orlando: Harcourt, 1996. (An elderly woman who has outlived everyone close to her names anything and everything that she feels confident will outlive her. The book conveys a theme of resilience and acceptance.) *Why is it important to remember our family members?*

Rylant, C. *The Relatives Came.* New York: Aladdin, 1985. (An extended family comes up from Virginia to visit and fills the house with their presence.) *How does meeting with extended family bring change to one's household?*

Schreck, K. H. *Lucy's Family Tree.* Gardiner, ME: Tilbury House, 2006. (The book describes the identity issues with which many adoptees struggle.) *What is a family?*

Skutch, R. *Who's in a Family?* Berkeley, CA: Tricycle Press, 1995. (Using both humans and animals, this book portrays multicultural contemporary family structures to include mixed race families, single-parent, grandparent, gay and lesbian, etc.) *Are more families similar or different?*

Williams, V. *A Chair for My Mother.* New York: Greenwillow Books, 1988. (A young girl tells the story of how she, her mother, and her grandmother saved all their change to buy a new chair for her hardworking mother.) *How do family members care for each other?*

Woodson, J. *Our Gracie Aunt.* New York: Hyperion Books for Children, 2000. (A brother and sister stay with their aunt because of their mother's neglect. They wonder, will they ever see Mother again?) *Are families still families when one member has to be away for an extended time period?*

Woodson, J. *Show Way.* New York: G.P. Putnam's Sons, 2005. (Based on Woodson's own history, the story of African American women across generations, from slavery and the civil rights movement to the present.) *How important are our family histories?*

Woodson, J. *Visiting Day.* New York: Scholastic Press, 2002. (A young girl and her grandmother visit the girl's father in prison.) *Are families still families when one member has to be away for an extended time period?*

Zolotow, C. *The Old Dog.* New York: HarperCollins, 1995. (This book describes the death of a beloved pet.) *How can we cope with loss in our families?*

Diversity

Alko, S. *I'm Your Peanut Butter Big Brother.* New York: Knopf Books for Young Readers, 2009. (A child in an interracial family wonders what his yet-to-be-born little brother will look like.) *How important are our differences in appearance?*

Brown, T. *Salaam: A Muslim American Boy's Story.* New York: Henry Holt Books for Young Readers, 2006. (This book describes Imran's life as a Muslim American child; includes photographs.) *Are we more similar or more different?*

David, M. *Bedwin.* Frederick, MD: Publish America, 2009. (Bedwin is a shy dragon who refuses to frighten other creatures, causing him to be shunned by the other dragons. One day, he encounters strange creatures called Greeples, and they soon learn to overcome their differences.) *Are people more similar or more different?*

Dooley, N. *Everybody Cooks Rice.* Minneapolis, MN: Lerner, 1995. (A girl looking for her little brother at dinnertime is introduced to a variety of cultures as she encounters the many different ways rice is prepared by her neighbors.) *Are we more similar or different?*

Fleischman, P. *Glass Slipper, Gold Sandal: A Worldwide Cinderella.* New York: Henry Holt, 2007. (Cinderella tales from seventeen cultures are woven together.) *How do the different Cinderella stories from around the world reflect the cultures of their countries?*

Fox, M. *Whoever You Are.* San Diego: Harcourt Brace, 1997. (There are children all over the world who may look different, live different kinds of lives, speak a different language, or do different things. But all children love, smile, laugh, and cry—under our skin, we are all the same.) *Are people more similar or different?*

Garcia, C. *The Adventures of Connie and Diego.* San Francisco: Children's Book Press, 1997. (Tired of being laughed at because they are different, a pair of multicolored twins run away to ask the animals where they really belong.) *How important are our differences in appearance?*

Hamanaka, S. *All the Colors of the Earth.* New York: Mulberry Books, 1999. (This simple text describes children's skin tones and hair in terms of natural phenomena.) *How important are our differences in appearance?*

Headley, J. C. *The Patch.* Watertown, MA: Charlesbridge, 2007. (A five-year-old girl with amblyopia fears being teased for her eye patch.) *How important are our differences in appearance?*

Hicks, B. J. *Jitterbug Jam.* New York: Random House, 2004. (A monster is frightened of a little boy.) *How does fear of the unknown contribute to prejudice?*

Hudson, W. (ed.). *Pass It On: African American Poetry for Children.* New York: Scholastic Press, 1993. (Anthology of light and serious poems by African America poets about different aspects of African America heritage.) *What can we learn about culture from poetry?*

Katz, L. *The Colors of Us.* New York: Henry Holt, 1999. (A seven-year-old and her mother view the variations in the colors of her friends' skin, comparing them to different colors of various foods.) *How important are our differences in appearance?*

Knight, M. B. *Talking Walls.* Gardiner, ME: Tilbury House, 1992. (An illustrated description of walls around the world and their significance.) *How do the walls we build reflect our different cultures?*

Lester, J. *Let's Talk About Race.* New York: HarperCollins, 2005. (This book discusses how race is only one part of each person's story.) *How important are our differences in appearance?*

Pinkney, M., and Pinkney, S. L. *I Am Latino: The Beauty in Me.* New York: Little, Brown Books for Young Readers, 2007. (A celebration of Latino children in all of their various shades, cultures, and customs.) *Are we more similar or more different?*

Pinkney, S. L. *Shades of Black: A Celebration of Our Children.* New York: Scholastic, 2000. (Photos and poetic text celebrate the beauty and diversity of African American children.) *Are we more similar or different?*

Seuss, Dr. *The Sneetches and Other Stories.* New York: Random House, 1961. (A parable of prejudice, based on stars, or lack thereof, on bellies.) *How important are our differences in appearance?*

Swope, S. *The Araboolies of Liberty Street.* New York: Potter, distributed by Crown, 1989. (An irrepressible, multicolored family moves into and changes a neighborhood bullied by conformists.) *To what extent should a community support the cultural pluralism of its residents?*

Waber, B. *You Look Ridiculous Said the Rhinoceros to the Hippopotamus.* New York: Houghton Mifflin Company, 1976. (An insecure hippo suffers from an inferiority complex until she realizes she's just fine the way she is.) *How important are our differences in appearance?*

Friendship

Feiffer, J. *The House Across the Street.* New York: Hyperion Books, 2002. (A boy watches the house across the street from his smaller house and imagines that the boy inside leads a fantastic life. Ultimately, he imagines they are friends.) *Can people of different backgrounds be friends?*

Fox, M. *Wilfrid Gordon McDonald Partridge.* La Jolla, CA: Kane/Miller Book Publishers, 1985. (A boy tries to discover the meaning of memory so he can help an elderly friend who is losing hers.) *Can people of different generations be friends?*

Hatkoff, I., Hatkoff, C., and Kahumbu, Dr. P. *Owen and Mzee: The Language of Friendship.* New York: Scholastic Press, 2006. (A young hippo, separated from its family in the 2004 tsunami, adopts an ancient tortoise as his mother, and the two become inseparable.) *Do friends need to be alike?*

McKissack, P. *Goin' Someplace Special.* New York: Atheneum Books for Young Readers, 2001. (A girl in segregated Nashville goes to the library.) *How can children from different backgrounds find things in common to build friendships?*

Woodson, J. *The Other Side.* New York: G.P. Putnam's Son, 2001. (A story of friendship across a racial divide.) *How can children from different backgrounds find friendship?*

References

Anti-Defamation League. "Talking to Your Child About Hatred and Prejudice." http://www.adl.org/issue_education/hateprejudice/print.asp (cited September 22, 2009).

Rogovin, P. *Classroom Interviews: A World of Learning.* Portsmouth, NH: Heinemann, 1998.

Chapter 3

Time, Continuity, and Change

When I Was Five by Arthur Howard is an obvious choice for the study of memoir. In the book, a six-year-old boy describes things he liked when he was five and compares them to the things he likes now: "When Jeremy was five he wanted to be an astronaut or a cowboy or both." And while he now has new favorites when it comes to cars and dinosaurs, his best friend last year is *still* his best friend this year. As he says, "Some things never change."

A less obvious use of this book is in the study of time, continuity, and change. A timeline of one's life is one way to get at the issue; we like to extend our students' thinking beyond sequencing the events of their lives to identifying the changes that have occurred and then analyzing and evaluating those changes. In the spirit of *When I Was Five,* we have students chart what has stayed the same in their lives in the past few years and what has changed. In the last column of the chart, we have students identify whether the changes were positive or negative and why. Our students, young though they are, still have experiences that they can classify as positive (getting my own room, a new friend moved onto my block, I can read, I can tie my own shoes) and negative (we moved and I had to go to a new school, I have to share my room with my new little brother, the neighborhood park was closed, I don't like having lunch so early this year). We discuss with our students how the experiences that they classify as negative might be shaped into more positive ones (e.g., sharing a room with a sibling might have both positive and negative aspects—the lack of privacy may be outweighed by the increased opportunities for living with a perpetual playmate). We invite students to make predictions about future changes in their lives. Although *When I Was Five* examines continuity and change in a limited slice of life, students learn the importance of analyzing events, small and large, to make judgments about quality of life and to improve circumstances that affect it.

When Everybody Wore a Hat by William Steig, *A Street Through Time* by Anne Millard, and *Someday* by Alison McGhee and Peter Reynolds enable students to evaluate the changes that occur over time.

Essential Questions

To what extent does change lead to progress and progress lead to change?

To what extent does technological innovation lead to progress for all?

What makes an event a turning point or turning point in (personal, local, national, global) history?

How are the past and present both similar and different? What are the positives and negatives of each?

When Everybody Wore a Hat by William Steig

In the story *When Everybody Wore a Hat*, William Steig tells about the time when he was a young boy, a time that was very different from today. Women wore corsets, people listened to phonographs, and horses pulled the fire engines. This is a wonderful tale to use to teach about memoir and voice, and teachers typically ask students how their lives are different from that of the character in the book.

The book can also be a springboard for students to generate questions to investigate their grandparents' lives and as a model for students to write their own stories about their grandparents' lives. Students discover that oral history is authentic history. They also discover the similarities and differences among people of the same generation and can compare those experiences to their own. As we engage students in a discussion using the questions in the chart that follows, we compile their answers in a Venn diagram that enables them to compare life in the early twentieth century with their lives today.

Social Studies Concepts and Discussion Questions

(We did not include an exhaustive list of questions here because the activity below involves students generating questions based on the book.)

Social studies concepts	Questions to ask based on the text
Time	When does this book take place? What events were going on in the world at this time?
Change	What are some of the changes that have occurred since the time period in which this book is set? What was most surprising to you about the way things were done back then? Which changes do you think are most significant? Why?
Location	Where does this story take place? How does location influence how people live?
Family	How was the author's family life similar and different from your own?
Gender	What kinds of things did girls do that were different from what the boys did? What kinds of things did moms do that were different from what dads did?
Social class	How did you know if someone was wealthy or poor? What do you think is the economic status of the main character? What evidence do you have for your answer?

Activity

After reading the book together, we use the text to help students generate and compile questions to ask their grandparents or older friends of the family. These questions are the basis for an oral history each student will write about his or her grandparent or older friend of the family. Because this is a story about a person who was born in 1908, the activity may lead students to ask questions that may not be relevant to people born in the United States in the 1940s or '50s but may be relevant to people who came from another country. Not all the questions students generate have to be asked; each of the questions will help students gain insights into what life was like years ago.

We model this activity first with the first page of text, then the whole class brainstorms questions based on the second page of text. Finally, student pairs are given a worksheet that has text from a page of the book, from which they generate questions. Once the group work is complete, we compile the questions on chart paper in front of the room.

Name _____ Date _____

Student Handout:
Generating Questions from *When Everybody Wore a Hat*

Directions: Based on the text below, write a list of questions you could ask your grandparents about their life when they were young.

Text from *When Everybody Wore a Hat*	Questions generated by the text
"In 1916, when I was eight years old there were almost no electric lights, cars or telephones—and definitely not TV. Even fire engines were pulled by horses. Kids went to LIBRARIES for books. There were lots of immigrants. *"This is me climbing a tree in the Bronx, where I spent most of my childhood."* [Photograph on opposite page.]	• When were you born? • Where did you grow up? • Do you have a picture from when you were young? • Did you have electric lights? A car? A telephone? A TV? • Did those things look the same as they do today? • Did you go to the library a lot? • Were there lots of immigrants where you grew up? • Did you climb trees? What did you do for fun?
"Mom and Pop came to America from the Old Country. This is my family at the supper table. I was the second youngest." *"We all lived in a small apartment. It was impossible to be alone."* *"Sometimes Mom and Pop quarreled."* *"They spoke four languages; German, Polish, Yiddish and English. They spoke Polish a lot. Who knew what they were saying? But we learned the important words."* *"When there wasn't enough heat, Pop even fought with the radiator."*	**Your Questions**

After the pairs of students finish writing their questions, we compile a class list. Students analyze the list and prioritize or eliminate questions; they also work to identify gaps or questions that they would like to ask that did not come out of the book. To help students with this task, we identified all of the themes in the book about which questions could be written. These include: location, housing, entertainment, play, family, clothing, roles of boys and girls, cost of things, social class, shopping, transportation, communication, events of the time, medical care, common sicknesses, technology, and future dreams. To supplement the list of questions, we also recommend websites (About.com: Genealogy). The completed list of interview questions can be sent home with students to conduct in-person or phone interviews. (Interview questions can also be posted on a teacher web page for easy access from a variety of locations.) We recommend that students videotape or audiotape the interviews, both so that they can recall what was said for the writing of their stories, and, perhaps more important, so that they have permanent records of their grandparents speaking of their lives.

Strategies for teachers to help students conduct effective interviews are discussed in Chapter 2; additional ideas can be found on oral history websites (Texas A & M, no date).

Applying the Concepts

Using William Steig's story as their model, students will compose and illustrate a story (using photos and/or drawings) of their grandparents' lives, based on the interviews they have conducted. The needs and the ability levels of your students will dictate the amount of structure you need to provide. Some students will need only blank paper to create a wonderful work. For some of our students who need more support, we use the following two templates (see Appendix A for full-page templates).

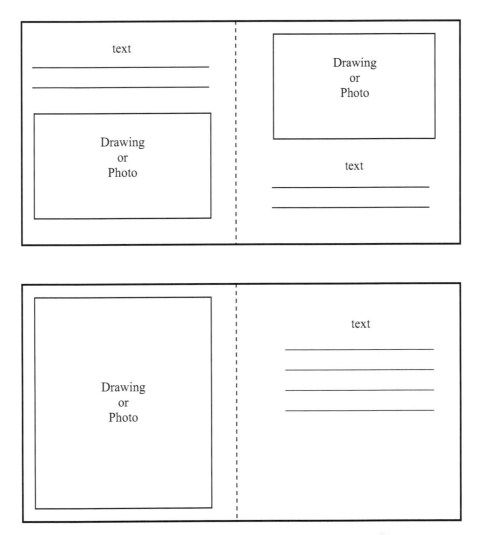

After students have finished their books, they read the work of at least two of their classmates. We then engage students in a whole class discussion; their books serve as a reference.

Discussion Questions

- *What did you learn about your grandparents' lives that surprised you?*

- *What were the most significant differences between their childhoods and your own?*

- *What were the similarities and differences between the stories of your grandparents' lives and William Steig's story?*

- *What were the similarities and differences between your story and your classmates' stories? What accounts for the similarities and differences in your stories?*

- *How did the photographs and/or illustrations enhance your understanding of the time period?*

- *To what extent did location and culture affect how people lived back then?*

- *Would you want to have lived back then? Why or why not?*

Extending the concepts in your class . . .

Read other memoirs and compare them to William Steig's.

Identify other people to interview for oral histories.

Conduct a group interview with three people from your school and write a book collectively.

Interview older members of your school community to ascertain their stories.

Collaborate with an art teacher to help students illustrate their books.

A Street Through Time by Anne Millard

This oversized, nonfiction book sketches the evolution of one street from the Stone Age to the present day, showing how people lived. Each double-page illustration conveys information about the major accomplishments of each highlighted period. This book may be thought of as a vehicle to teach about world history: however, it may also be used to introduce younger students to the concepts of continuity and change over time.

A Street Through Time enables students to see how the passage of time affects many aspects of life, including homes, jobs, clothing, food, architecture, modes of transportation, population density, technological developments, interaction between people, land usage, the environment and the emergence of leisure time activities.

Social Studies Concepts and Discussion Questions

(Because of its detailed illustrations, *A Street Through Time* is best examined by students in small groups. We keep four copies of the book in our classroom for just this purpose.)

Social studies concepts	Questions to ask based on the text
Time	What is the time span covered by this book?
Location	What are the advantages of living along a river?
Environment	How did people modify to their environment in each time period? How did people adapt to their environment in each time period? What are the implications of increased population density?
Technology	What were some of the major technological innovations over time? What is the impact of technological innovation on: the architectural landscape, transportation, livelihood, leisure time, and population density along the street?
Health and Medicine	Describe how sanitation and plumbing change over time. How does this influence the development of cities? How does medical care change over time?
Gender	How do the roles of men and women seem to change or stay the same over time? Does social class have an impact on the roles of men and women? On children?
Social class	How do the lives of the rich and poor seem to differ in each time period? (Consider housing, jobs, clothing, etc.)
Government	As life along the street evolves, how does the government seem to change? Why? At what point does an army seem to develop? Why?
Change	Which changes do you think are most significant? Why? What do you think led to those changes?

Activity

After discussing the book, students are ready to conduct a study of their own town over time. To help students in this endeavor, we begin our study with a class analysis of our school over time. We brainstorm the sources we will use to gather data, including Google maps, newspaper archives, old yearbooks and other school publications, local historical societies, town hall records, long-time town residents.

When we conduct this study with our students, they produce a museum-like display that includes four or five photos of the school in different decades. Teams of students are assigned one of the photos for which they create a narrative that describes the exterior and interior of the school, the grade level of students who attended the school, the landscape and playground equipment around the school, the clothing and hair length of the students, the presence and type of vehicles near the school, and the demographics of the school.

Students use a research guide like the one that follows to help them write the narrative for their assigned photo. Although much of the information will be derived from photos and old school publications, some might come from long-time residents of the community. These multiple sources of information provide us with a nice opportunity to discuss the reliability of different kinds of sources.

The photos and accompanying narratives are displayed in the classroom. Students walk around their "museum" and complete a viewing guide to help them identify the attributes of the school during each time period. Following the research guide is a sample viewing guide (with one category completed). Ultimately, students write a paragraph about the continuity and changes of their school through time.

Name _____ Date _____

Student Handout:
School Through Time **Research Guide**

Directions: Use the research guide below to record information about our school for the year you have been assigned.

YEAR YOU ARE INVESTIGATING: _____

Topic	Description	Source of information
Exterior of school		
Interior of school		
Grade level of students		
Landscape/playground		
Clothing/hair		
Vehicles		
Demographics		

	1954 School	1965 School	1977 School	2000 School	Continuity and Change
Exterior of school					
Interior of school					
Grade level of students					
Landscape/playground	*Slide, swings, small trees, no fences*	Slide, swings, metal jungle gym, ball field, bigger trees, four-square boxes	Wooden jungle gym with swings, slides, seesaws, pebble ground underneath, fort-like structure, basketball court, two ball fields	Metal wooden structure on foam-like ground, located in a new spot with new trees planted, painted map on playground, basketball court and two ball fields, big shade trees, new fences	*· Still have a playground but it is more developed and made of safer materials* *· More opportunity to play organized sports* *· Learning opportunity in the playground* *· Teachers said kids have less recess time than fifteen years ago* *· An extension on the building forced the playground to be relocated*
Clothing/hair					
Vehicles					
Demographics					

Applying the Concepts

Students expand on their investigation of their school through time by investigating other aspects of their town through time. Groups of students go through the same process to research Main Street, their block, the park, the firehouse, the police station, the post office, Town Hall, the library, the bank, the high school, the cemetery, a supermarket, a mall, etc. At the end of their investigation, they create a museum installation, "Our Town Through Time," for the lobby of the school.

Discussion Questions

- *How have changes in technology shaped the town over time?*

- *How has the environment been modified over time?*

- *What were the most striking changes in our town over time?*

- *What accounts for the changes over time?*

- *What are the positives and negatives of living in each time period?*

- *In which time period do you think it would be most advantageous to live?*

Extending the concepts in your class . . .

Invite a village historian to speak with your class.

Based on the historical information you have gathered, create a podcast for a walking tour of the town.

Digitize your museum displays for the town website.

Someday by Alison McGhee and Peter Reynolds

In *Someday*, by Alison McGhee, a mother imagines all of the milestones that her child will experience during life, from enjoying her first snowfall to brushing her own child's hair one day. This book provides a wonderful model of writing that offers sentence prompts for students, such as *One day . . ., Sometimes. . .,* and *Someday . . . .* It will help students begin to think about the significant events in their own lives and what makes them so important.

Because the book is about a child's life, teachers may not initially think of this book as a vehicle for teaching American history. However, because the book goes beyond traditional milestones, such as a child's first day of school or losing one's first tooth, it is an excellent model for children to think about milestones throughout history. Students can think beyond the traditional milestones in American history, such as wars and elections of presidents, to include a wider range of events, including those from social, cultural, and economic history.

Social Studies Concepts and Discussion Questions

Social studies concepts	Questions to ask based on the text
Time	How does the author use language in the book to denote passage of time? Why do you think the events included in this story are significant to the author?
Change	What are some of the changes that take place in the story? Which changes do you think are most significant? Why? How does the mother anticipate that her little girl's perception of their home will change, as she gets older? ["Someday you will look at this house and wonder how something that feels so big can look so small."]
Continuity	How is the past similar to how the mother imagines the future will be?
Environment	What role does the environment play in the significant events of the little girl's life?

Activity

Have students think about their own lives to date and list at least ten significant milestones. (A milestone is a significant event or stage in the development or life of a person, nation, etc. For a child, it may be a first snowfall; for a nation, it may be the inauguration of a president.) From that list of ten milestones, students select at least three that they believe are the most significant events for the changes that they brought to their lives. These significant events are called "turning points." (A turning point is an important division of time that indicates that a significant change has occurred. For a child, it may be the birth of a sibling; for a nation, it may be a war.) This assignment should be given with time for students to go home and get input from their family.

Questions to Prompt Students to Think of Milestones in Their Lives

- *Remind yourself of all of the "firsts" in the book. Are any of those events ones that were milestones in your life?*

- *Think about your experiences in the environment. (Remember the girl's first snowfall.) Would you classify any of those as milestones?*

- *Think about any religious celebration (e.g., Holy Communion, Bar or Bat Mitzvah) that denotes passage. Would you classify any of those as milestones?*

- *Think about any school "firsts."*

- *Think about any extracurricular activities (recitals, big games). Would you classify any of those as milestones?*

Questions to Prompt Students to Think of Turning Points in Their Lives

- *Did any of the events you listed as milestones bring great change to your life? (If so, classify them as turning points.)*

- *How many of you have moved? Did that make a significant change in your life?*

- *Did any of you have a new brother or sister arrive? How did that affect your life?*

- *Have any of you read a book that made you fall in love with reading?*

- *Did anything happen to you that made you think that you were a good student or a bad one? To what extent did it change your behavior?*

- *Did anything happen to you in any aspect of your life that made you think about yourself and behave differently?*

Students create a timeline that includes all of the milestones and turning points of their lives. (This is an excellent opportunity to reinforce the concept that a timeline is not just a line with events on it; rather, it is divided into equal-length segments denoting the same periods of time.) For each turning point, students write an explanation accompanying the event, explaining how it changed their lives. Children post timelines around the room.

Milestones and Turning Point Events

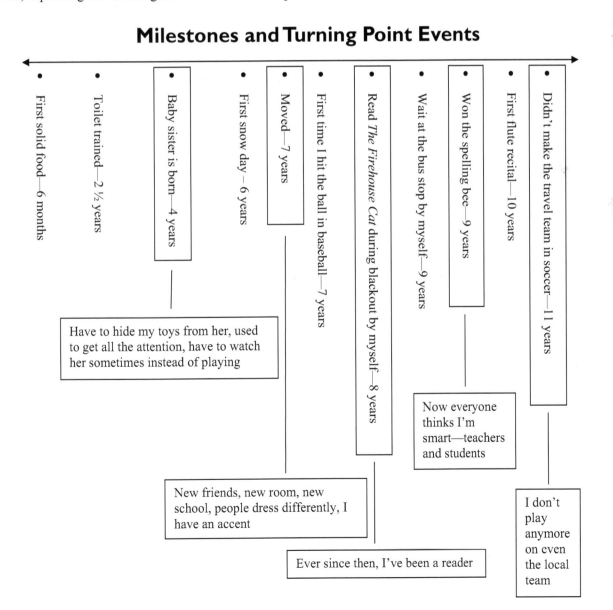

First solid food—6 months

Toilet trained—2 ½ years

Baby sister is born—4 years

First snow day – 6 years

Moved—7 years

First time I hit the ball in baseball—7 years

Read *The Firehouse Cat* during blackout by myself—8 years

Wait at the bus stop by myself—9 years

Won the spelling bee—9 years

First flute recital—10 years

Didn't make the travel team in soccer—11 years

Have to hide my toys from her, used to get all the attention, have to watch her sometimes instead of playing

Now everyone thinks I'm smart—teachers and students

New friends, new room, new school, people dress differently, I have an accent

Ever since then, I've been a reader

I don't play anymore on even the local team

Discussion Questions

- *How much difficulty did you have distinguishing between milestones and turning points in your life?*

- *What events did you see on a variety of classmates' timelines that were labeled as turning points?*

Applying the Concepts

Students will transfer what they have learned about identifying turning points in their own lives to identify turning points in American history. We begin by asking students to brainstorm a list of events in American history that they have heard of. We compile the events as a class and begin to assess whether they would qualify as turning points in American history.

Questions

- *What makes an event important? What makes an event a turning point?*

- *Are there any inventions that you would consider to be turning points?*

- *Are there any wars that you would consider to be turning points?*

- *Are there any social or political movements (e.g., civil rights, suffrage, etc.) that you would consider to be turning points?*

- *Are there any geographic movements of people that you would consider to be turning points?*

- *Are there any economic changes that you would consider to be turning points?*

- *Are there any health advances that you would consider to be turning points?*

To broaden students' thinking about the kinds of events that might be turning points, we compare the list that we have compiled to the "Stacked Timeline" on the next page, asking students what kinds of events appear on the "Stacked Timeline" that do not appear on ours. Students then add events to our list that reflect their new thinking.

"Stacked" Timeline

1900	Women's life expectancy is 48 years
1903	Wright brothers' flight
1907	First radio broadcast
1915	Telephone connects New York to San Francisco
1917	United States enters WWI Electric vacuum cleaner invented
1920	19th Amendment: women get vote Women comprise 20% of labor force Women's fashion allows greater freedom of movement Electrification of homes begins Majority of population lives in cities rather than farms Mass production of automobiles
1924	New immigration restrictions are enacted
1925	Electric refrigerators, frozen foods
1927	Phonograph is invented
1928	First sound movie is shown
1929	Stock market crashes
1930	Electric dishwasher is invented
1933	FDR is president—New Deal
1938	Nylon is invented
1941	Penicillin is available for disease control
1941–45	United States enters Word War II; 6 million women enter labor force
1944	Forerunner of the digital computer is invented
1945	The atomic bomb explodes on Hiroshima
1946	The automatic washing machine appears
1947	GI Bill spurs move to the suburbs
1950	United States enters Korean War
1950s	Baby boom Explosion of prepared food Containment of communist policy
1951	Television launched
1953	Women comprise 30 percent of labor force
1954–55	Supreme Court ends legalized school segregation
1950s	Civil Rights Movement seeks equality for blacks Rock and roll culture begins
1958	The jet engine makes its first flight
1962	Women's liberation movement seeks equality for women
1964	Title VII of Civil Rights Act forbids sex-based job discrimination U.S. is involved in Vietnam
1971	Women's life expectancy is 74 years
1974	Women comprise 45% of the labor force
1975	10 million Americans attend college

Adapted from Citizenship Education for the 21st Century: Gender Equity and Social Studies.

From *Every Book Is a Social Studies Book: How to Meet Standards with Picture Books, K–6* by Andrea S. Libresco, Jeannette Balantic, and Jonie C. Kipling. Santa Barbara, CA: Libraries Unlimited. Copyright © 2011.

To add to our list, we then survey friends and family (of at least high school age) about the ten most important events in American history. The survey appears on the next page and reflects the expanded thinking of our students as to what kinds of events in history might be considered turning points. Each student is responsible for at least three completed surveys. (It should be noted that one of the issues that arises in the course of our discussion is when American history begins: With the migration of nomadic people to the Western Hemisphere? With Columbus' voyage? With Jamestown? With the Declaration of Independence? As is the case with most rich discussions, the conversation is more important than coming to consensus.)

Name _____ Date _____

Student Handout: What Do You Think Are the Ten Most Important Events in American History?

Directions: Make a list of the ten most important events in American history. (Be sure to think about this question broadly by considering inventions, wars, political and social movements, geographic movements of people, economic changes, health advances, etc.) The events do not have to be listed in any particular order. If you wish to give any explanation for your selections, please feel free to do so.

1. _____

_____

2. _____

_____

3. _____

_____

4. _____

_____

5. _____

_____

6. _____

_____

7. _____

_____

8. _____

_____

9. _____

_____

10. _____

_____

From *Every Book Is a Social Studies Book: How to Meet Standards with Picture Books, K–6* by Andrea S. Libresco, Jeannette Balantic, and Jonie C. Kipling. Santa Barbara, CA: Libraries Unlimited. Copyright © 2011.

In groups, students examine the surveys and make a list, compiling all of the events in American history that they listed, which are then combined into one master class list. We list all of the events at the bottom of a long blackboard or a long strip of bulletin board paper. Students then place a Post-It note over the events that appear on each survey, which creates a bar graph of Post-It notes, reflecting the number of people who chose each event as most important. We also have students actually draw the bar graph on graph paper so that they practice this skill. We select the top ten or so events (depending on how many students there are in the class), and each pair of students selects one event to research, using books, websites, and *Cobblestone* (a historical journal for elementary students). They gather and record as much information about their event as possible, including dates, people, interesting details, and what made it such a significant event.

Because students' goal in researching the event is to find out why the event is considered a turning point in American history, they need to discover what changed and for whom as a result of the event. The organizer we give students has this emphasis. Following are two of the events students selected.

Turning Points in American History

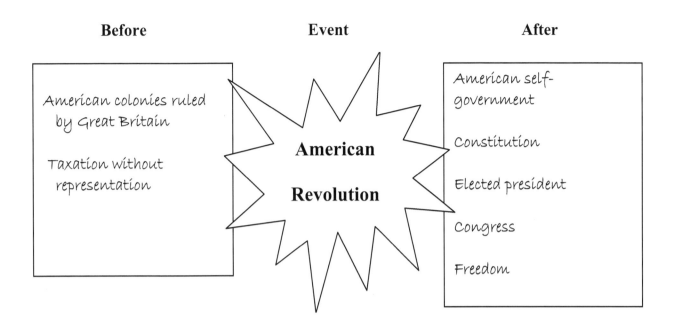

	Before	Event	After

Before

American colonies ruled by Great Britain

Taxation without representation

Event

American Revolution

After

American self-government

Constitution

Elected president

Congress

Freedom

After the American Revolution, the colonists controlled themselves. They no longer had to ask the king's permission to do anything. They were a new country and created their own government with elected leaders and freedoms.

Turning Points in American History

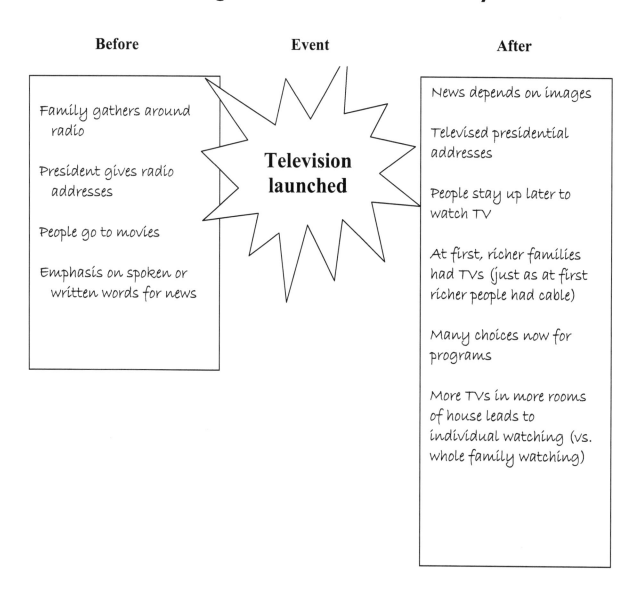

Before

Family gathers around radio

President gives radio addresses

People go to movies

Emphasis on spoken or written words for news

Event

Television launched

After

News depends on images

Televised presidential addresses

People stay up later to watch TV

At first, richer families had TVs (just as at first richer people had cable)

Many choices now for programs

More TVs in more rooms of house leads to individual watching (vs. whole family watching)

When television appeared, everyone wanted one. Eventually, almost everyone had one. People get their news from TV, see every major event (Olympics, elections, sports, wars) on TV. It also changed how people spend their time (just like the Internet changed how people spend their time today).

Student Handout: Turning Points in American History

Name _____ Date _____

Directions: Write the name of the event you are researching on the center starburst. Include information about what life was like before and after the event. Explain why the event should be considered a turning point in history. As a result of the event, what changed and for whom?

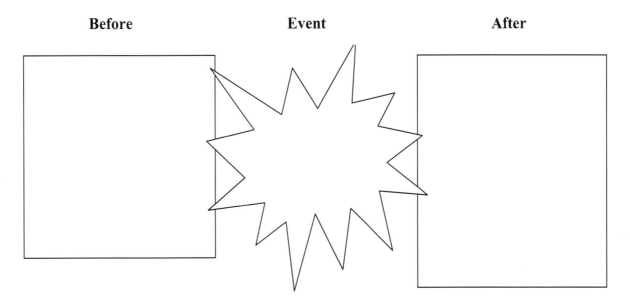

Before   **Event**   **After**

Explain why the event should be considered a turning point in history. As a result of the event, what changed and for whom?

After pairs of students record their research on their chosen event, they share the events with the class in a format of their own choosing (written report, PowerPoint, dramatic representation, etc.), one per day. We use this as an opportunity to teach the skill of note-taking, in which students take their own notes, then compare with those of their classmates. As homework, they retell the event in writing, using their notes from class. At the end of several weeks of sharing of the turning points, the students know all of the events well. Finally, we create a large illustrated class timeline that goes all around the room and stays up all year as a class reference tool.

Extending the concepts in your class . . .

Have students use the information from their classmates' reports to create poems titled "Turning Points."

Run a class discussion on what event created the greatest change.

Have students interview family members to discover turning points in their own family history.

While reading biographies of significant people, have students identify turning points in those people's lives.

Recommended Books

For a list of books that explore the changes that technology has brought, please see *Technology and Change* in the Recommended Books list at the end of Chapter 9: "Science, Technology, and Society."

Change and Continuity

Baker, J. *Window.* New York: Greenwillow Books, 1991. (This book chronicles the events and changes in a young boy's life and his environment, from babyhood to grownup, through wordless scenes observed from the window of his room.) *How are the past and present both similar and different? What are the positives and negatives of each?*

Burton, V. L. *The Little House.* Boston: Houghton Mifflin, 1969. (A country house is unhappy when the city, with all its buildings and traffic, grows up around it.) *How are the past and present both similar and different? What are the positives and negatives of each?*

Davies, J. *Tricking the Tallyman: The Great Census Shenanigans of 1790.* New York: Alfred A. Knopf, 2009. (This introduction to the census is set in 1790, when skeptical residents of a small Vermont town try to trick the man who has been sent to count their population for the first United States Census.) *To what extent are the issues raised in this book about the first census still with us today?*

Harrington, J. *Going North.* New York: Farrar, Straus & Giroux, 2004. (In this lyrical text, a young African American girl and her family leave their home in Alabama and head for Lincoln, Nebraska, where they hope to escape segregation and find a better life.) *How difficult is it to move away from your birthplace? To what extent has the situation in the South changed since this family moved?*

Henson, H. *That Book Woman.* New York: Atheneum Books for Young Readers, 2008. (A family living in the Appalachian Mountains in the 1930s gets books to read during the regular visits from the traveling librarian, who rides a pack horse through the mountains, lending books to isolated residents.) *To what extent is a service like this still needed today?*

Hopkinson, D. *A Packet of Seeds*. New York: Greenwillow Books, 2004. (When a pioneer family moves west, the mother misses home so much that she will not even name the new baby until her daughter thinks of just the right thing to cheer her up.) *How difficult is change, and how can we work through the difficulties?*

Howard, A. *When I Was Five*. New York: Harcourt Brace, 1996. (A six-year-old boy describes the things that he liked when he was five and compares them to the things that he likes now.) *How are the past and present both similar and different?*

Johnson, A. *I Dream of Trains*. New York: Simon and Schuster Books for Young Readers, 2003. (This story of a sharecropper's son emphasizes the role of the train in the Great Northern Migration.) *To what extent did trains represent change for African Americans in the South?*

Jones, L. *Mrs. Lincoln's Dressmaker The Unlikely Friendship of Elizabeth Keckley and Mary Todd Lincoln*. New York: Dutton, 2009. (Details the relationship of Elizabeth Keckley, an experienced seamstress born into slavery, and the First Lady. Their stories are told in alternating chapters and make excellent use of quotes, photos, and art of the period.) *How did changes in society change the relationship of Mrs. Lincoln and her dressmaker?*

Lawrence, J. *The Great Migration*. New York: HarperCollins, 1995. (Paintings by Jacob Lawrence with a concluding poem by Walter Dean Myers show the causes, process, and outcome of the Great Migration.) *To what extent did the Great Migration bring about positive change for all Americans?*

McGhee, A., and Reynolds, P. *Someday*. New York: Atheneum, 2007. (A mother speaks to her young daughter of milestones to come in her life.) *What are the most important milestones in a person' life?*

Millard, A. *A Port Through Time*. New York: DK Publishing, 2006. (A harbor town traced through history, from fishing village to bustling present day.) *What can the changes of a port over time tell us about the civilizations that shaped its history?*

Millard, A. *A Street Through Time*. New York: DK Publishing, 1998. (A riverside European location in fourteen periods, from the Stone Age to modern times.) *What can the changes of a street over time tell us about the civilizations that shaped its history?*

Miller, B. M. *Buffalo Gals: Women of the Old West*. Minneapolis, MN: Lerner Publications, 1995. (Between the 1830s and the 1890s, thousands of women moved West seeking economic prosperity and religious freedom, traveling alone or with their families by railroad, wagon train, and even on foot. The author brings these pioneers' stories to life through quotations from diaries, letters, and photographs.) *How are the past and present both similar and different? What are the positives and negatives of each?*

Provenson, A. *My Fellow Americans: A Family Album*. Orlando, FL: Browndeer Press (Harcourt Brace), 1995. (An album featuring free spirits, rebels, villains, radicals, and others in American history.) *Who effected the most change in American history?*

Ruelle, K. J. *The Tree*. New York: Holiday House Books, 2008. (An elm tree in New York City stands witness to yellow fever, the Civil War, the railroad, the Statue of Liberty, and countless events spanning more than 250 years.) *What were the most important changes of the last 250 years?*

Sidman, J. *Red Sings from Treetops: A Year in Colors*. Boston: Houghton Mifflin Harcourt, 2009. (Nature displays different colors to announce the seasons of the year.) *In what ways does the world change and yet still stay the same?*

Steig, W. *When Everybody Wore a Hat*. New York: HarperCollins, 2005. (Memoir of Steig's immigrant childhood in the Bronx nearly a hundred years ago.) *How are the past and present both similar and different? What are the positives and negatives of each?*

Swain, R. F. *Underwear: What We Wear Under There*. New York: Holiday House Books, 2008. (A history of underwear.) *How has people's thinking about underwear evolved over time?*

Wilson, J. *Imagine That!* Markham, Canada: Fitzhenry & Whiteside, Ltd, 2000. (On her 100th birthday, an aunt reminisces with her great-grandniece about her life and all of the changes in the past century.) *What were the most important changes of the twentieth century?*

Remembering and Understanding the Past

Bunting, E. *Dandelions.* San Diego: Harcourt Brace, 1995. (Zoe and her family find strength in each other as they make a new home in the Nebraska territory.) *How can remembering the past help us face the future?*

Bunting, E. *Once Upon a Time.* Katonah, NY: R. C. Owen, 1995. (This autobiography explores influences that shaped the author's life.) *How do events of the past influence who we are today?*

Dragonwagon, C. *Home Place.* New York: Macmillan/McGraw-Hill, 1990. (While out hiking, a family comes upon the site of an old house and finds some clues about the people who once lived there.) *How can we find out what happened in the past?*

Fox, M. *Wilfrid Gordon McDonald Partridge.* Brooklyn: Kane/Miller Book Publishers, 1985. (A boy tries to discover the "meaning of memory" so he can help an elderly friend who is losing hers.) *How important is it to know our own history?*

Halpern, M. *Railroad Fever: Building the Transcontinental Railroad, 1830–1870.* Washington, DC: National Geographic, 2003. (This book presents a history of the building of the Transcontinental Railroad and its effects on American life.) *How can understanding the past help us prepare for the future?*

Lange, K. *1607: A New Look at Jamestown.* Washington, DC: National Geographic, 2007. (This book takes a look back at what we now know about the Jamestown Colony.) *To what extent does change lead to progress and progress lead to change?*

Mochizuki, K. *Baseball Saved Us.* New York: Lee & Low Books, 1993. (A Japanese American boy learns to play baseball when he and his family are forced to live in an internment camp during World War II.) *To what extent has the U.S. government learned from its wartime policies of the past?*

Nelson, S. R., and Aronson, M. *Ain't Nothing but a Man: My Quest to Find John Henry.* Washington, DC: National Geographic Children's Books, 2008. (Exploration of the myth and the history of John Henry through primary source documents.) *How do historians know what they know?*

Perkins, L. R. *Pictures from Our Vacation.* New York: Greenwillow Books, 2007. (Given a camera that takes and prints tiny pictures just before leaving for the family farm in Canada, a young girl records a vacation that gets off to a slow start but winds up being a family reunion filled with good memories.) *How can we record today's events for tomorrow's memories?*

Polacco, P. *Pink and Say.* New York: Philomel Books, 1994. (A story of interracial friendship during the Civil War between two fifteen-year-old Union soldiers.) *How important is it to know about difficult episodes in our history?*

Rudolf, C. *I Am Sacajawea, I Am York: Our Journey with Lewis and Clark.* New York: Walker Books for Young Readers, 2005. (The story of this important journey is told from the point of view of two people who did not go on this expedition of their own free will. York was Clark's slave, and Sacajawea was considered to be the property of the expedition's translator. Yet these two were essential to the success of the trip.) *What makes an event a watershed or turning point in (personal, local, national, global) history?*

Rylant, C. *When I Was Young in the Mountains.* New York: Dutton, 1982. (Reminiscences of the pleasures of life in the mountains as a child.) *How do things from the past influence the present?*

Stanley, J. *Hurry Freedom: African Americans in Gold Rush California.* New York: Crown Publishers, 2000. (Recounts the history of African Americans in California during the Gold Rush while focusing on the life and work of Mifflin Gibbs.) *What makes an event a watershed or turning point in (personal, local, national, global) history?*

Steckel, R., and Steckel, M. *The Milestones Project: Celebrating Childhood Around the World.* Berkeley, CA: Tricycle Press, 2007. (Photographs and quotes from children all over the world, as well as recollections from authors and illustrators, experiencing similar milestones, such as losing a tooth.) *Are the milestones we experience more alike or more different?*

Weitzman, D. *Brown Paper School Book: My Backyard History Book.* Boston: Little, Brown & Company, 1975. (Complete and entertaining guide for "doing" local history using objects, photographs, places and people that might otherwise be overlooked.) *How can we find out what happened in the past?*

Yolen, J., and Stemple, H. E. Y. *Roanoke The Lost Colony: An Unsolved Mystery from History.* New York: Simon & Schuster Books, 2003. (Analysis of what happened to the lost colony that preceded Jamestown.) *What makes an event a watershed or turning point in (personal, local, national, global) history?*

References

About.com: Genealogy. "Fifty Questions for Family History Interviews: What to Ask the Relatives." http://genealogy.about.com/cs/oralhistory/a/interview.htm (cited September 30, 2009).

Cobblestone. Peterborough, NH: Cobblestone.

Crocco, M., and A. Libresco. "Citizenship Education for the 21st Century: Gender Equity and Social Studies." In D. Sadker and E. Silber (eds.), *Gender in the Classroom: Foundations, Skills, Methods and Strategies.* Mahwah, NJ: Lawrence Erlbaum Associates, 2006.

Texas A & M. "Oral History: Techniques and Questions." http://fcs.tamu.edu/families/aging/reminiscence/oral_history_techniques.php (cited September 30, 2009).

Chapter 4

People, Places, and Environments

Children love reading and rereading their favorite fairy tales. Fairy tales follow a predictable structure and typically end with a moral. For example, *Red Riding Hood* teaches children to listen to their parents when they tell them not to talk to strangers; *Goldilocks and the Three Bears* tells children not to wander into strange houses and take what isn't theirs. Based on the lessons they have learned, students are often asked to rewrite fairy tales.

In addition to teaching important life lessons and promoting creative writing, fairy tales provide an opportunity for students to develop their geography skills. Drawing a map of the place in which a story is set helps students pay attention to details in the story. For example, when we teach *Red Riding Hood,* we have students map the setting and the possible routes she could take to her grandmother's house. In addition, students analyze the pros and cons of going through the forest (it's more direct and faster, has better views, has flowers to pick for Grandma; but it holds the danger of meeting the wolf or other strangers) or around it (it takes longer, is less interesting, but it is safer and more familiar).

This activity develops the visualization and comprehension skills essential for literacy, and it also develops an understanding of the social studies concepts of location and place. This strategy can be applied to any book to help students better understand the story and the implications of its setting.

The Wartville Wizard by Don Madden, *My New York* by Kathy Jakobsen, and *What You Know First* by Patricia MacLachlan enable students to explore issues of geography and how they shape how people live.

Essential Questions

To what extent do geography and climate shape the way people live?

How do people shape their environments?

Whose responsibility is the environment?

Are rural, suburban, and urban environments more similar or different?

How does where we come from shape who we are?

The Wartville Wizard by Don Madden

An old man comes to realize that the town he loves is inundated with trash. At first, he tries to clean it up himself but realizes that he cannot solve the problem alone. He casts a spell on his fellow townsfolk, through which the garbage that they thoughtlessly discarded comes to stick to their bodies and stay with them wherever they go. Ultimately, the people develop an environmental consciousness and change their behavior, and the old man lifts the spell.

Teachers often introduce environmental lessons around Earth Day; however, it is important to establish a sense of environmental responsibility all year long. Earth Day ought to be every day. *The Wartville Wizard,* with its humorous take on this vital issue, provides an opportunity to continue the discussion throughout the year with a variety of ongoing activities.

Social Studies Concepts and Discussion Questions

Social studies concepts	Questions to ask based on the text
Environment	Describe the place the old man lives.
	How does looking closer affect the old man's perception of his environment?
	Whose responsibility is the environment?
Citizenship	What does the old man do to clean up the environment? Is he successful?
	To what extent would the old man have more allies if he were nicer to his fellow citizens?
	Do people who make a difference in the world have to be perfect citizens in all aspects of their lives?
Resources	Which items of garbage do you think could be recycled rather than thrown away?
	What happens to garbage when it leaves your garbage can? Does garbage ever really go away?
Change	To what extent is consciousness the first step to change?
	How does the citizens' shame affect their willingness to change their behavior?
	How and why does the epidemic end?
Power	What power does the old man have to change the environment by himself?
	How does the old man's visit with Mother Nature give him the "power over trash"?
	What is the event that causes the old man first to use his magical power?
	Why doesn't the doctor have the power to cure people's trash epidemic?
	What powers do the townspeople discover that they have?
Wants and needs	Examine the different items of trash sticking to the townspeople. Which do you think are wants and which do you think are needs?

Activity

To help our students develop a consciousness about the amount of garbage that they generate each day and each week, our class undertakes a project in which we all carry around the garbage we individually create with us for an entire week. Each child is given a big, heavy-duty garbage bag and must throw everything into it, including leftover food (which, for health reasons, might be placed in a zip-lock bag). We weigh each student's bag after the first day of collecting garbage, and the students make predictions, based on this initial weigh-in, as to how many pounds of garbage they expect to generate at the end of the week, as well as how many pounds the class as a whole will generate. When we weigh the garbage bags again at week's end, it is interesting to see whether students, by virtue of their participation in this experiment, have already begun to change their behavior and diminish their generation of garbage.

How Much Garbage Do We Generate?

Student name	Initial weigh-in	Prediction (in lbs.) for week of garbage	Final weigh-in	How'd we do?
Whole class				

Discussion Questions

- *What did you observe from the final weigh-in? Did you generate more or less garbage than you expected?*

- *How did the class as a whole do over the course of the week?*

- *To what extent do you feel like one of the townspeople in* The Wartville Wizard?

- *How is it possible to have power over trash without using magic?*

- *Do you have any recommendations for how to change our behavior to create less garbage in our world?*

Applying the Activity

After students discuss the amount of garbage they have generated in a week, have them make it more visual by transferring the data into the form of a bar graph. In addition, we ask students to take their final weigh-in results from one week of garbage collection and use the result to determine how much garbage they individually and everyone as a whole class would produce in a month, a year, and ten years.

Name _____ Date _____

Directions: Based on the weight of garbage that you generated in a week, calculate how much garbage you would generate in one month, in one year, and in one decade.

Student Handout:
How Much Garbage Is in Our Future?

Your final weigh-in x 4 = one month of garbage

_____ x 4 = _____

Your month's worth of garbage x 12 = one year of garbage

_____ x 12 = _____

Your year's worth of garbage x 10 = one decade of garbage

_____ x 10 = _____

What is your reaction to the above data?

Now that students have a consciousness about the amount of garbage that they each might produce over time, it is important to develop a sense of power over this trash. We brainstorm questions we have about all of the ways we might reduce the amount of garbage generated. Our list includes the following:

- *What can be recycled in our trash at school?*

- *What happens to the trash when it leaves our school?*

- *What can be recycled in our trash at home?*

- *What happens to the trash when it leaves our home?*

- *What items could we eliminate in the first place by not buying them? (Which items are not "needs"?)*

- *Could manufacturers package things differently to reduce trash?*

- *What can shoppers do to help stores eliminate unnecessary packaging and trash?*

- *How can we use composting to reduce our food garbage?*

- *Are there any laws that could be passed to help reduce the amount of trash we generate as a society?*

- *Can we create a garbage-free society?*

After brainstorming these questions, small groups of students select the question they would like to research. They may do so by reading books and articles and by interviewing store managers, local legislators, environmental activists, waste management experts, and local farmers. Students share their findings with the class, including how they acquired their information, and make recommendations for a plan of action. These plans may include writing letters to legislators and manufacturers; raising the consciousness of the community by bringing the garbage simulation to other classes; writing letters to the editor, making signs, and developing public announcements for a local radio station or the school public address system; and starting compost and recycling projects at home and at school. Students report back to the class within a month on the progress of their projects.

Extending the concepts in your class...

In the lunchroom, students can scrape all of their uneaten food into a clear container, which is then weighed, so that the entire school can see how much food is wasted every day and every week.

For younger students, you may elect to run the experiment only with trash generated during the school day.

Involve other classrooms in the experiment. Can they beat your students by generating even less garbage?

Encourage families to conduct the experiment and report their results to the class.

Students and their families can calculate their ecological footprints at http://www.myfootprint.org, compare the size of their footprints to the average for their country or other countries, and then research and choose steps to reduce them.

My New York by Kathy Jakobsen

This book, written in the form of a letter from a young girl to her friend, describes favorite places in New York City that she would like to show her friend when he moves there. She writes about the Statue of Liberty, the Museum of Natural History, the Empire State Building, the subway, the Central Park Zoo, the Plaza Hotel, a new building under construction, the Intrepid, and the harbor. The illustrations are vibrant and include pages that fold out to reflect the size of dinosaurs at the museum and tall buildings around town.

Our students love this book because they have been to, or want to visit, many of the sights depicted here, and many teachers, near to and at a distance from New York City, use the book to allow children to envision this urban center, bursting with people and teeming with energy. However, if this is the only book that teachers use, students will get a limited picture of New York City. Thus, in this lesson we use a variety of books about it that provide many perspectives on the city and its people, including the many subcultures that comprise it. Teachers who do not live near a city can use the same model to explore their own town, allowing students to gain a fuller and more accurate picture of the place they live.

Before reading *My New York,* we ask students to brainstorm what they think of when they hear the word "city." Their lists include tall buildings, sidewalks, and lots of people rushing around; they rarely include trees, parks, open spaces, the variety of jobs people hold, or the different types of people who make the city their home.

Social Studies Concepts and Discussion Questions

Social studies concepts	Questions to ask based on the text
Movement	What forms of transportation do you see in New York City? Why is public transportation so important in a city? For what reasons might people from all over the country and the world come to New York City?
Population density	Where does a city with little space put its telephone wires? What other examples of population density are evident in the design of the city?
Place	What physical (natural) features are found in the city? Why is it important to have parks in a city? What human-made features are found in the city? What is a borough? How does the fact that Manhattan (one of the five boroughs of New York City) is an island affect its history and its character?
Diversity	What evidence do you find that different cultures live together in New York City? How does the diversity of cultures provide advantages to the residents of the city?
Economics	What is the Stock Exchange? What are the different kinds of businesses shown in the story?
Culture	What different options exist in New York City for people who want to be entertained or learn about something? What symbols of, or monuments to, American ideas and culture are found in the city?

Activity

We engage students in a discussion of how their conception of a city may have changed or grown after reading the book. This is a springboard to introducing students to a wide variety of other books that are set in cities. Groups of students each read a different book set in New York City. They then complete a graphic organizer that helps them focus on aspects of the city found in their book, some of which they may not have originally associated with New York City. Different books will have more information about some of the aspects than others. The books include the following:

Barber, Barbara. *Saturday at the New You.* (A girl accompanies her mother to work at the beauty shop.)

Collier, Bryan. *Uptown.* (A tour of the sights of Harlem.)

DiSalvo-Ryan, Dyanne. *City Green.* (A girl helps plant a garden in a vacant lot.)

Hall, Bruce. *Henry and the Kite Dragon.* (Immigrant children from China and Italy clash over sharing space in the city.)

Hartland, Jessie. *Night Shift.* (Tells the stories of people whose jobs require them to work when everyone else is asleep.)

Mak, Kam. *My Chinatown.* (The author shares a year of growing up in a city within a city.)

Nunes, Susan Miho. *The Last Dragon.* (A boy learns about the people and culture of Chinatown.)

Percoli, Matteo. *See the City.* (Architectural view of the East Side and West Side of New York as seen from the harbor.)

Platt, Richard, and Hartas, Leo. *The Apartment.* (A day in the life of the residents of an apartment building.)

Rylant, Cynthia. *An Angel for Solomon Singer.* (A lonely New York City man finds companionship at a café.)

Sis, Peter. *Madlenka.* (A girl's trip around her New York City block is like a trip around the world.)

Another view of the city … as seen in *An Angel for Solomon Singer*

(Name of Book)

(Sample Student Responses)

Aspects of the city	What you found in your book
Physical features found in this view of the city	*lack of crickets* *lack of stars in the sky* *lack of open fields*
Human features found in this view of the city	*streets and avenues* *hotels* *Westway Café* *tall buildings* *lights that shine like stars*
Positive aspects of life in this view of the city	*Caring people like Angel who waits tables at the café "with brown eyes that were lined in the corners from a life of smiling"* *"the lights in the buildings twinkled and shone like stars"* *"the voices of all who passed sounded like conversations of friendly crickets"*
Negative aspects of life in this view of the city	*people can feel lonely, even with a lot of people nearby* *the room has no balcony and no fireplace* *no porch swing* *no picture window for watching the birds* *can't have a cat or dog in the apartment* *not allowed to paint apartment walls another color*
Aspects of culture found in this view of the city	*Angel appears to be Hispanic*
Evidence of population density found in this view of the city	*large buildings* *crowds of people on the streets—too many people to greet individually*
Different jobs found in this view of the city	*waiter*
Write your own idea here: *People come from lots of different places to live in the city*	*Solomon Singer comes from Indiana*

Name _____ Date _____

Student Handout: Different Views of New York City

Directions: Record the name of the book you read about New York City. Based on the book, jot down information you learned about different aspects of the city.

Another view of the city . . . as seen in _____
                                                        (Name of Book)

Aspects of the city	What you found in your book
Physical features found in this view of the city	
Human features found in this view of the city	
Positive aspects of life in this view of the city	
Negative aspects of life in this view of the city	
Aspects of culture found in this view of the city	
Evidence of population density found in this view of the city	
Different jobs found in this view of the city	
Write your own idea here:	

Discussion Questions

- *What did you discover from your book that expanded your idea of what we might find in a city?*
- *What did you discover from your book that expanded your idea of what kinds of people live in a city?*
- *How many "different" New York Cities are there within the one New York City?*
- *How much of what you discovered about how people live in the City depends on their income?*
- *Did you find more positive or negative aspects of the City in your book?*
- *What do people give up when they come to live in the City?*
- *What do people gain when they come to live in the City?*

Applying the Concepts

After students see the great variety of perspectives on New York City, they are ready to depict this variety of views in a class mural. Each group is given a large panel of paper. Using the information on their graphic organizers, they illustrate the aspects of the City that they discovered in their book. The panels are assembled together on a wall. Students view the different panels and decide whether there are aspects of the City absent from the panels. If so, they create other panels that capture these missing aspects.

Extending the concepts in your class . . .

Find out what the five boroughs of New York City are and draw them on a map. Compare how your locale is divided into sections with the borough system in New York.

Go on a field trip in your own community and interview community members to ascertain different points of view to gain a fuller picture of your town.

Make a mural of your town, having students create different panels based on the different parts of town they explore.

What You Know First by Patricia MacLachlan

A child comes to terms with the painful fact that she and her family are leaving their home on the prairie. Initially, she reflects on all of the reasons that she does not want to leave her prairie home. Her parents attempt to console their daughter by talking about all the new things she will see in her new home, like the ocean and trees. Ultimately, she is comforted by the idea that she will help her baby brother know the place where he was born. Although she recognizes that she "cannot take the sky," she realizes that she can bring a little bit of the prairie with her in the form of "a twig of the cottonwood tree, . . . a little bag of prairie dirt."

What You Know First is typically used for language arts lessons in teaching about memoir and emphasizing the literary device of repeated lines. The poetic language of the book details the landscape of the prairie with its "ocean of grass" that is so big, the narrator "can't see where the land begins or where it ends." This book can also provide a link to a social studies lesson on the concept of place and how geographic features can have an impact on people's lives.

Social Studies Concepts and Discussion Questions

Social studies concepts	Questions to ask based on the text
Place	Describe the place where the little girl lives. Describe the place where the little girl is moving. What are the things specific to her prairie home that are important to the little girl? How are people's livelihoods determined by the place where they live?
Climate	What are the season-specific memories the little girl has? What do Uncle Bly's songs reveal about the climate of the prairie?
Identity	Why doesn't the little girl want to move? Why is the cottonwood tree important to the little girl and her family?
Change	How is the cottonwood tree a symbol of change to the little girl and her family? How does the family feel about the move to a new place?
History	What do Uncle Bly's songs reveal about the history of the prairie? How will the little girl become the memory-keeper for her baby brother? What does the little girl's papa mean when he says, "What you know first stays with you?" What artifacts does the little girl choose to take with her and why?

Activity

We use this book as a springboard to analyze and evaluate the impact that geography can have on people's lives. We want our students to recognize that geography is not a list of states and capitals to be memorized; rather, geography helps us understand how and why people live the way they do. The chart that follows provides a framework for this analysis; we begin with the geographic features mentioned in the book and expand the discussion to include a variety of other features. Students analyze how each feature could have both positive and negative effects on the way people live. We provide students with a blank map of the United States that we help them label (with a topographical map as our guide) as we discuss each feature. In the end, they have identified major mountain ranges, rivers, flatlands, and so on.

Name _____ Date _____

Student Handout:
The Impact of Geographic Features

Directions: For each geographic feature listed below, describe and illustrate it in the left-hand column, and then list what might be positive and negative about each feature. As you discuss each feature, label its location on a map of the United States.

Geographic feature description and illustration	Potential positive impact	Potential negative impact
Prairie		
Coastal Region		
Mountains		
Rivers		
Woodlands		

X marks the spot: Look at the physical map of the United States that you have created. Consider the impact of each of the features and draw an X on the area that you believe is the best place to live and be prepared to explain why.

The Impact of Geographic Features (Sample Student Responses)

Directions: For each geographic feature listed below, describe and illustrate it in the left-hand column, and then list what might be positive and negative about each feature. As you discuss each feature, label its location on a map of the United States.

Geographic feature description and illustration	Potential positive impact	Potential negative impact
Prairie *Flat grassy land*	· Good for farming and raising cattle · A lot of open land · Beautiful big sky country	· Extreme weather (lightning storms, tornados, blizzards) · No protection from invaders
Coastal region *Area that borders the ocean*	· Fun water activities (surfing, waterskiing, swimming, etc.) · Fishing jobs · Harbors and ships and boats to trade and travel	· Erosion · Hurricanes or tsunamis · Crowded (high population density) · People fight over control of the ports
Mountains *Land that is high up with big slopes*	· Fun activities (skiing, snowboarding, tubing, hiking) · Beautiful views · Hard to invade (natural barrier)	· Hard to farm · Hard to get to; isolated · Cold winters with a lot of snow
Rivers *A moving body of water that flows into another body of water*	· Provides fertile land (irrigation) · Drinking water, fish · Trade and transportation (if there are no waterfalls) · Water sports: kayaking, canoeing	· Flooding · Drowning · Crowded · People fight for control of the land where the rivers are
Woodlands *Forested area*	· Logging jobs · Wood for building · Quiet and beautiful · Hiking · Wildlife · Fresh air (good for breathing)	· Forest fires · Dangerous animals · Lonely (isolated) · Hard to build roads · Sometimes people cut them down

X marks the spot: Look at the physical map of the United States that you have created. Consider the impact of each of the features and draw an X on the area that you believe is the best place to live and be prepared to explain why.

Applying the Concepts

After we have completed this introductory activity about the impact of geographic features on people's lives, we ask students to analyze and evaluate the impact of the geographic features on the region in which they live. This application activity allows students to realize that the decisions they make about where to live are not always purely geographically based.

Name _____ Date _____

Student Handout:
The Impact of Geographic Features on Your Region

Directions: Use a map to identify the key geographic features in your region. Name and describe the features in the left-hand column (e.g., the Catskill Mountains). Then identify the positives and negatives about each place. Remember: There might be features in your region that were not on the class chart of the United States, such as lakes, valleys, plateaus, climate, and others.

Specific geographic feature and description	Potential positive impact	Potential negative impact

X marks the spot: Consider the impact of each of the features you have found in your region and draw an X on the area that you believe is the best place to live. Write a paragraph that explains why.

Discussion Questions

- *Which factor had the greatest impact on your decision? Why?*

- *How have people in your region adapted to or altered the geographic features around them?*

- *What other factors besides geography and climate would you consider when deciding where to live (access to public transportation, certain stores, school district reputation, job possibilities, population density, proximity to family, etc.)?*

Extending the concepts in your class . . .

Survey students about other places they have lived and their memories, both positive and negative, of those places.

Have students compose poems that focus on the details (a favorite tree, season, person) of the places they live (home, classroom, school, town).

Have students use the same kind of features analysis to evaluate the best room in their house, the best place to hang out in the classroom, and the best place to live in their town.

Compile data on other factors that might influence where people choose to live, for example, access to public transportation, certain stores, school district reputation, job possibilities, population density, and so on.

Think about the different ways we can be memory-keepers today—scrapbooks, digital archives, videos, and so on.

Recommended Books

For a list of books that explore the concept of *Community*, please see the Recommended Books list at the end of Chapter 6: "Individuals, Communities, and Institutions."

Doing Geography

Chesanow, N. *Where Do I Live?* Hauppauge, NY: Barron's Educational Series, 1995. (Chesanow's book shows home, neighborhood, town . . . all the way out to the galaxy.) *How are all places interrelated?*

Hartman, G. *As the Crow Flies: A First Book of Maps.* New York: HarperCollins, 1991. (This book takes a look at different geographic areas from the perspectives of an eagle, rabbit, crow, horse, and gull.) *How do people make sense of the world around them?*

Hopkinson, D. *Sweet Clara and the Freedom Quilt.* New York: Alfred A. Knopf, 1995. (A quilt is used as a representation of the land that will lead escaping slaves to freedom.) *To what extent can a quilt act as a map?*

Leedy, L. *Mapping Penny's World.* New York: Henry Holt, 2000. (After studying maps at school, a girl maps all of her dog's favorite places.) *How do people make sense of where they live?*

Marshall, J. *Red Riding Hood.* New York: Penguin Putnam, 1987. (Marshall offers a retelling of the classic fairy tale.) *How can mapping your world help you understand it?*

Pericoli, M. *See the City.* New York: Alfred A. Knopf, 2004. (Architectural view of the East Side and West Side of New York City.) *How does mapping your "home-place" give you insight into where you live?*

Spier, P. *Gobble, Growl, Grunt.* Garden City, NY: Doubleday, 1971. (The only text is sounds that animals make, but the animals are organized according to the *place* where they live. Most teachers only use it for teaching onomatopoeia, but it would be a great resource to introduce young children to the concept of place.) *What do you notice about the place that each type of animal lives?*

Sweeney, J. *Me on the Map.* New York: Crown, 1996. A girl explains maps, beginning with her bedroom and expanding to street, hometown, state, country, and world, and back again to her bedroom.) *How do people make sense of the world around them?*

Winter, J. *Follow the Drinking Gourd.* New York: Alfred A. Knopf, 1988. (Slaves escape by following the constellations, as described in the Drinking Gourd song.) *How does the sky's geography help us to understand our own world?*

Where We Live Influences How We Live

Aardema, V. *Why Mosquitoes Buzz in People's Ears.* New York: Puffin/Dial, 2004. (A chain of events is traced back to a mosquito's buzzing.) *How do folktales reflect their places of origin?*

Aillaud, C. L. *Recess at 20 Below.* Portland, OR: Alaska Northwest Books/Graphic Arts Center Publishing Company, 2005. (This book includes photographs of children at recess in an elementary school in Alaska.) *How does where we live affect how we live?*

D'Aluisio, F. *What the World Eats.* Berkeley, CA: Tricycle Press, 2008. (This photographic collection explores what the world eats, featuring portraits of twenty-three families from twenty-one countries.) *How does where people live affect what they eat?*

Fleischman, P. *Glass Slippers, Gold Sandals.* New York: Henry Holt, 2007. (This inspired retelling blends many versions of "Cinderella" into a single, extraordinary tale that is a pan-cultural, universally pleasing interweaving of variants from seventeen distinct cultures.) *How does place influence culture?*

Flood, N. B. *The Navajo Year, Walk Through Many Seasons.* Flagstaff, AZ: Salina Bookshelf, 2006. (The yearly cycle of weather, tasks, and customs in a traditional Navajo family.) *How does a place influence culture?*

Heide, F. P., and Gillibrand, J. H. *The Day of Ahmed's Secret.* New York: Mulberry Books, 1990. (The sights and sounds of the streets of Cairo where a boy uses a donkey cart to deliver cans of fuel.) *How does place influence culture?*

Heydlauff, L. *Going to School in India.* Watertown, MA: Charlesbridge, 2005. (Photographs and artwork capture the daily lives of children in India, along with the challenges many must overcome to attend school. *How does place influence culture?*

Hollyer, B. *Let's Eat! What Children Eat Around the World.* New York: Henry Holt, 2004. (Explores the way people eat and live around the world.) *How does what we eat tell us about where we live?*

Hollyer, B. *Wake Up, World! A Day in the Life of Children Around the World.* New York: Henry Holt, 1999. (Take a look inside eight homes in eight countries to see where children sleep, what they eat, how they learn, and how they play.) *How does place influence culture?*

Jackson, E. *It's Back to School We Go! First Day Stories from Around the World.* Minneapolis, MN: The Millbrook Press, 2003. (The first day of school is described for children from eleven countries.) *How does place influence culture?*

Jakobsen, K. *My New York.* Boston: Little, Brown & Company, 2003. (A girl writes a letter to a friend who will soon be moving from the Midwest to New York, detailing all of the sights to see.) *How does place influence culture?*

Kessler, C. *The Best Beekeeper in Lalibela: A Tale from Africa*. New York: Holiday House, 2006. (Ethiopian tale of a girl's quest to challenge societal roles to be the best beekeeper in her village.) *How does where we live influence how we live?*

Lowe, A. *Come and Play: Children of Our World Having Fun*. New York: Bloomsbury, 2008. (Beautiful black-and-white photos show children across the world at play. Opposite each picture are a few simple lines of free verse, which are based on "wordriffs" by students in the editor's New York City grade-school classes.) *How do climate and geography affect how we play? Are children from different places more similar or different?*

MacLachlan, P. *What You Know First*. New York: HarperTrophy, 1998. (As a family prepares to move away from its farm, the daughter reflects on all the things she loves there so that she can tell her baby brother when he grows up.) *What is special about where we live?*

McDermott, G. *Anansi the Spider: A Tale from the Ashanti*. New York: Henry Holt, 1972. (Six sons help their spider father and then discuss who helped the most.) *How do folktales reflect their places of origin?*

Platt, R. *The Apartment Book: A Day in Five Stories*. New York: DK Publishing, 1995. (Illustrates a day in the life of an apartment building by showing activities going on in different units between 7:00 AM and 1:00 AM.) *How does where we live influence our activities?*

Ringgold, F. *Tar Beach*. New York: Crown, 1991. (An African American family's dreams from the roof of their building.) *How does where we live influence how we live?*

Schuett, S. *Somewhere in the World Right Now*. New York: Alfred A. Knopf, 1995. (Schuett describes what is happening in different places around the world at a particular time.) *How does where we live influence how we live?*

Shulevitz, U. *How I Learned Geography*. New York: Farrar, Straus & Giroux, 2008. (As he spends hours studying his father's map, a boy escapes the hunger and misery of refugee life.) *How can a map help us imagine other people and their lives?*

Siebert, D. *Mississippi*. New York: HarperCollins Children's Books, 2001. (The flow of the Mississippi River's history is traced in poem and painting.) *How does a river location influence how we live?*

Singer, M. *On the Same Day in March: A Tour of the World's Weather*. New York: HarperCollins Children's Books, 2000. (A meteorological trip around the globe points out the drastically different weather conditions that can occur in various places, all on the same day.) *How does where we live influence how we live?*

UNICEF. *Celebrations! Festivals, Carnivals, and Feast Days from Around the World*. New York: DK Publishing and UNICEF, 1997. (This book explores celebrations around the world.) *How does where we live affect how we live?*

UNICEF. *Children Just Like Me: A Unique Celebration of Children Around the World*. New York: DK Publishing and UNICEF, 1995. (This is an exploration of how children live around the world.) *How does where we live affect how we live?*

UNICEF. *A Life Like Mine: How Children Live Around the World*. New York: DK Publishing and UNICEF, 2003. (This book explores the rights of children in different countries as well as their living situations.) *How does where we live affect how we live?*

UNICEF. *A School Like Mine: A Unique Celebration of Schools Around the World*. New York: DK Publishing and UNICEF, 2007. (Classrooms around the world are featured in this text.) *How does where we live affect how we live?*

Viorst, J. *Alexander Who Is Not (Do You Hear Me? I Mean It!) Going to Move*. St. Louis, MO: Turtleback Books, 1999. (A boy resists his family's move to a new location.) *What is distinctive about where you live?*

Yolen, J. *The Greyling*. New York: Philomel Books, 1991. (A selchie, a seal transformed into human form, lives on land with a lonely fisherman and his wife, until the day a great storm threatens the fisherman's life.) *How does where we live influence how we live?*

Zemach, M. *It Could Always Be* Worse. New York: Farrar, Straus & Giroux, 1990. (A rabbi's clever advice leads a husband and wife, ultimately, to appreciate what they have.) *How do folktales reflect their places of origin?*

Environment

Asch, F. *The Earth and I.* Orlando, FL: Harcourt Brace, 1994. (A boy talks about the myriad ways he and the planet benefit and enjoy each other.) *How can we live in harmony with nature?*

Baker, J. *Home.* New York: Greenwillow/HarperCollins, 2004. (This wordless book with its beautiful collage illustrations shows a view through a window that changes over a generation from smog and sprawl to trees, birds, and sky.) *How can people reclaim the environment in their communities?*

Bang, M. *Common Ground: The Water, Earth and Air We Share.* New York: Blue Sky Press, 1998. (A parable of overgrazing the land long ago raises issues of preserving and sharing the earth today.) *How can we satisfy our needs without overusing the earth's resources?*

Base, G. *Uno's Garden.* New York: Abrams Books for Young Readers, 2006. (Uno loves the forest and creates a garden, but development crowds it out; ultimately, Uno's descendants nurture the forest back into balance with human life.) *How can we find a balance between human development and nature?*

Baylor, B. *The Other Way to Listen.* New York: Scribner, 1978. (A little girl learns how to listen to the natural world around her.) *How can paying attention to our environment affect our attitude toward our environment?*

Bethel, E. *Michael Recycle.* London: Worthwhile Books, 2008. (The adventures of a young superhero whose powers allow him to teach people about recycling.) *What responsibility do we have for our environment?*

Burk, S. *Let the River Run Silver Again! How One School Helped Return the American Shad to the Potomac River—and How You Too Can Help Protect and Restore Our Living Waters.* Granville, OH: McDonald & Woodward, 2005. (An environmental conservation success story of elementary students who helped restore the fish population in the Chesapeake Bay watershed.) *To what extent can young people have an impact on the environment?*

Cherry, L. *A River Ran Wild.* San Diego: Harcourt Brace Jovanovich, 2002. (An environmental history of the Nashua River, ending with the cleanup that revitalized it.) *To what extent can citizens reclaim a river?*

Cooney, B. *Miss Rumphius.* New York: Viking Press, 1982. (As she travels, a woman makes the world more beautiful.) *Whose responsibility is it to beautify the environment?*

DiSalvo-Ryan, D. *City Green.* New York: Morrow Junior Books, 1994. (A girl and her neighbor start a campaign to clean up an empty lot and turn it into a community garden.) *What responsibility do we have for our environment?*

Doner, K. *On a Road in Africa.* Berkeley, CA: Tricycle Press, 2008. (The story of an animal rescuer—the real-life "Mama orphanage"—who collects donations of food from the community to feed the animals at the Nairobi Animal Orphanage.) *Whose responsibility is it to preserve and nurture the animal populations in our communities?*

Fleming, D. *Where There Once Was a Wood.* New York: Henry Holt, 1996. (Fleming describes how wildlife is displaced by development.) *Whose responsibility is it to preserve the environment and the animals that live in it?*

Frasier, D. *On the Day You Were Born.* Orlando, FL: Harcourt Brace & Company, 2005. (Frasier tells the story of what went on in the universe on the day a child was born.) *How is a birth a significant part of the cycle of the environment?*

George, J. C. *The Wolves Are Back*. New York: Dutton Children's Books, 2008. (How wolves were brought back from near extinction in our country.) *Whose responsibility is it to preserve different species?*

Gibbons, G. *Recycle: A Handbook for Kids*. Boston: Little, Brown & Company, 1996. (Explains the process of recycling from start to finish and how it helps make our planet a safer and healthier place to live.) *How important is recycling for the health of our planet?*

Inches, A. *The Adventures of an Aluminum Can: A Story About Recycling*. New York: Little Simon (Simon & Schuster for Young Readers), 2009. (Journey with a can from its origin in a bauxite rock, to a manufacturing line, to the store shelf, to the garbage can and then to the recycling plant where it is reincarnated as an aluminum bat.) *What responsibility do we have for our environment?*

Inches, A. *The Adventures of a Plastic Bottle: A Story About Recycling*. New York: Little Simon (Simon & Schuster for Young Readers), 2009. (Readers learn about recycling from the free-spirited perspective of a plastic bottle.) *What responsibility do we have for our environment?*

Lasky, K. *John Muir: America's First Environmentalist*. Cambridge, MA: Candlewick Press, 2008. (The story of John Muir, who was passionate about nature and conservation and was instrumental in the development of Yosemite Park and the creation of the Sierra Club.) *How can one individual make a difference in the preservation of the environment?*

Lasky, K. *She's Wearing a Dead Bird on Her Head*. New York: Hyperion Books for Children, 1995. (Historical fiction picture book chronicling two proper Boston women who became disgusted over the fashion trend of wearing bird feathers—and sometimes even whole, stuffed birds—on the hats of "stylish" ladies. The women educated the public and helped to form the Audubon Society to pass protective legislation.) *Whose responsibility is it to preserve and nurture the animal populations in our communities?*

Madden, D. *The Wartville Wizard*. New York: Macmillan, 1986. (A spell attaches people's litter to them for all to see.) *What role do we or should we play in cleaning up our environment?*

McLerran, A. *Roxaboxen*. New York: Lothrop, Lee & Shepard, 1991. (A hill covered with rocks and wooden boxes becomes an imaginary town for a girl, her sisters, and her friends.) *How do people shape their environments?*

Rockwell, A. *What's So Bad About Gasoline? Fossil Fuels and What They Do*. New York: HarperCollins, 2009. (Presents basic facts about gasoline—how it was discovered, how it used and produced—and then goes on to explain that because it is used so widely, it pollutes the environment.) *How can we find the balance between human development and protecting our environment?*

Schnetzler, P. *Earth Day Birthday*. Nevada City, CA: Dawn, 2004. (A great way to inform kids about Earth Day and what they can do to help the environment.) What responsibility do we have for our environment?

Schulman, J. *Pale Male: Citizen Hawk of New York City*. New York: Alfred A. Knopf, 2008. (The real-life story of the hawk and his mate who built their nest near the top of a Fifth Avenue apartment building and the residents' differing reactions to them.) *Who should be responsible for making decisions about wildlife in cities?*

Wong, J. *The Dumpster Diver*. Cambridge, MA: Candlewick Press, 2007. (A story about a quirky neighborhood man who recruits the local kids to help him figure out ways to reuse and reincarnate the things he finds in the garbage.) *To what extent can "junk" be recycled?*

Reference

Center for Sustainable Economy, "How Big Is Your Ecological Footprint?" http://www.myfootprint.org/ (cited July 22, 2009).

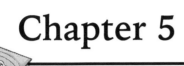

Chapter 5

Individual Development and Identity

Often used as a model for good writing techniques in the elementary grades, *When I Was Young in the Mountains* by Cynthia Rylant is the story of her childhood in the Appalachian Mountains. Its repeated line, "When I was young in the mountains . . ." provides an excellent prompt for students to begin their own pieces. Through its detailed descriptions ("When I was young in the mountains, Grandfather came home in the evening covered with the black dust of the coal mine. Only his lips were clean, and he used them to kiss the top of my head"), students come to understand how to "show, not tell" in their own work.

We use this beautifully written book to emphasize that we are the sum total of our experiences. The events of our lives, where we were born, how we were brought up, the people we remember, the joys and the difficulties—all make us who we are. To this end, we ask our students to go back through the book and identify all of the different influences that made Cynthia Rylant who she is. Students notice the hard work (her grandfather coming back dirty and tired from his job in the mine), the chores (carrying and heating water for baths), the simple way of having fun (swimming in the swimming hole) and the loving relationships with her family members (the kiss on the top of her head from her grandfather). Our students discover that the parts of their lives that they often take for granted, the quotidian details of their lives, are the experiences that shape them as people. All of the experiences in the story help us create categories we can use to examine the influences on our own families' lives. Students use these categories when they interview parents and grandparents to see what made them the people they are, what gave them their identity. This activity prepares our students to study the lives of people who made a difference and analyze the experiences that led them to become influential figures that shaped their societies.

Seven Blind Mice by Ed Young, *The Araboolies of Liberty Street* by Sam Swope, and *I've Seen the Promised Land: The Life of Dr. Martin Luther King, Jr.* by Walter Dean Myers enable students to explore the different perspectives that are shaped by individuals' upbringings and environments.

Essential Questions

How do we become the people we are?

How does our identity affect what we see and do?

How do you balance individual identity with societal pressures to conform?

To what extent do early life experiences shape our actions as adults?

Seven Blind Mice by Ed Young

Ed Young retells the famous Indian fable of the seven blind men who individually investigate the different parts of an elephant and argue about what they each have found. In this story, seven blind mice replace the seven blind men. Upon encountering an elephant, six of the seven mice each believe that they have found something different—a snake, a fan, a cliff, and so on—because they "see" from their own vantage point The seventh mouse, however, goes all the way up, down, and around the "Something," and she discovers the truth: that all of the parts together make up an elephant.

Students love the mystery in trying to figure out what each mouse thinks he "sees." We value this book because it provides us with the opportunity to lay the foundation for what is essential in our classes: that students consider perspective and seek out reliable information before drawing conclusions.

Activity

(Social studies concepts and discussion questions follow this opening activity).

Several days before reading the book, we have students write in class about a memorable event in their lives. Students often write about being in a family wedding, getting a new pet, a religious rite of passage, a block party, or a family vacation. We collect the students' papers and then assign them to interview someone else who was present at the same event (often a relative). In class the next day, students compare their version of the event with that of their relative, making a list of similarities and differences. Students often discover that their recollection has a totally different emphasis than their relative's. For example, one student recalled a block party and the fun and excitement of riding her scooter up and down the street all day long, while her mother remembered the headache and expense of ordering all of the food. The comparisons also can reveal factual differences between the two versions. One of our students told about the fishing trip he took with his father. In the boy's version, he caught ten fish; in his father's version, only seven were caught.

Stories where there are factual discrepancies, like the fishing trip, provide us with the opportunity to discuss how such different versions could exist and how we can figure out where the truth lies. We ask students what information they would need to figure out whose recollection about the number of fish caught was accurate. Students brainstorm alternate sources of information: photos of the fish caught, videos from the day, the bait seller's receipts about how much bait was sold, the recollection of the person who rented them the boat, the person who cooked the fish, the diary entry by the child who caught the fish, the number of fish in the freezer, and some kids even suggest reconstructing the fish bones in the garbage to ascertain the true number of fish caught. After these sources of information are generated, we ask students to consider the reliability of each. Perhaps the most interesting discussion revolves around the diary, as students explore why diaries may or may not be reliable sources. In this activity, students go through the same process as historians; they amass a variety of sources and try to assess their accuracy. This is also an opportune time to introduce students to the terms, "primary source" and "secondary source."

After this activity, we read *Seven Blind Mice* aloud.

Before we get to the end of the book, we ask students to figure out what the moral of the story is. We also ask them about the connection between the book and the memorable event activity.

Social Studies Concepts and Discussion Questions

Social studies concepts	Questions to ask based on the text
Identity	In what color does each mouse "see" the part of the elephant it encounters? Why do you think the author does this? To what extent do you think people see things through their own eyes?
Change	Why do the mice change their views about what they have "seen"? How did the white mouse help the other mice reconsider their initial impressions?
Historical evidence	What's the moral of the story? What is the connection between the moral of this tale and the study of history?

Applying the Concepts

This is a perfect time to engage students in an analysis of current events. Students work in groups to investigate a current events topic that interests them, for example, a presidential speech, the passing of a law, a traffic accident, international events/crises, even a sporting event. Students use the chart on the next page to record how the event is reported in a variety of sources, including newspapers and news broadcasts. We encourage students to use the Internet to access headlines from newspapers across the country. For example, in sports, hometown papers may have wildly different emphases and tone in their coverage of the same game. After a Yankee loss, New York papers might proclaim, "We Wuz Robbed," whereas the other team's hometown paper might write, "Angels Crush Yanks." The New York paper blamed a few bad rulings by the umpires for the loss, whereas the California paper credited the talent of its team for the win.

Name _____   Date _____

Student Handout: Analyzing the News

Directions: Use the chart below to analyze how three different news sources report the same event.

Current Events Topic:_____			
	Source 1:	Source 2:	Source 3:
Headline			
Facts of the story			
Tone of the story			
Sources quoted in the story			

What differences did you discover in the way the three sources covered the same story?

Which source do you think is most reliable and why?

From *Every Book Is a Social Studies Book: How to Meet Standards with Picture Books, K–6* by Andrea S. Libresco, Jeannette Balantic, and Jonie C. Kipling. Santa Barbara, CA: Libraries Unlimited. Copyright © 2011.

Discussion Questions

- *What is the value in consulting three different news sources?*

- *To what extent did where the news was published or broadcast affect its coverage?*

- *What questions does the coverage of this story raise in your mind?*

- *To what extent does this comparison affect what papers you might read and news channels you might watch in the future?*

- *It is often said that "Journalism is the first draft of history." What do you think this means? If it's true, why do the lessons learned from this activity matter?*

Extending the concepts in your class ...

Compare *The True Story of the Three Little Pigs* with "The Three Little Pigs" fairy tale and brainstorm sources that would help students figure out who's telling the truth.

After a special event in the school or your class, have all of the students write their own accounts of what happened. When students share their accounts, discuss how the versions differ.

Invite in a reporter to discuss how she or he tries to gather facts for a story, as well as how she or he tries to keep personal biases out of the story.

After reading *The Pain and the Great One*, have students with siblings talk about the different perspectives they and their siblings may have about their families.

The Araboolies of Liberty Street by Sam Swope

General Pinch and his wife rule the residents of Liberty Street, preventing all laughter and nonconformity. When the Araboolies move in, with their colorful sense of individuality and gaiety, everything begins to change. As the General tries to force the family out, the children of the town come to their defense in a creative show of support.

The Araboolies of Liberty Street might be used as an example of how to write with humor or in an antibullying unit, as the townsfolk stand up to the mean General Pinch and his wife. We use the book to emphasize the importance and power of being one's own person and celebrating individuality. All different kinds of people contribute to their communities; thus, communities should make room for diversity.

Social Studies Concepts and Discussion Questions

Social studies concepts	Questions to ask based on the text
Identity	Why do you think the author named the General "General Pinch?" Describe the Araboolie family. Why do you think the author named the little girl who organizes the resistance "Joy"? Who is the hero/heroine of the book? How does the identity of the town change overnight? How do you suppose the people of the town change as the look of their town changes? To what extent should newcomers to a town assimilate? To what extent should a town support the cultural pluralism of its residents?
Freedom	What would you expect to find on a street named "Liberty"? What is ironic about what actually happens on "Liberty" Street? Was it OK for Joy and the other children to sneak out from their houses to execute their plan? Throughout the book, how much freedom is there on Liberty Street?
Conformity	Before the Araboolies move in, how is Liberty Street an example of conformity? What are the positives and negatives of this conformity? Why do you think the townsfolk go along with every house looking the same? How does the Araboolie family respond to General Pinch's threats? How do the townspeople respond to the presence of the Araboolies? Describe the town the morning that the army was to arrive.
Power	What behaviors are upsetting to the Pinches? What do they threaten to do in response to those behaviors? How do the parents and children feel about General Pinch's rules? Why do they go along with the rules? Why are the Pinches so upset when "things were getting out of control?" What is the purpose of an army? Was General Pinch's order to the army just? What is ironic about how the story ends?
Tolerance	Why do the Pinches find the colorful Araboolies and their habits to be "revolting"? How would you feel if the Araboolies lived next door to you? How do you respond to people who look or act different from you? Do you think the Pinches should have been allowed to stay?

Activity

The Araboolies of Liberty Street presents two extremes. At the beginning of the story, total conformity reigns. By the end of the book, the street has become completely wacky, and those who crave order have been removed. The questions below frame a class discussion that helps our students explore issues of self-expression and conformity, as they seek to find their own balance.

Discussion Questions

- *What does it mean to express yourself?*
- *How do we express ourselves (e.g., clothes, hairstyle, cars, houses, jewelry, etc.)?*
- *Can self-expression ever lead to problems for others?*
- *How can people retain their individuality and live together peacefully with others in a community?*
- *How could* The Araboolies of Liberty Street *have had a better outcome for all of its residents?*
- *Can community rules allow the Araboolies and the Pinches to be who they are and live happily together on the same block?*
- *Who should develop community rules that govern behavior?*

We reread the story from the beginning to the point where the Araboolies' ball comes through the Pinches' window, and General Pinch declares, "This means war." At this point, we ask students to work in groups to complete one of the following activities that results in the Araboolies and the Pinches being able both to preserve their individuality and to coexist on their street. Each of the activities requires that students consider the points of view of both the Araboolies and the Pinches, as well as the balance between self-expression and community needs.

- Act out a skit of the discussion that might ensue between the Araboolies and the Pinches as they try to arrive at consensus regarding the balance between individuality and community rules.

- Rewrite the story so that it reflects the Araboolies' and the Pinches' efforts to arrive at consensus regarding the balance between individuality and community rules.

- Draw a revised picture of the final page of the book, showing what the community would look like if the Araboolies and the Pinches were to arrive at consensus regarding the balance between individuality and community rules.

Discussion Questions

- *In doing the rewrite, how difficult was it to find a balance between individual expression and community rules?*
- *In which skit, story, or picture do you think the group found the best balance between individual expression and community rules?*

Applying the Concepts

So that students can see the real-life application of the balance between individuality and community rules, we read an article with our students and have them either write a letter to the editor or draw a political cartoon, expressing their views on the issue. An article we often use is "Novelist's Purple Palette Is Not to Everyone's

Taste" by Sara Rimer, published in the *New York Times* on Monday, July 13, 1998 (available at http://www.nytimes.com/1998/07/13/us/san-antonio-journal-novelist-s-purple-palette-is-not-to-everyone-s-taste.html). It discusses the poet and novelist Sandra Cisneros's controversial purple house in San Antonio and the reaction it causes among her neighbors.

We ask students to weigh in on this real-life scenario in which Sandra Cisneros's community seeks to balance individual expression and community standards. We engage students in a "four corners" activity. Each corner of the room is labeled with a sign: *Strongly agree, Agree, Disagree, Strongly disagree.* Students react to the statement, "Sandra Cisneros should have to repaint her house a color more acceptable to the community" by moving to the corner of the room that reflects their view. We discuss the different positions. Students have the opportunity to change their opinion based on the discussion; if they do so, they move to the corner of the room that reflects their new position.

The culminating activity requires students to draw a cartoon or write a letter to the editor in which they express their opinion as to whether Sandra Cisneros should have to repaint her house. Letters and cartoons must reflect their position on how to balance individual expression and community standards. (For an activity that introduces students to the skill of political cartoon analysis, see Appendix B.)

Name _____   Date _____

Student Handout:
The Purple House—A Response Letter to the Editor

Directions: Use the template below to write a letter to the editor that expresses your opinion as to whether or not Sandra Cisneros should have to repaint her house.

To the Editor:

With regard to "San Antonio Journal; Novelist's Purple Palette is not to Everyone's Taste" (July 13, 1998), Sandra Cisneros should/should not have to repaint her house because _____

_____

_____

_____

_____

_____

_____

_____

_____

_____

_____

_____

_____

Sincerely,

From *Every Book Is a Social Studies Book: How to Meet Standards with Picture Books, K–6* by Andrea S. Libresco, Jeannette Balantic, and Jonie C. Kipling. Santa Barbara, CA: Libraries Unlimited. Copyright © 2011.

Name _____ Date _____

Student Handout:
The Purple House—A Cartoon Response

Directions: Think about what your position or opinion is on whether Sandra Cisneros should be allowed to paint her house, then draw a political cartoon that reflects your view.

As you begin to consider what you want to draw, ask yourself the following questions:

- What is your topic/issue? (Sandra Cisneros's house)

- What is your opinion/position on the topic/issue?

- Who are the people you want to portray?

- Where will the scene take place? Does it have to be the real setting related to the topic/issue?

- What symbols can you use to represent the issues and/or people?

- If you can't draw people, how will we know who is in your picture?

After you have answered the questions, sketch something out. This will help you develop your idea. Then draw your cartoon on good paper. Try to fill the entire page with your cartoon (don't make the people, objects, or words too tiny), and feel free to add color.

You MUST get your message across to people—it is hard to do, but it is the point of drawing a cartoon! You are not simply *illustrating* an event; you must convey a message (your opinion!).

Go for it! Once your cartoon is completed, show it to someone to see if he or she "gets it"—is your opinion clearly represented?

Remember: You don't have to be able to draw well; you just have to have a point of view!

From *Every Book Is a Social Studies Book: How to Meet Standards with Picture Books, K–6* by Andrea S. Libresco, Jeannette Balantic, and Jonie C. Kipling. Santa Barbara, CA: Libraries Unlimited. Copyright © 2011.

Extending the concepts in your class . . .

Research how Sandra Cisneros's purple house story turned out. Do you agree with the outcome?

Play the song, "Little Boxes" and analyze the connections between the message of the lyrics and the message of *The Araboolies of Liberty Street*. Available at: people.wkv.edu/charles.smith/MALVINA/mr094.htm

Explore the zoning laws in your community with regard to fence height, house color, house extensions, tree removal, and so on. Discuss the extent to which the community supports the laws.

I've Seen the Promised Land: The Life of Dr. Martin Luther King, Jr. by Walter Dean Myers

Every teacher has a favorite biography of Martin Luther King, Jr. that he or she probably uses each January 15 or during Black History Month (February). Many elementary teachers read *Martin's Big Words* by Doreen Rappaport, which highlights quotes that shaped or reflected King's life as a civil rights activist. This document-based picture book is an excellent choice to engage students in an analysis of Dr. King's words. However, there are myriad books on Dr. King that give insight into other aspects of his work and life.

Walter Dean Myers's *I've Seen the Promised Land: The Life of Dr. Martin Luther King, Jr.* complements *Martin's Big Words* in that it provides rich detail of the actions taken by Dr. King and other protesters and the reactions they met with from other citizens. Myers's book traces the chronology of Dr. King's life and participation in the Civil Rights Movement, including the conflicts among civil rights activists regarding tactics. The juxtaposition of the two books enables students to see the value of multiple sources in the investigation of any individual or event.

Social Studies Concepts and Discussion Questions

Social studies concepts	Questions to ask based on the text
Justice and rights	How did Dr. King's early life in the South affect his later actions? How did people react to Dr. King's call for equality? How did local police and governments react to civil rights protesters? How far were Dr. King and his family willing to go to achieve equality and justice in America? Would you have been willing to go as far? What was the significance of the "I have a dream" speech?
Change	How important was Dr. King's leadership in effecting change in America? Why did Dr. King insist on the philosophy and tactics of nonviolence? What were the arguments of those who disagreed? Which arguments do you find most persuasive? Why do you think that Dr. King remained committed to the belief that justice would win out over evil (even in the face of bombings, jailings, and assassinations)?
Economic justice	Why did Dr. King march with the striking sanitation workers in Memphis? Why did Dr. King speak out against poverty?
Democracy	What role did Dr. King believe individuals should play in our democracy? What do you think Dr. King thought was the promise of America?
Power	What role did the United States government play in the Civil Rights Movement? To what extent did individuals make a difference in this movement?

Activity

The reading and discussion of *I've Seen the Promised Land* takes place after students have read *Martin's Big Words*. The benefit of reading the two books one after the other enables students to see the importance of consulting multiple sources in order to gain a deeper understanding of a person's life and impact on history. The analysis of these two biographies serves as a model for students to read and share biographies on different historical activists in their own literature circles.

We frame our class analysis of the Martin Luther King, Jr. biographies around the same questions that will ultimately guide students' subsequent literature circles on different activists. Each question is written on a separate piece of chart paper. Students first respond to the questions based on our reading of *Martin's Big Words*; we record those answers in blue. After we read *I've Seen the Promised Land,* we go back and answer the questions again; we record those answers in red (we've used different fonts to indicate this in the chart below). Thus, students can see that different books yield different information on the same historical figure.

What societal need did the individual discover, and how did this discovery shape her or his motivation to be a change agent?	What characteristics (personal, family, societal) shaped the individual's ability to be a change agent?
<ul><li>"Whites only" signs in his home town</li><li>Poverty in society and low income jobs</li><li>Segregation on buses and in other areas of society</li><li>*Heard his father called "boy"*</li></ul>	<ul><li>Hearing his father (a minister) preach</li><li>Father a highly respected minister</li><li>His parents and the Bible—everyone can be great!</li><li>The teachings of Gandhi—love over hate</li><li>Born in the Atlanta</li><li>His wife Coretta Scott King supported him even though she had a small baby</li><li>Traveled to India to study Gandhi's teachings of nonviolence</li><li>*A law in one city that blacks and whites could not play checkers or dominoes together*</li></ul>
What obstacles did the individual face in his or her struggle for change?	How did the individual contribute to the society in which she or he lived?
<ul><li>During the Montgomery bus boycott—and numerous other times—he was arrested</li><li>Different ideas about how you change things (fists vs. love)</li><li>Malcolm X differed with King over methods to achieve equality</li><li>Assaulted with firehoses, bitten by dogs</li><li>Mayors, police, and courts who told them to stop marching</li><li>Bombing of 16th Street Baptist Church: four little girls killed</li><li>Northern riots</li><li>Death threats and house bombings</li><li>Assassinated</li><li>JFK, friend to Civil Rights Movement, assassinated</li><li>Malcolm X murdered</li><li>*FBI ignores warnings of white mob action—let violence happen*</li></ul>	<ul><li>A well-known minister in Montgomery, he was asked to lead the boycott</li><li>Helped lead the Montgomery Bus Boycott, which lasted 381 days</li><li>Supreme court declared bus segregation unconstitutional</li><li>Participated in marches, gave speeches, spoke out against poverty</li><li>"I Have a Dream" speech inspired people.</li><li>April 3, 1968, speech: "I have been to the mountain top and seen the Promised Land"</li><li>"Whites only" signs came down</li><li>Won Nobel Peace Prize</li><li>Helped garbage collectors</li><li>MLK Day—federal holiday</li><li>Voting Rights Act of 1965</li><li>*Spoke out against Vietnam War*</li></ul>

Some of our students got so excited about the comparison that they read other books on Dr. King to try to find out more information; we added their new information to our chart paper. The entries in purple reflect a sampling of information from . . . *If You Lived at the Time of Martin Luther King* by Ellen Levine.

The final part of the analysis of Dr. King's life is an examination of the monuments that have been erected to honor his leadership in the Civil Rights Movement. On the next page are two images from Maya Lin's famous civil rights monument in Montgomery, Alabama, but there are many monuments designed to honor Dr. King in a variety of communities (Google Images, Martin Luther King, Jr. Monuments).

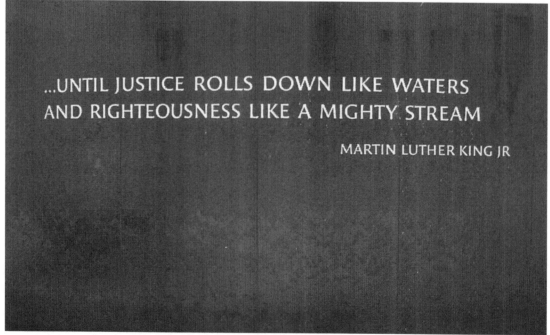

The Civil Rights Monument in Montgomery, Alabama, designed by Maya Lin.

- *What elements of Dr. King's life and teachings are reflected in the monuments?*

- *What symbols do the artists use? Why?*

- *Which words from Dr. King have the artists selected? Why?*

Applying the Concepts

Now that students see the value of reading multiple works on the same person, they are ready to participate in literature circles to analyze biographies of citizens who made a difference in America. Teachers often use literature circles to have students analyze works of fiction. In the literature circles detailed below, students in each circle read nonfiction works; each student reads a different biography about the same person, and they share what they discover.

Students work in small groups to complete this assignment. First, they select an individual who made a difference from the list below. At the library, each student in the group selects a biography at her or his reading level. As students read their biographies, they focus on the four questions that guided their reading of the Martin Luther King, Jr. books.

- *What societal need did the individual discover, and how did this discovery shape her or his motivation to be a change agent?*

- *What characteristics (personal, family, societal) shaped the individual's ability to be a change agent?*

- *What obstacles did the individual face in his or her struggle for change?*

- *How did your individual contribute to the society in which she or he lived?*

Students then come together to share and compare what they learned from their respective biographies. Each group also designs a monument to honor the leadership of the person researched. Below is the list of citizens who made a difference that we give our students:

Abigail Adams	Benjamin Franklin
Susan B. Anthony	Dolores Huerta
Mary McLeod Bethune	Langston Hughes
Elizabeth Blackwell	Thomas Jefferson
Nelly Bly	Thurgood Marshall
John Brown	Malcolm X
Rachel Carson	Jackie Robinson
Cesar Chavez	Eleanor Roosevelt
Frederick Douglass	Ida B. Wells-Barnett

Students present their monument ideas or sketches to the class. During these presentations, students must answer the question, *How did your individual contribute to the society in which she or he lived?* Ultimately, the sketches are hung around the classroom with a museum card (index card) that explains how the individual contributed to society.

Our class discussion revolves around the extent to which individuals can make a difference in society. In addition, we have students consider how reading life stories of significant individuals affects the way they want to live their own lives. Finally, we ask students to assess their books as biographies and elicit from them the attributes of a good biography.

Extending the concepts in your class . . .

Enlist art teachers to help with the design of the monuments.

In lieu of full-class presentations, jigsaw the students so that they share biographies of different individuals in small groups to develop a list of attributes common to activists.

Have students create a poster for the library that outlines the qualities of a good biography.

Have students write "Student's Selection" blurbs for the biographies they have read to be posted on the shelves in the library à la Barnes and Noble employee picks.

If you use a textbook in your class, students can check to see if these activists get their due in the text. If not, information about the person can be inserted in the textbook on a Post-it note.

Recommended Books

For a list of books that explore heritage, please see *Immigration* on the Recommended Books list at the end of Chapter 2: "Culture."

Identity

Beaumont, K. *I Like Myself!* Orlando: Harcourt, 2004. (A curly-haired African American girl always emphatically proclaims "I like myself!" despite what she is doing or what others may think.) *Who defines who we are?*

Bunting, E. *Young Cheyenne.* New York: Houghton Mifflin, 1995. (A young American Indian boy named Young Bull struggles to hold on to his cultural identity when he is forced to go to an all-white school off the reservation.) *Who defines who we are?*

Common. *I Like You but I Love Me.* Chicago: Hip Hop School House, 2006. (When a young African American boy tries to change himself to win the affections of a girl, he learns an important lesson about self-love.) *How important is a sense of self?*

Cotton, C. *Abbie in Stitches.* New York: Farrar, Straus & Giroux, 2006. (In the 1800s, Abbie would rather read than work on the needlework her mother expects her to master. She finds creative ways to express her dislike for this work.) *What are different ways that people can express their identities?*

Henkes, K. *Chrysanthemum.* New York: Greenwillow Books, 2007. (In this classic tale, a young female mouse learns to take pride in and love her unique and beautiful name.) *How much a part of our identity are our names?*

Hoffman, M. *Amazing Grace.* New York: Dial Books for Young Readers, 1991. (Although classmates say that she cannot play Peter Pan because she is Black and a girl, Grace discovers that she can do anything she puts her mind to.) *Who defines who we are?*

Kessler, L. *Mr. Pine's Purple House.* Cynthiana, KY: Purple House Press, 1965. (On a street with all white houses, Mr. Pine decides to break with conformity and paint his house a different color.) *How do you balance individual identity with societal pressures to conform?*

Kuskin, K. *I Am Me.* New York: Simon & Schuster Books for Young Children, 2000. (A story about a girl who learns that despite bearing remarkable resemblances to many of her family members she remains her own unique person.) *How much is family background a part of identity?*

Lionni, L. *A Color of His Own*. New York: Knopf Books for Young Readers, 2006. (The story of a chameleon that is displeased with his changeable appearance because he has no color of his own like every other animal, but he learns there are more important things in life than this.) *What is the relationship between identity and friendship?*

Lionni, L. *Pezzetino*. New York: Knopf Books for Young Readers, 2006. (Pezzetino is so small, he is convinced that he must be a part of someone else, until he meets a wise man who tells him the truth.) *How important is a sense of self?*

Lynn, L. R. *The Mirror and Me*. Chicago: Hip Hop School House, 2005. (A young African American boy is teased at his new school in New York City and attempts to change his identity to fit in. He learns that to earn the respect of others, he must first learn to respect himself.) *Who defines who we are?*

Meltzer, A. *A Mezuzah on the Door*. Minneapolis: Kar-Ben, 2007. (A young boy learns about his Jewish identity when he and his family move to the suburbs.) *What role does religion play in our identity?*

Parr, T. *It's Okay to be Different*. New York: Hachette Book Group, 2001. (Not only does this book show children that it's okay to be different, it also goes a step further and makes readers feel like anything goes as long as you are being honest with yourself.) *To what extent are our differences strengths?*

Payne, T. *The Hippo-Not-Amus*. New York: Orchard Books, 2003. (A young hippopotamus, tired of being a hippo, sets off on a journey to find his true self.) *How important is a sense of self?*

Reynolds, P. *Ish*. Cambridge, MA: Candlewick Press, 2004. (Ramon loses confidence in his ability to draw, but his sister gives him a new perspective on things.) *How do others' ideas about us affect our identities?*

Rousaki, M. *Unique Monique*. San Diego: Kane/Miller Book Publishers, 2008. (An engaging story about a girl who wants and learns to be different by following the rules.) *To what extent is what we wear part of our identity?*

Rylant, C. *When I Was Young in the Mountains*. New York: Dutton, 1982. (Reminiscences of the pleasures of life in the mountains as a child.) *How does where we grow up influence who we become?*

Scieszka, J. *Math Curse*. New York: Viking, 1995. (When the teacher tells her students that they can think of almost everything as a math problem, the narrator is afflicted with a "math curse" that affects how every facet of the day is viewed.) *How does our identity affect what we see and do?*

Swope, S. *The Araboolies of Liberty Street*. New York: Potter; distributed by Crown, 1989. (An irrepressible, multicolored family moves into and changes a neighborhood bullied by conformists.) *To what extent should a community support the individualism of its residents?*

Tarpley, N. *I Love My Hair*. Boston: Little, Brown & Company, 1998. (A young African American girl describes the different, wonderful ways she can wear her hair.) *What are different ways people can express their own identities?*

Tyler, M. *The Skin You Live In*. Chicago: Chicago Children's Museum, 2005. (By using an easy vocabulary and a nice rhythm, this story shows children the importance of celebrating diversity and accepting who they are.) *How important are our looks as part of our identity?*

Vail, R. *Sometimes I'm Bombaloo*. New York: Scholastic Press, 2002. (A girl gets angry but learns how to calm herself.) *How much control do we have about how we behave?*

Waber, B. *"You Look Ridiculous," Said the Rhinoceros to the Hippopotamus*. New York: Houghton Mifflin, 1973. (It is best to be yourself, even if you're a big, fat hippopotamus.) *How important are our looks as part of our identity?*

Perspective

Banyai, I. *Zoom*. New York: Viking, 1995. (This wordless picture book re-creates the effect of a camera lens zooming out, letting the reader realize that our vision of what is real is always a tiny piece of what really is.) *How does our angle of vision help shape our perspective?*

Browne, A. *Voices in the Park*. New York: DK Publishing, 1998. (A trip to the park is viewed from four different perspectives.) *How do our backgrounds shape our perspectives?*

Catrow, D., and Cuyler, M. *That's Good!, That's Bad!* New York: Henry Holt, 1993. (A little boy has a series of adventures and misadventures.) *How can the same event be looked at as both positive and negative?*

Crow, K. *Middle Child Blues*. New York: G.P. Putnam's Sons, 2009. (A boy named Lee sings about all the miserable aspects of being a middle child.) *To what extent do early-life experiences shape our actions as adults?*

L'Engle, M. *The Other Dog*. New York: Sea Star Books, 2001. (The family poodle protests at first when the family brings home a new "dog" to share the household.) *How does our identity affect what we see and do?*

Sciescka, J. *Math Curse*. New York: Viking, 1995. (A boy's teacher suggests that everything can be seen as a math problem, and then he starts to see daily activities through the prism of mathematical equations.) *How might everything be seen as a social studies issue?*

Young, E. *Seven Blind Mice*. New York: Putnam, 2002. (Retells the Indian tale of seven blind men who try to decide what an elephant is like based on examining only one part of it.) *How does our angle of vision help shape our perspective?*

Biographies

Bardhan-Quallen, S. *Ballots for Belva: The True Story of a Woman's Race for the Presidency*. New York: Abrams Books for Young Readers, 2008. (The story of Belva Lockwood, who fought to go to college, law school, and to be a candidate for president.) *How do our backgrounds and experiences shape the people we become?*

Bass, H. *The Secret World of Walter Anderson*. Cambridge, MA: Candlewick Press, 2009. (The life story of an eccentric naturalist/painter along the Mississippi Gulf Coast, best known for his watercolors of uninhabited Horn Island. The illustrations capture the beauty and solitude of his existence and his art.) *How do our experiences shape who we become?*

Borden, L. and Kroeger, M. K. *Fly High*. New York: Margaret K. McElderry, 2001. (Discusses the life of the determined African American woman, Bess Coleman, who went all the way to France in order to earn her pilot's license in 1921.) *How can individuals influence their communities?*

Brighton, C. *Keep Your Eye on the Kid: The Early Years of Buster Keaton*. New York: Flash Point, 2008. (The tumbling skills he learned as a child played a big role in shaping one of America's most beloved silent film stars.) *How do our experiences shape who we become?*

Bryan, J. *A River of Words: The Story of William Carlos Williams*. Grand Rapids, MI: Eerdmans Books for Young Readers, 2008. (An introduction to the poet that connects his appreciation of nature and the ordinary experiences of life to the free forms and rhythms he chose for his poems.) *How do our experiences shape who we become?*

Cooney, B. *Eleanor*. New York: Puffin, 1999. (The story of Eleanor Roosevelt's transformation from shy girl to one of the most influential women of the twentieth century.) *How do our backgrounds and experiences shape the people we become?*

DePaola, T. *On My Way.* New York: Putnam's, 2001. (This memoir describes dePaola's fifth year of life with great feeling and detail. Interesting historical and cultural details enlighten the reader, and a zest for life's special moments is captured throughout.) *To what extent do early life experiences shape our actions as adults?*

Dray, P. *Yours for Justice, Ida B. Wells: The Daring Life of a Crusading Journalist.* Atlanta, GA: Peachtree, 2008. (Biography of the activist for rights and justice whose stories and data on lynching helped bring attention to, and ultimately outlaw, the practice.) *How did her background and experiences lead Ida Wells to become determined and daring?*

Fletcher, R. *Leon's Story.* New York: Farrar, Straus & Giroux, 1997. (The son of a North Carolina sharecropper recalls the hard times his family and other African Americans faced in the first half of the twentieth century and the changes that the Civil Rights Movement helped bring about.) *To what extent do early life experiences shape our actions as adults?*

Fritz, J. *Will You Sign Here, John Hancock?* New York: Paperstar Books, 1997. (Biography of the first signer of the Declaration of Independence.) *How important was John Hancock to American independence?*

Greenfield, E. *Mary McLeod Bethune.* New York: Crowell, 1977. (Biography of Mary Jane McLeod Bethune who made numerous contributions to education for African Americans.) *How did her background and experiences lead Mary McLeod Bethune to be a change agent in education?*

Krull, K. *Harvesting Hope: The Story of Cesar Chavez.* San Diego: Harcourt Children's Books, 2003. (This biography describes the migrant farm worker's life, from boyhood to his activism as an adult .) *How did his background and experiences lead Cesar Chavez to fight for justice?*

Lasky, K. *Vision of Beauty: The Story of Sarah Breedlove Walker.* Cambridge, MA: Candlewick, 2003. (Biography of the young woman who would become Madame C. J. Walker, an entrepreneur whose hair and beauty products contributed to the well-being of African America women and the community.) *How do our backgrounds and experiences shape the people we become?*

Locker, T. *Rachel Carson: Preserving a Sense of Wonder.* Golden, CO: Fulcrum, 2004. (The enchantment of nature as seen through the eyes of a budding scientist and environmentalist.) *How do our backgrounds and experiences shape the people we become?*

Macy, S. *Bylines: A Photobiography of Nellie Bly.* Washington, DC: National Geographic Society, 2009. (Replete with photos, quotes, and maps, this chronological biography of the muckraking journalist, globetrotter, and women's right advocate presents Nellie Bly as a woman who was eager to engage in the controversial issues of her day.) *How did her background and experiences lead Nellie Bly to become so determined and daring?*

Myers, W. D. *I've Seen the Promised Land: The Life of Dr. Martin Luther King, Jr.* New York: HarperCollins, 2004. (The focus here is on his public image, from the bus boycott to the sanitation strike in Memphis. The book ends with King"s assassination, but words and pictures show his strength and his enduring message against racism and for peace.) *How do our backgrounds and experiences shape the people we become?*

Myers, W. D. *Malcolm X: A Fire Burning Brightly.* New York: HarperCollins, 2000. (Retells the experiences of Malcolm X.) *How do our backgrounds and experiences shape the people we become?*

Nobleman, M. T. *Boys of Steel: The Creators of Superman.* New York: Alfred A. Knopf, 2008. (The nerdy outcasts who created the character of Superman.) *How do our experiences shape who we become?*

Rappaport, D. *Martin's Big Words: The Life of Dr. Martin Luther King, Jr.* New York: Jump at the Sun/ Hyperion, 2007. (This picture-book biography juxtaposes original text with quotes from King's writing and speeches.) *How do our backgrounds and experiences shape the people we become?*

Rockwell, A. *Only Passing Through: The Story of Sojourner Truth.* New York: Alfred A. Knopf, 2000. (Rockwell describes how a young slave girl grew into a strong, brave woman who spoke out on the evils of slavery.) *How do our backgrounds and experiences shape the people we become?*

Stone, T. L. *Elizabeth Leads the Way: Elizabeth Cady Stanton and the Right to Vote.* New York: Henry Holt, 2008. (Biography of women's rights activist that traces her sense of injustice back to childhood.) *How do our backgrounds and experiences shape the people we become?*

White, L. A. *I Could Do That: Esther Morris Gets Women the Vote.* New York: Farrar, Straus & Giroux, 2005. (In 1869, a woman's can-do attitude shapes her life, makes her instrumental in making Wyoming the first territory to allow women to vote. She later becomes the first woman to hold public office in the United States.) *How do our backgrounds and experiences shape the people we become?*

References

Google Images: Martin Luther King, Jr. monuments. http://images.google.com/images?hl=en&um=1&sa=1&q=Martin+Luther+King%2C+Jr.+monuments&btnG=Search+images&aq=f&oq=&aqi=&start=0 (cited August 22, 2009).

Google Images: Maya Lin Civil Rights Memorial. http://images.google.com/images?um=1&hl=en&tbs=isch%3A1&sa=1&q=maya+lin+civil+rights+memorial&aq=3&aqi=g7&aql=f&oq=Maya+Lin&gs_rfai=&start=0 (cited August 22, 2009).

Malvina Reynolds: Songs, Lyrics and Poems: "Little Boxes." http://web2.wku.edu/~smithch/MALVINA/mr094.htm (cited November 19, 2009).

Rimer, Sara. "Novelist's Purple Palette Is Not to Everyone's Taste." *New York Times,* July 13, 1998. http://www.nytimes.com/1998/07/13/us/san-antonio-journal-novelist-s-purple-palette-is-not-to-everyones-taste.html (cited November 19, 2009).

Chapter 6

Individuals, Groups, and Institutions

In the primary grades, teachers emphasize to students the importance of being oneself. *Ferdinand* by Munro Leaf is often used for this purpose. Ferdinand, a young bull, does not behave like the other young bulls, who butt, snort, and spar with each other to get picked for the bullfights. He prefers to sit and smell the flowers. In an ironic twist, he accidentally sits on a bee, which makes him temporarily crazy, is selected as the maddest bull, and finds himself in the center of the bullfight ring, expected to fight the matador. He refuses to fight; instead, he sits and smells the flowers on the hats of the ladies in the crowd. Ultimately, he is returned home where he can continue to do what he loves best.

In addition to someone who stays true to himself, Ferdinand can also be seen as a figure who refuses to participate in violence and forces people to question their long-held expectations of bulls. This book raises the issue of how one individual can take a stand for what he or she believes in, perhaps changing the hearts and minds of others. We discuss with students the elements of activism (understanding what you believe in, developing a strategy for conveying that belief, deciding if you need to defy society to express your belief, deciding if you feel strongly enough to break society's rules), the possible actions one can take, as well as the possible consequences for taking those actions. We often draw parallels between Ferdinand and the students who orchestrated the sit-ins in Greensboro during the Civil Rights Movement. They, too, refused to move. Unlike Ferdinand, who got sent home, they were beaten and sent to jail. Of course, civil right activists didn't change hearts and minds immediately; however, over time, people in society came to question their long-held beliefs about racial differences and equality. The Civil Rights Movement may seem like ancient history to our students; the rights issue of their time may well be gay rights and the extent to which the actions of individuals standing up for the right to be themselves can change long-held societal beliefs.

The Librarian of Basra: A True Story from Iraq by Jeanette Winter, *Freedom on the Menu: The Greensboro Sit-Ins* by C. B. Weatherford, and *Something Beautiful* by Sharon Dennis Wyeth enable students to explore what kind of power individuals have to shape their communities.

Essential Questions

Do communities shape individuals, or do individuals shape communities?

How does being a wide-awake citizen affect how you view your community?

Who is important to a community?

Who has the power to shape a community?

Is it ever OK for citizens to break the law? Under what conditions?

How do you build community?

The Librarian of Basra: A True Story from Iraq by Jeanette Winter

On the eve of war, Alia Muhammad Baker, the chief librarian in Basra, Iraq, moves all the books in the library to private homes for safe keeping. Within days, the library is destroyed, but the books are protected. This true story shows how one individual's courage and determination can help sustain the community.

Teachers are sometimes reluctant to use picture books that are set in war-torn nations, because they may assume that children will be frightened to learn about war. However, children are aware of the world around them through hearing snippets of conversations and seeing images on 24/7 news channels. Instead of shying away from issues of war, we use this book to highlight a person who behaves heroically in a difficult situation. It is often the case that books set in times of war focus on the courageous acts of soldiers. This book spotlights an unlikely hero, a librarian, who is a model of a courageous civilian. It is important for children to have models of average people who are shapers of communities so that they can think of themselves as important contributors to their own communities.

Social Studies Concepts and Discussion Questions

Social studies concepts	Questions to ask based on the text
Community	Why is a librarian an important member of the community?
	What are the important roles in our community that we don't always notice?
Citizenship	Alia speaks of preserving the books that are "more precious to her than mountains of gold." Why does she feel this way?
	How is reading books connected to being a good citizen?
	Who do you think are the good (and not so good) citizens in this story?
	Why do you think the governor did not give Alia permission to save the books? Could he have had a good reason?
	To what extent is Alia's responsibility as a citizen over once she has saved the books?
Power	Who does Alia think has the power to make the decision to save the books? Who does she ultimately decide has the power to make this decision?
	[When] is it ever appropriate to disobey those in charge?

Activity

Because *The Librarian of Basra* is based on the true story of Alya Abdul Hussein, who took it upon herself to save the volumes of her library during the Iraq War that began in 2003, we want students to know more about this courageous citizen. We have students read "Rebuilding of Baghdad Library Speaks Volumes on Tenacity" (Mahmoud, 2005), the newspaper account of her actions and those of her fellow community members to preserve the library books. The organizer on the next page helped our students to identify more aspects of the story that highlight the powerful contributions that citizens made to save this important part of their community and add that information to the original book.

Name _____ Date _____

Student Handout: Basra Library

Directions: Use the news article "Rebuilding of Baghdad Library Speaks Volumes on Tenacity" by Mona Mahmoud and *The Librarian of Basra* to complete the handout below. The article can be found at on the *USA Today* website at: http://www.usatoday.com/news/world/2005-07-14-baghdad-books_x.htm#.

People who made a difference in preserving the library in Basra

People from the book	Actions to preserve their library

People from the newspaper article	New information about their actions to preserve their library

People Who Made a Difference in Preserving the Library in Basra (Sample Student Responses)

People from the Book	Actions to preserve their library
Alia	· Has the idea to remove the books and put them in a safe place · Involves others
Anis Mohammed	· Takes the curtains from the restaurant to wrap the books · Takes crates from her shop · Stores the books in her restaurant
Truck driver	· Drives books to Alia's and friends' homes for safe keeping
Friends of Alia	· Store the books in their homes
People from the newspaper article	New information about their actions to preserve their library
Alya	· Uses her paycheck from the city to repair the fence in front of the library
Alya's husband	· Stood guard over the library, protecting it from looters
Mohammed Qassim, government official	· Tried to reopen the library with grant money
The U.S. government	· Provided grant money for the library (although the U.S. military also put the hole in the fence, etc.)
Two Italian women— Simona Pari, Simona Torretta	· Volunteered to help restore the library (although they were kidnapped and later released and so could not follow through)
Two librarians and a gardener	· Kept watch over the library after its restoration

Discussion Questions

- *How important was Alya's contribution in saving the library? How important were the other members of the community's contributions in saving the library?*

- *Why do you think the author chose to include some contributions and not others? Would you have made different choices?*

- *Using data from the chart, "Baghdad books by the numbers," assess the health of Baghdad's libraries today.*

- *Why do you suppose that librarians' salaries in Baghdad have greatly increased?*

After students identify the other people who preserved the community library from the article, they use templates like the following to create their own original pages to add to *The Librarian of Basra* to honor these contributors. (See Appendix A for full page templates.)

Applying the Concepts

After completing the new pages for *The Librarian of Basra,* student groups are ready to create their own book about people who make a difference. Each group will select one of the following options for its project:

- Scour local newspapers for stories about people who make a difference in your town or who restore the community (e.g., Habitat for Humanity, protestors for a cause, those who care for animals at shelters, etc.)
- Using nonfiction books, research kids who have made a difference by engaging in service projects. Some helpful sources may include:

  It's Our World, Too!: Young People Who Are Making a Difference: How They Do It—How You Can, Too! by Phillip Hoose

  The Kid's Guide to Social Action: How to Solve the Social Problems You Choose—and Turn Creative Thinking into Positive Action by Barbara A. Lewis

  The Kid's Guide to Service Projects: Over 500 Service Ideas for Young People Who Want to Make a Difference by Barbara A. Lewis

  Kids with Courage: True Stories About Young People Making a Difference by Barbara A. Lewis.

After doing the research, each group will create pages (using the template in Appendix A) about each person who makes (or made) a difference. We bind the books and use them in our classroom library as reading books. The group who studies people in the community who make a difference may wish to invite them in to be honored at a tea.

Extending the concepts in your class . . .

See what needs to be done around your community and take action. Figure out what allies you will need.

Research what people do to help their countries. For example, research what women did to help the war effort during World War II, symbolized by Rosie the Riveter.

Invite speakers who work for social service agencies to your class to see how people help support other people in your community.

Freedom on the Menu:
The Greensboro Sit-Ins by C. B. Weatherford

C. B. Weatherford's *Freedom on the Menu* offers a child's-eye view of how ordinary citizens stood up for their rights and changed society, both locally and nationally. An eight-year-old girl watches her older brother get involved in the Greensboro sit-ins to integrate the lunch counter at Woolworth's and helps in her own way.

Teaching about the Civil Rights Movement is often confined to certain months of the school year and focuses on a few select individuals, including Martin Luther King Jr., Rosa Parks, and, perhaps, Ruby Bridges. Although it is important to study the acts of these important and courageous figures as patriots and role models for children, the pool of civil rights figures is too small and children often do not realize the roles that ordinary citizens played in the struggles for civil rights. *Freedom on the Menu* enables us to focus on these extraordinary ordinary individuals.

Social Studies Concepts and Discussion Questions

Social studies concepts	Questions to ask based on the text
Equality and justice	How does Connie's brother explain to her why his friends sat in at the lunch counter?
	What is the constitutional and moral basis for African Americans' demand and desire for equal rights?
Power	Who made the law that said that African Americans couldn't eat at the lunch counter?
	Who has the power to make rules and laws in society?
	How did Connie's family try to change the segregation laws?
	What role did Martin Luther King Jr. play in the fight for equal rights?
	What role did the NAACP play in the fight for equal rights?
	Who has the power to change rules and laws in society?
Citizenship	Explain the meaning of the newspaper headline: "Negro Students Stand Up by Sitting Down."
	Why was making the picket signs an important job for Connie to do?
	When Connie's sister goes to jail, is she being a good citizen?
	Is it ever OK for citizens to break the law? Under what conditions?
Change	Why did some people think that segregation would last forever, while some believed that they could end it?
	How long should people be willing to wait for change?
	How do the Greensboro sit-ins influence other communities in the South?

Activity

A study of civil rights provides a nice opportunity for students to engage in a research assignment; however, we do not want students simply to write a generic cut-and-pasted biography. We have had a great deal of success having students compose biographical poems about famous activists and ordinary citizens who did extraordinary things in the struggle for equal rights. The format for the bio-poem is as follows:

Format:

Line 1   First name
Line 2   Title
Line 3   Three words that describe that person
Line 4   Lover of (two things or ideas)
Line 5   Who believed (one or more ideas)
Line 6   Who wanted (two things)
Line 7   Who used (two methods or things)
Line 8   Who worked with (one or more people or organizations)
Line 9   Who said, " . . . " (a quote)
Line 10 Last name

After we read a book about Rosa Parks, we model the bio-poem writing process by composing a class poem on Rosa Parks.

BIO-POEM—TEMPLATE

Line 1 First name *Rosa*

Line 2 Title *Seamstress*

Line 3 Three words that describe the person *Courageous, determined, organizer*

Line 4 Lover of *equality and justice*

Line 5 Who believed *it was worth getting arrested to get equal rights*

Line 6 Who wanted *to be able to sit in any seat on the Montgomery bus and to be treated as a human being*

Line 7 Who used *civil disobedience and publicity*

Line 8 Who worked with *the NAACP*

Line 9 Who said, *"People always say that I didn't give up my seat because I was tired, but that isn't true. I was not tired physically, or no more tired than I usually was at the end of a working day. I was not old, although some people have an image of me as being old then. I was forty-two. No, the only tired I was, was tired of giving in."*

Line 10 Last Name *Parks*

Rosa

Seamstress

Courageous, determined, organizer

Lover of equality and justice

Who believed it was worth getting arrested to gain equal rights

Who wanted to be able to sit in any seat on the Montgomery bus and to be treated as a human being

Who used civil disobedience and publicity

Who worked with the NAACP

Who said, "People always say that I didn't give up my seat because I was tired, but that isn't true. I was not tired physically, or no more tired than I usually was at the end of a working day. I was not old, although some people have an image of me as being old then. I was forty-two. No, the only tired I was, was tired of giving in."

Parks

Applying the Concepts

We provide pairs of students with a list of people for their bio-poem that includes abolitionists from the mid-1800s and civil rights activists from the mid-1900s. We include reformers from different time periods so students can see the continuity of themes throughout American history. We are also mindful that many students do not realize that the Abolition and Civil Rights Movements occurred over one hundred years apart. Thus, as part of this assignment, students place their bio-poems on the illustrated timeline that we maintain in our classroom and contribute to it throughout the year. The illustrated timeline enables students to see that abolitionist Harriet Tubman and civil rights activist Rosa Parks lived one hundred years apart and that their specific goals were products of the time period in which they lived. Students can now identify that Tubman's primary goal in the nineteenth century was to free slaves and put an end to the institution of slavery, whereas Parks' primary goal in the twentieth century was to end segregation.

After students complete their bio-poems, they read them to the class. After each poem is read, students place them and pictures of the activists on the timeline. The visual conglomeration of images in both time periods makes it apparent to students that there were many courageous actors in each movement and that when the most famous actor on the scene, Martin Luther King Jr., was violently removed from the stage, the play was far from over.

Name _____ Date _____

Student Handout: Bio-Poem

Directions: You will be assigned an abolitionist or civil rights activist. Your job is to research the person with an emphasis on discovering and understanding the contributions of your person. After you complete your research, you will write a bio-poem—a ten-line poem that captures the essence of your person and what she or he fought for. There are two challenges:

1. Be creative in your use of language—vary your word choice, make an impact.

2. For line 9, find a quote that really reflects your person's thoughts and is in line with your poem. There are many online sources for quotes (for example, see http://www.brainyquote.com/, http://www.thinkexist.com).

Use the form below to write your poem. The details may be one word or a phrase or two. Try to be as accurate and complete in your description as possible. Try several words before you decide which to use—read your poem out loud to see how it sounds!

Format

Line 1   First name

Line 2   Title

Line 3   Three words that describe that person

Line 4   Lover of (2 things or ideas)

Line 5   Who believed (1 or more ideas)

Line 6   Who wanted (2 things)

Line 7   Who used (2 methods or things)

Line 8   Who worked with (1 or more people or organizations)

Line 9   Who said, " . . . " (a quote)

Line 10 Last Name

Mount your bio-poem on a piece of construction paper and include a picture of your abolitionist or civil rights activist. Following are some subject ideas for your bio-poem.

John Brown	Nat Turner	John Lewis
Frederick Douglass	Muhammad Ali	Malcolm X
William Lloyd Garrison	Daisy Bates	Thurgood Marshall
Angelina and Sarah Grimke	Stokely Carmichael	James Meredith
Abraham Lincoln	Elizabeth Eckford	Diane Nash
Lucretia Mott	Medgar Evers	Rosa Parks
Harriet Beecher Stowe	Fannie Lou Hamer	Minnie Jean Brown Trickey
Sojourner Truth	Martin Luther King Jr.	
Harriet Tubman	Westley Law	

Name _____ Date _____

Student Handout: Bio-Poem (*Continued*)

Line 1   First name _____

Line 2   Title _____

Line 3   Three words that describe the person _____

_____

Line 4   Lover of _____

_____

Line 5   Who believed _____

_____

Line 6   Who wanted _____

_____

Line 7   Who used _____

_____

Line 8   Who worked with _____

_____

Line 9   Who said, _____

_____

_____

_____

_____

_____

_____

Line 10 Last Name _____

Discussion Questions

- *How are the abolitionists similar? How are they different?*

- *How are the civil rights activists similar? How are they different?*

- *How are the abolitionists similar to or different from the civil rights activists?*

- *What conclusions can you draw from looking at the clusters of activists on the timeline?*

- *To what extent can individuals shape history? To what extent are individuals products of their time periods in history?*

- *Do communities shape individuals, or do individuals shape communities?*

Extending the concepts in your class . . .

Are there any rights activists in your community whom you can invite in to speak with your students?

Are there articles in the news about civil rights issues today? Start a current events bulletin board to display contemporary civil rights issues.

Examine the extent to which the election of President Obama is a long-term effect of the Civil Rights Movement.

Something Beautiful by Sharon Dennis Wyeth

When her teacher writes the word "beautiful" on the blackboard, a little girl in Sharon Dennis Wyeth's *Something Beautiful* resolves to look for what is beautiful in her neighborhood. In the course of doing so, she finds ugly graffiti, trash, and broken glass around her home, which, initially, gets her down. She takes action to beautify some aspects of her neighborhood and comes to realize that beautiful means "something that when you have it, your heart is happy."

Language arts teachers may use this book as an example of a personal narrative. In social studies, we emphasize the power of individuals to shape their communities, which must begin with a consciousness of the world around them.

Social Studies Concepts and Discussion Questions

Social studies concepts	Questions to ask based on the text
Community	What does the little girl see as she looks out her window and walks through her neighborhood?
	How do you think she feels about what she sees? How do you know?
	How does the little girl define "beautiful?"
	What do different members of the girl's community see as beautiful?
	How is beauty experienced through each of the five senses?
Power	How are the little girl's eyes opened to her community as a result of her conversations with the people who live in it?
	How do these conversations empower the girl?
	How does she discover that she has the power to make change?
Citizenship	What does the little girl do to beautify her home and her neighborhood?
	What if everyone in her community took action similar to the little girl's?
	How do we help others see the beauty in the world around them?
Change	How or why does the little girl come to realize that she can be an agent of change in her community?

Activity

We read the book aloud once to the class. The second time we read the book, we ask students to imagine that they are the little girl; we stop our reading periodically so that students can complete diary entries from the perspective of the little girl. Before students complete the first diary entry, we discuss what might be included in the girl's diary. We encourage our students to illustrate their diary entries.

The points at which to pause in the text and the questions to ask follow. Remind students that they are responding to the questions and writing in their diaries from the perspective of the little girl.

- *For the first diary entry, stop at the line, "Where is my something beautiful?" Ask students: What do you see in your community, and how does it make you feel?*

- *For the second diary entry, stop at the line, "My baby's laugh is something beautiful, says Aunt Carolyn." Ask students: After you chat with people in the neighborhood, what do you begin to realize?*

- *For the third diary entry, read to the end of the book. Ask students: What actions did you take, and how do you feel about your actions?*

- *For the fourth diary entry, ask students: What do you envision for the future of your community?*

A sample diary entry follows:

Date _____

Dear Diary,

Today I saw trash in the courtyard and a broken bottle. I also noticed writing in the halls of my building. Someone wrote the word, "Die." I saw a woman sleeping on the streets. I ran past a scary alley. There was a garden without any flowers.

It made me feel scared – Mommy says I should never stop by the alley. It also made me feel sad because I don't feel that there is anything that's beautiful in my neighborhood. It kind of made me feel mad, too, because I deserve something beautiful to see every day.

Name _____   Date _____

Student Handout:
Something Beautiful—Diary Entries

Directions: Imagine you are the little girl. You will write four different diary entries at different points in the book.

Diary #1: Consider the question: *What do you see in your community, and how does it make you feel?*

Date _____

Dear Diary,

Today I saw _____

_____

_____

_____

_____

_____

_____.

It made me feel _____

_____

_____

_____

_____

_____.

From *Every Book Is a Social Studies Book: How to Meet Standards with Picture Books, K–6* by Andrea S. Libresco, Jeannette Balantic, and Jonie C. Kipling. Santa Barbara, CA: Libraries Unlimited. Copyright © 2011.

Name _____ Date _____

Student Handout:
Something Beautiful—Diary Entries

Directions: Imagine you are the little girl. You will write four diary entries at different points in the book.

Diary #2: Consider the question: *After you chat with people in the neighborhood, what do you begin to realize?*

Date _____

Dear Diary,

Today I saw _____

_____

_____

_____

_____

_____.

It made me feel _____

_____

_____

_____

_____

_____

_____.

Name _____ Date _____

Student Handout:
Something Beautiful—Diary Entries

Directions: Imagine you are the little girl. You will write four diary entries at different points in the book.

Diary #3: Consider the question: *What actions did you take, and how do you feel about your actions?*

Date _____

Dear Diary,

Today I saw _____

_____

_____

_____

_____

_____

_____ .

It made me feel _____

_____

_____

_____

_____

_____ .

Name _____   Date _____

Student Handout:
Something Beautiful—Diary Entries

Directions: Imagine you are the little girl. You will write four diary entries at different points in the book.

Diary #4: Consider the question: *What do you envision for the future of your community?*

Date _____

Dear Diary,

Today I saw _____

_____

_____

_____

_____

_____.

It made me feel _____

_____

_____

_____

_____

_____.

Discussion Questions

Based on the students' diary entries and their reaction to the text, discuss the following questions as a class:

- *What were the relatively easy problems on which the little girl could take action in her community?*

- *What were the more difficult problems to solve? What makes them more difficult to solve?*

- *How could the little girl go about solving those problems?*

Applying the Concepts

Just as the little girl has her eyes opened to the beauty in her community, so do we want our students to open their eyes to the good, the bad, and ugly in their own communities. Students continue to use the diary format to record, in writing and illustration, the things they see in their community and how they feel about what they see. We model this activity by taking a walk inside and outside of the school.

Name _____ Date _____

Student Handout:
Things I See in My Community

Directions: After your walk around your community, use the diary template below to record your observations and reflections.

Date _____

Dear Diary,

Today I walked around my community, I saw _____

_____

_____

_____

_____

_____ .

It made me feel _____

_____

_____

_____

_____

_____ .

For homework, students continue their investigations of their own neighborhoods. After students have closely examined their school and neighborhoods, together we generate a list of the beautiful aspects of our community, as well as a list of the aspects that need improvement.

We prioritize the list of things that need improvement and identify things that can be addressed by individual students and projects that our class might undertake together. In our class, students worked together in groups to improve their school community. One group observed that many of the water fountains had gum in the drains, and some did not work; they spoke to the principal to try to get the drains cleaned and the broken fountains fixed. They also put up posters to encourage students to keep the water fountains clean. Another group created and maintained a garden in the back of our school to help beautify the grounds. In an effort to stop local high school students from smoking on the corner, a third group started an antismoking campaign. Although students in the third group were less successful in their efforts, they did raise awareness in their school about the dangers of smoking.

Students maintain a diary throughout the process recording their actions, feelings, successes, and frustrations as they go about beautifying their community.

Extending the concepts in your class . . .

Students can take pictures and write articles about their community improvement projects for the local newspaper.

Investigate news stories that address the concerns of the nation and the world to see what issues need attention and how students might contribute.

Investigate feature stories in the news that celebrate individuals and groups who address issues in their communities and make the world a better place.

Recommended Books

For a list of books that explore people who fought for civil rights, please see *Biographies* in the Recommended Books list at the end of Chapter 5: "Individual Development and Identity." In addition, for books about women who fought for their rights, see Chapter 7: "Power, Authority, and Governance."

Making a Difference

Amstel, M. *Sybil Ludington's Midnight Ride.* Minneapolis: Lerner Publishing Group, 2000. (Amstel tells the story of Ludington's horseback ride to rouse American soldiers to fight against the British during the America Revolution.) *How can one determined individual make a difference?*

Bass, J. *Herb, the Vegetarian Dragon.* Cambridge, MA: Barefoot Books, 2008. (Herb is the only vegetarian dragon in a land full of carnivores. When the townspeople decide to protect themselves from the meat-eating dragons, they capture Herb instead and plan to execute him, until a young girl steps in to prove his innocence. An agreement is eventually made between the people and the dragons so that meat-eaters and vegetarians can live together in peace.) *Who has the power to shape a community?*

Buckley, S., and Leacock, E. *Kids Make History: A New Look at America's Story.* Boston: Houghton Mifflin Company, 2006. (The authors describe the role of young people in history, from Pocahontas to September 11, 2001.) *How can young people make a difference?*

Burk, S. *Let the River Run Silver Again! How One School Helped Return the American Shad to the Potomac River—and How You Too Can Help Protect and Restore Our Living Waters.* Granville, OH: McDonald & Woodward, 2005. (An environmental conservation success story of elementary students who helped restore the fish population in the Chesapeake Bay watershed.) *To what extent can young people have an impact on the environment?*

Cherry, L. *A River Ran Wild.* Boston: Harcourt/Sandpiper, 2002. (An environmental history of the Nashua River, ending with the cleanup that revitalized it.) *To what extent can citizens reclaim a river?*

Christensen, B. *Woody Guthrie: Poet of the People.* New York: Alfred A. Knopf/Random House Children's Books, 2009. (This book details the songwriter's experience during the Great Depression as seen in the lyrics of his song, "This Land Is Your Land.") *What responsibility do individuals have to speak out about injustice?*

Cooney, B. *Miss Rumphius.* New York: Viking Press, 1982. (A woman makes the world more beautiful as she travels.) *How can one citizen affect how people see the world around them?*

Deedy, C. A. *The Yellow Star: The Legend of King Christian X of Denmark.* Atlanta, GA: Peachtree, 2000. (Deedy tells the story of King Christian and the Danes' resistance to the Nazis during World War II.) *How can people come together to fight injustice?*

Gibbons, G. *Recycle: A Handbook for Kids.* Boston: Little, Brown & Company, 1996. (Explains the process of recycling from start to finish and how it helps make our planet a safer and healthier place to live.) *How important is recycling for the health of our planet?*

Hoose, P. *It's Our World, Too!: Young People Who Are Making a Difference: How They Do It—How You Can, Too!* Boston: Little, Brown & Company, 1993. (This is a collection of brief essays about children who have made notable achievements, accompanied by a handbook for young activists.) *How can children make a difference in our world?*

Krensky, Stephen. *Sisters of the Scituate Light.* New York: Dutton Children's Books, 2008. (In 1814, when their father leaves them in charge of the Scituate, Massachusetts, lighthouse, two teenage sisters devise a clever way to avert attack by a British warship patrolling the coast.) *How can average people make a difference in wartime?*

Leaf, M. *The Story of Ferdinand.* New York: The Penguin Group, 2007. (This is the story of a bull who loved to smell flowers, not fight like the other bulls do.) *How can being true to who we are as individuals promote peace in the world?*

Lewis, B. *Kids with Courage: True Stories About Young People Making a Difference.* Minneapolis, MN: Free Spirit, 1992. (This book features stories of kids who make a difference in their neighborhood, community, or world.) *How can young people make a difference in our world?*

Lewis, B. *The Kid's Guide to Social Action: How to Solve the Social Problems You Choose—And Turn Creative Thinking into Positive Action.* Minneapolis, MN: Free Spirit, 1998. (This resource guide for children teaches political action skills that can help them in addressing social problems at the community, state, and national levels.) *How can young people make a difference in our world?*

Lewis, B. *The Kid's Guide to Service Projects: Over 500 Service Ideas for Young People Who Want to Make a Difference.* Minneapolis, MN: Free Spirit, 2009. (This book features more than five hundred service ideas for young people.) *How can young people make a difference in our world?*

Morrow, B. O. *A Good Night for Freedom.* New York: Holiday House, 2003. (A girl has to make a choice between turning in the runaway slaves whom she has found or helping them escape.) *What responsibility do individuals have to their fellow human beings?*

Munsch, R. *The Paper Bag Princess.* Toronto: Annick Press, 1980. (A princess saves her fiancé prince with her wits, but then he claims she isn't feminine enough. She decides not to marry him after all.) *What are the most important qualities of individuals?*

Shetterly, R. *Americans Who Tell the Truth.* New York: Dutton Children's Books, 2008. (Quotes and portraits of fifty Americans, such as Muhammad Ali, Emma Goldman, and Paul Robeson, who have spoken out and challenged the status quo.) *What responsibility do individuals have to speak out about injustice?*

Winter, J. *The Librarian of Basra: A True Story from Iraq.* San Diego, CA: Harcourt, 2005. (In war-stricken Iraq, a librarian in Basra struggles to save her community's priceless collection of books.) *How can one person's actions make a difference in her community?*

Community

Barber, B. E. *Saturday at the New You.* New York: Lee & Low Books, 1994. (Shauna, a young African American girl, wishes she could do more to help Momma with her customers at her beauty salon. Then one day she gets her chance.) *Who is important to a community?*

Barrett, J. *Cloudy with a Chance of Meatballs.* New York: Macmillan, 1978. (In the town of Chewandswallow, where it rains soup and juice, snows mashed potatoes, and blows storms of hamburgers—life is delicious . . . that is, until the weather takes a turn for the worse, and the whole community must leave together.) *How does being a wide-awake citizen affect how you view your community?*

Brown, M. *Stone Soup.* New York: Atheneum Books for Young Readers, 1947. (Soldiers know how to bring the community together to feed them.) *Who has the power to shape a community?*

Collier, B. *Uptown.* New York: Henry Holt, 2000. (This book takes readers on a tour of Harlem.) *What makes a place a community?*

Cooney, B. *Roxaboxen.* New York: Lothrop, Lee & Shepard, 1991. (Kids create an imaginary town on a hill covered with rocks and wooden boxes.) *What makes a place a community?*

Cowen-Fletcher, J. *It Takes a Village.* New York: Scholastic, 1994. (An entire village watches out for a small child.) *Does community shape individuals, or do individuals shape communities?*

Dooley, N. *Everybody Cooks Rice.* Minneapolis, MN: Carolrhoda Books, 1991. (In this book, various households make different cultural versions of a dish. A child is sent to find a younger brother at dinnertime and is introduced to a variety of cultures by encountering the many ways rice is prepared at the different households visited.) *What unites a community?*

Fine, E. H., and Josephson, J. P. *Armando and the Blue Tarp School.* New York: Lee & Low Books, 2007. (Armando and his father are trash-lickers in Mexico, but when a "school" comes—a blue tarp set down near the garbage dump—Armando's father decides that Armando must attend classes and learn. This book is based on a true story.) *How much power does one person have to make a difference?*

Fleischman, P. *Weslandia.* Cambridge, MA: Candlewick Press, 1999. (Oddball boy creates his own civilization that draws in his classmates.) *Who has the power to shape a community?*

Fleming, D. *Where Once There Was a Wood.* New York: Henry Holt, 1996. (Wildlife is displaced by development.) *What responsibility do people have to the animal community?*

Greenburg, J., and Gordon, S. *Christo and Jeanne-Claude: Through the Gates and Beyond.* New York: Flashpoint, 2008. (An overview of the careers of the husband-and-wife team that has been creating large outdoor art installations since the 1960s.) *How important is public art to society? Does it need to be permanent to be important?*

Guthrie, W., and Jacobsen, K. *This Land Is Your Land.* Boston: Little, Brown & Company, 1998. (The lyrics to the famous song by Woody Guthrie, illustrated.) *What makes a place a community?*

Hall, D. *Ox-Cart Man.* New York: Viking Press, 1979. (This book details the daily life of an early-nineteenth-century New England family over changing seasons.) *How do communities both change and stay the same?*

Jakobsen, K. *My New York.* Boston: Little, Brown & Company, 2003. (Take a tour of a girl's favorite places in New York City.) *What makes a community special?*

Knight, M. B. *Talking Walls.* Gardiner, ME: Tilbury House, 1992. (The author takes a look at walls around the world and their significance.) *How do you build community?*

Krull, K. *Supermarket.* New York: Holiday House, 2001. (How does food get to a community?) *How do communities meet their needs?*

Kurusa. *The Streets Are Free.* Toronto: Annick Press, 1985. (This book is based on the true story of children in the barrio in Caracas, Venezuela, who came together to advocate for a playground.) *How can groups of people come together to make a difference in their communities?*

McBrier, P. *Beatrice's Goat.* New York: Atheneum Books for Young Readers, 2001. (The gift of an income-producing goat helps a family and the community). *Who has the power to shape a community?*

McGovern, A. *The Lady in the Box.* New York: Turtle Books, 1997. (When children discover a homeless woman in their neighborhood, they must reconcile their desire to help with their mother's admonition not to talk to strangers.) *What responsibility do we have to economically disadvantaged members of our community?*

Nunes, S. M. *The Last Dragon.* New York: Clarion Books, 1995. (A boy learns about the people and culture of Chinatown.) *Does community shape individuals, or do individuals shape communities?*

Pfister, M. *The Rainbow Fish.* New York: North South Books, 2000. (A story about becoming part of a community.) *What makes a place a community?*

Polacco, P. *Applemando's Dreams.* New York: Putnam & Grosset Group, 1991. (The town believes that a young boy is dreaming his life away, but the boy's dreams change the village and its people.) *How important are dreamers and artists to a community?*

Powell, A. *America's Promise.* New York: HarperCollins, 2003. (A woman creates a clubhouse in her basement to provide a safe place for the children of her community.) *How much power does one individual have to shape a community?*

Ruelle, K. G., and DeSaix, D. D. *The Grand Mosque of Paris: A Story of How Muslims Rescued Jews During the Holocaust.* New York: Holiday House, 2009. (In Nazi-occupied France, when no Jew was safe from deportation to a concentration camp, many Jews found refuge and community in the sprawling complex of the Grand Mosque of Paris.) *What should the role of religious or community institutions be toward community members with different cultural backgrounds?*

Rylant, C. *An Angel for Solomon Singer.* New York: Orchard Books, 1992. (A lonely New York City man finds companionship at a café.) *How can community be more than just a place?*

Sendak, M., & Kushner, T. *Brundibar.* New York: Hyperion Books for Children, 2003. (Banding together, children defeat a bully in this parable about the Holocaust.) *How can community members protect everyone's rights?*

Silverstein, S. *The Giving Tree.* New York: HarperCollins, 1992. (A tree gives a boy all of herself.) *What do we owe our fellow community members?*

Sis, P. *Madlenka.* New York: Farrar, Straus & Giroux, 2000. (A girl's trip around her New York City block is like a trip around the world.) *What unites a community?*

Smith, D. J. *If America Were a Village: A Book About the People of the United States.* Toronto, Canada: Kids Can Press, 2009. (Stats on an America as a village of one hundred people.) *How does being a wide-awake citizen affect how you view your community?*

Smith, D. J. *If the World Were a Village.* Toronto, Canada: Kids Can Press, 2002. (Stats on the world as a village of 100 people.) *How does being a wide-awake citizen affect how you view your community?*

Stanley, E. *Deliverance of Dancing Bears.* La Jolla, CA: Kane/Miller Book Publishers, 2004. (A poor man spends all his money to free two mistreated dancing bears and in doing so reminds onlookers that the dignity of all living creatures must be respected.) *How can individuals protect the rights of all community members?*

Stewart, S. *The Library.* New York: Farrar, Straus & Giroux, 1995. (A woman who loves to read opens a library for the town.) *Who has the power to shape a community?*

Thurber, J. *The Great Quillow.* New York: Harcourt, Brace & World, 1944. (A toy maker defeats a giant and saves his town.) *Who is important to a community?*

UNICEF. *A Life Like Mine: How Children Live Around the World.* New York: Dorling Kindersley, 2002. (This nonfiction book profiles eighteen children from all over the globe, from developed and developing nations, leading their lives in different and fascinating ways.) *Are communities more alike or different?*

Williams, V. B. *A Chair for My Mother.* New York: Greenwillow Books, 1982. (A community helps a family start over after a fire.) *How do people in a community work together to solve problems?*

Wyeth, S. D. *Something Beautiful.* New York: Dragonfly Books, 1998. (When she goes looking for "something beautiful" in her community, a young girl finds beauty in many forms.) *How does being a wide-awake citizen affect how you view your community?*

Civil Rights

Adler, D. *A Picture Book of Thurgood Marshall.* New York: Holiday House, 1999. (Follows the life of the first African American to serve as a judge on the United States Supreme Court.) *How can one person influence a nation?*

Freedman, F. *Freedom Walkers: The Story of the Montgomery Bus Boycott.* New York: Holiday House, 2008. (Stories and photographs of average citizens, local crusaders, and prominent civil rights lawyers portray the 381-day boycott to end racial segregation on buses.) *How can groups of determined people effect change?*

Freedman, F. *The Voice That Challenged a Nation: Marian Anderson and the Struggle for Civil Rights.* New York: Clarion, 2004. (This is the biography of the African American singer who challenged where she was allowed to sing.) *How can an individual make a difference?*

Giovanni, N. *Rosa.* New York: Square Fish, 2005. (Chronicles the quiet determination of Rosa Parks and the bus boycotters.) *How can one individual and then a whole community make a difference?*

Haskins, J. *Delivering Justice: W. W. Law and the Fight for Civil Rights.* Cambridge, MA: Candlewick Press, 2005. (The story of the mail carrier, an unsung hero, who orchestrated the Great Savannah Boycott and was instrumental in bringing equality to his community.) *Who has the power to shape a community?*

Johnson, A. *A Sweet Smell of Roses.* New York: Simon and Schuster Books for Young Readers, 2005. (The Civil Rights Movement through the eyes of two young sisters who witness a march for equality organized by Martin Luther King Jr.) *To what extent can a young person fight injustice?*

Johnson, J. W. *Lift Ev'ry Voice and Sing.* New York: Scholastic, 1990. (This volume features the African American national anthem.) *How does this anthem help unite people in the cause of civil rights?*

Jordan, J. *Fannie Lou Hamer.* New York: Crowell, 1972. (A biography of one of the first black organizers of voter registration in Mississippi.) *What power do individuals have to influence their communities?*

King, C., and Osborne, L. B. *Oh, Freedom!: Kids Talk About the Civil Rights Movement With the People Who Made It Happen.* New York: Alfred A. Knopf, 1997. (In thirty-one interviews, children ask people what they did during the Civil Rights Movement.) *What can we learn from people who have helped shape communities in the past?*

Krull, K. *Harvesting Hope: The Story of Cesar Chavez*. San Diego, CA: Harcourt, 2003. (A biography of Cesar Chavez, from age ten when he and his family lived happily on their Arizona ranch, to age thirty-eight when he led a peaceful protest against California migrant workers' miserable working conditions.) *What power do individuals have to influence their communities?*

Levine, E. *If You Lived at the Time of Martin Luther King*. New York: Scholastic, 1990. (Explains the important changes brought about by the civil rights movement in question and answer format.) *What can we learn from people who have helped shape communities in the past?*

Littlesugar, A. *Freedom School, Yes!* New York: Philomel Books, 2001. (A fictionalized account of the 1964 Mississippi Summer Project, in which more than 600 volunteers risked their lives to teach black children in the deep South.) *Who has the power to shape a community?*

Lorbiecki, M. *Jackie's Bat*. New York: Simon & Schuster Children's Publishing, 2006. (Jackie Robinson's first year in the major leagues and his struggle to break the color barrier is told through the eyes of a bat boy who learns to overcome his own prejudice.) *To what extent can a young person fight injustice?*

McKissack, P. *Goin' Someplace Special*. New York: Atheneum Books for Young Readers, 2001. (In segregated 1950s Nashville, a young African American girl braves a series of indignities and obstacles to enter one of the few integrated places in town: the public library.) *What obligations do citizens have if government becomes unresponsive to their needs?*

Michelson, R. *As Good As Anybody: Martin Luther King and Abraham Joshua Heschel's Amazing March Toward Freedom*. New York: Knopf Books for Children, 2008. (A tribute to two great men, an American Baptist minister and a Polish-born rabbi who fled Nazi Germany, and their alliance to bring about civil rights.) *What motivates people to make a difference in the world around them?*

Miller, W. *Richard Wright and the Library Card*. New York: Lee & Low Books, 1997. (Based on a scene from Wright's autobiography, in which, as a 17 year old, he borrows a white man's library card and devours every book as a ticket to freedom.) *How does his education from library books shape Wright into a civil rights figure?*

Morrison, T. *Remember: The Journey to School Integration*. New York: Houghton Mifflin, 2004. (Photographs of ordinary young people and the role they played in school integration.) *To what extent can a young person fight injustice?*

Myers, W. D. *Ida B. Wells: Let the Truth Be Told*. New York: Amistad, 2008. (Biography of the anti-lynching crusader.) *How can we get the courage to make a stand for justice?*

Myers, W. D. *I've Seen the Promised Land: The Life of Dr. Martin Luther King, Jr*. New York: Amistad, 2003. (This is Myers' biography of the civil rights leader.) *To what extent was King successful?*

Pinkney, A. D. *Boycott Blues: How Rosa Parks Inspired a Nation*. New York: Amistad/Greenwillow Books, 2008. (This story recalls the December 1955 bus boycott in Montgomery, Alabama.) *When do individual events become a movement?*

Pinkney, A. D. *Sit-In: How Four Friends Stood Up by Sitting Down*. New York: Little Brown Books, 2010. (A celebration of the fiftieth anniversary of the Woolworth's lunch counter sit-in, when four college students staged a peaceful protest that became a defining moment in the struggle for racial equality.) *To what extent can a young person fight injustice?*

Rappaport, D. *Free at Last! Stories and Songs of Emancipation*. Cambridge, MA: Candlewick Press, 2006. (This is an anthology of poetry, songs, stories, testimony, letters, and more about work for African American rights from 1863–1954.) *How does an oppressed community find the strength and determination to resist?*

Rappaport, R. *Nobody Gonna Turn Me 'Round: Stories and Songs of the Civil Rights Movement*. Cambridge, MA: Candlewick Press, 2008. (Stories of key individuals and events of the civil rights movement.) *How can individuals make a difference?*

Rappaport, D. *The School Is Not White! A True Story of the Civil Rights Movement*. New York: Hyperion Books for Children, 2005. (An African American family in 1965 Mississippi pursues equal education for their children.) *How does education empower citizens?*

Ryan, P. M. *When Marian Sang: The True Recital of Marian Anderson*. New York: Scholastic Press, 2002. (The life of Marian Anderson, the beautiful singer who broke racial barriers to become a world-renowned performer.) *How can an individual make a difference?*

Shelton, P. Y. *Child of the Civil Rights Movement*. New York: Schwartz & Wade, 2009. (Shelton describes childhood as the daughter of a civil rights leader, Andrew Young.) *How do children cope with injustice?*

Shore, D. Z. *This Is the Dream*. New York: Amistad, 2005. (Chronicle of the Civil Rights Movement through verse and illustration.) *What are different ways people can express a need for justice?*

Stotts, S. *We Shall Overcome: A Song That Changed the World*. New York: Clarion Books, 2010. (The roots of the lyrics and music and its power in labor, civil rights, and antiwar movements.) *To what extent can a song become an anthem for people power?*

Weatherford, C. B. *Dear Mr. Rosenwald*. New York: Scholastic Press, 2006. (An African American community in 1921 pulls together to build a new school with the help of a grant from Mr. Rosenwald, the president of Sears, Roebuck and Co.) *How can an individual make a difference?*

Weatherford, C. B. *Freedom on the Menu: The Greensboro Sit-Ins*. New York: Puffin Books, 2007. (The author tells of the 1960 lunch counter sit-ins.) *To what extent can a young person fight injustice?*

Wiles, D. *Freedom Summer*. New York: Aladdin Paperbacks, 2005. (A story of friendship across a racial divide set in 1964 Mississippi, following the passage of the Civil Rights Act.) *How can friendship be an act of courage?*

Woodson, J. *The Other Side*. New York: G. P. Putnam's Sons, 2001. (A story of friendship across a racial divide.) *How can friendship be an act of courage?*

Reference

Mahmoud, Mona. "Rebuilding of Baghdad Library Speaks Volumes on Tenacity." *USA TODAY,* July 14, 2005. http://www.usatoday.com/news/world/2005-07-14-baghdad-books_x.htm# (cited August 20, 2009).

Chapter 7

Power, Authority, and Governance

When classes do biography units, they often read about Jackie Robinson, who had an enormous impact on how people viewed African Americans. Many books examine his stoic reaction to the taunts on the field and the hate mail he received, reflecting his courage and dignity. *Teammates* by Peter Golenbock provides the opportunity to look at Pee Wee Reese, Robinson's teammate, who gave Robinson support when he joined the Brooklyn Dodgers and became the first black player in Major League baseball.

Pee Wee Reese, by virtue of his white skin color, was a member of the group that had held power in society since the beginning of American history. He could have stood back from the controversy and let Robinson fend for himself. Instead, in a game filled with taunts and derision, he left his position at shortstop, walked over to Robinson at first base, put his arm around Robinson's shoulder, chatted for a few moments, and then returned to his position. By putting his arm around his fellow player at a crucial moment, Reese chose to use his power as a white southerner to make a public statement about friendship and acceptance of his black teammate. When our students read this book, they understand that all people have some level of power that they can use to effect change. Whether it is using one's popularity to stick up for the bullied kid on the playground or to welcome a new student to the classroom, or using one's intellectual strengths to help students who take longer to understand, we want children to recognize that, young as they are, they have the power to help others. We encourage our students to identify where they have power and then to summon up the courage to act.

¡Si, Se Puede! Yes We Can! Janitor Strike in L.A. by Diana Cohn, *Bloomers* by Rhoda Blumberg, and *We the Kids* by David Catrow enable students to analyze how people and governments can and do wield power.

Essential Questions

How much power should people have, and how can they use it justly?

How can those with seemingly little power have a say in society?

What responsibility does government have to its citizens?

What obligation do citizens have if government becomes unresponsive to their needs?

When do individual events become a movement?

¡Si, Se Puede! Yes We Can! Janitor Strike in L.A. by Diana Cohn

In *¡Si, Se Puede! Yes We Can!*, Carlos, a young boy, born in Mexico, now lives with his mother and grandmother in Los Angeles. His mother works hard as a janitor, cleaning offices to support her family. Although she works nights and weekends, she is unable to pay for all of her family's needs. We witness the event in April 2000 in which eight thousand workers participated in the janitor strike in Los Angeles through Carlos's eyes. Carlos's mother explains to her son why the strike is necessary and what the strikers hope to gain. The book includes an explanation of labor unions and strikes, as well as a brief biography of the union organizer, Dolores Sanchez.

Because of its bilingual text, this book has been a mainstay in many ESL classes; however, it can also be an entree into a discussion of work, the workplace, unions, power, and economic justice. It is often difficult for children to understand why collective action by workers has played such an important part in American history; this book can help students explore tactics, as well as the importance of teamwork and cooperation, for effecting change.

Social Studies Concepts and Discussion Questions

Social studies concepts	Questions to ask based on the text
Justice and rights	How does Carlos's mamá react when she learns about the plan to strike?
	Do janitors have the right to strike?
	What is the significance of the title of the book?
	Do all workers have the right to strike?
Change	Why do the janitors strike?
	How long does the strike last?
	What changes occur as a result of the strike? Are they just?
	How do these changes affect Carlos's family?
Culture	Why is the book written in both Spanish and English?
	Where does this story take place?
	Why are the signs and messages on the T-shirts in two languages?
Family	Who makes up Carlos's family?
	What are the roles and responsibilities of each member of the family to each other?
	How does the strike affect the workers' families?
	How does Carlos help his mother and the striking workers?
Power	Do the janitors have power?
	How can low-wage workers improve their working conditions?
	What are unions, and what role can they play in improving working conditions?
	What strengthens the janitors' power in the strike?
	How does the janitors' visibility play a role in their support?
	How do the events of the book support Carlos's teacher Miss Lopez's statement, "When many people join together, they can make a strong force"?
Economics and social class	Why does Carlos's mamá work at night?
	Why does his mamá work other jobs on the weekends?
	What do you think is the economic status of the main character? What evidence do you have for your answer?

Activity

¡Si, Se Puede! Yes We Can! enables students to explore the societal and personal ramifications of a contemporary strike, but we also use the book to launch an investigation of strikes in American history. In the late 1800s, the United States underwent a period of industrial growth that had an enormous impact on the lives of workers. Labor songs can be a vehicle for examining historical content; they also enable us to show how songs appeal to and can be learned by literate and nonliterate workers alike. In addition, labor songs, and the people who sang them, provide models of activism for young people in their current and future working lives.

Students work in groups to listen to and analyze famous protest songs of the labor movement. While students listen to the songs and read the lyrics, they

- identify working conditions that led to the formation of organized labor unions and

- discuss how labor songs can be important in helping workers organize and become powerful.

After students analyze their songs, we compile a list of workers' complaints (bad health and safety conditions, low pay, no payment for injuries, long working hours, no respect, etc.) and the remedies they sought (laws regulating health and safety conditions, livable wages, workers compensation, laws regulating work hours, respect, etc.).

Name _____ Date _____

Student Handout: Analyzing Labor Songs

Directions: As you listen to and read the lyrics of each song, make a list of the conditions workers faced and the improvements they wanted. Underline the words in the song that helped you get this information.

"Drill, Ye Tarriers [railroad workers], Drill" by Thomas Casey

http://www.youtube.com/watch?v=jmQtqW4G28g

Song lyrics	Conditions/improvements wanted

Ev'ry morning at seven o'clock
There were twenty tarriers a working at the rock,
And the boss comes along, and he says, kape still,
And come down heavy on the cast-iron drill.
 	
Chorus:
 	
   Drill, ye tarriers, drill!
   It's work all day
   For sugar in your tay,
   Down beyond the railway,
   And drill, ye tarriers, drill.
   And blast! And fire!
 	
Our new foreman was Jim McCann.
By God, he was a blame mean man.
Last week a premature blast went off.
And a mile in the air went big Jim Goff.
And drill ye tarriers drill!
 	
Chorus
 	
Next time pay day came around,
Jim Goff a dollar short was found.
When he asked, "What for?" came this reply,
"You were docked* for the time you was up in the sky."
And drill, ye tarriers, drill!
 	
Chorus	

* *Docked = pay was withheld.*

Questions

- *What happened to Jim Goff on the job?*
- *How did Jim Goff's employer treat him following his accident?*
- *How could this song be seen as an argument for forming a union?*

Name _____ Date _____

Student Handout: Analyzing Labor Songs

Directions: As you listen to and read the lyrics of each song, make a list of the conditions workers faced and the improvements they wanted. Underline the words in the song that helped you get this information.

"Go to Work on Monday" by Si Kahn

http://www.youtube.com/watch?v=TA85SmHrMT4

Song lyrics	Conditions/improvements wanted

I did my part in World War Two,
Got wounded for the nation,
Now my lungs are all shut down,
There ain't no compensation.
Chorus:
    I'm gonna go to work on Monday one more time.
    I'm gonna go to work on Monday one more time, one more time.
    I'm gonna go to work on Monday one more time.
The doctor says I smoke too much,
He says that I ain't trying,
He says he don't know what I've got,
We both know that he's lying.
Chorus
The last time I went near my job,
I thought my lungs were broken,
Chest bound down with iron bands,
I couldn't breath for choking.
Chorus
The politicians in this state,
They're nothing short of rotten,
They buy us off with fancy words,
And sell us out to cotton.
Chorus
The doctor says both lungs are gone,
He says that I can't make it,
But I can't live without a job,
Somehow I've got to take it.
Chorus
They tell me I can't work at all,
There ain't no need of trying,
But living like some used up thing,
It's just this short of dying.
Chorus
Sitting on my front porch swing,
I'm like someone forgotten,
Head all filled with angry thoughts,
And lungs filled up with cotton.
Chorus	

Questions
- *What illness does the singer have?*
- *How is the singer's illness related to his job?*
- *How could this song be seen as an argument for forming a union?*

Name _____   Date _____

Student Handout: Analyzing Labor Songs

Directions: As you listen to and read the lyrics of each song, make a list of the conditions workers faced and the improvements they wanted. Underline the words in the song that helped you get this information.

"Look for the Union Label" by Union of Needletrades, Industrial and Textile Employees, AFL-CIO, CLC

http://www.youtube.com/watch?v=QO7VUklDlQw

http://unionsong.com/u103.html

This song is short. As you watch the video of the song, record the lyrics in the left column, then follow the instructions above. ("ILG" in the song refers to the International Ladies Garment Workers' Union.)

Song lyrics	Conditions/improvements wanted

Questions

- *Where does the song suggest we should look for a union label?*

- *According to the song, why is it important to buy a product made by a union member?*

- *How does this song help the public to understand the importance of unions?*

Student Handout: Analyzing Labor Songs

Directions: As you listen to and read the lyrics of each song, make a list of the conditions workers faced and the improvements they wanted. Underline the words in the song that helped you get this information.

"Solidarity Forever"

http://www.youtube.com/watch?v=kYiKdJoSsb8 (Pete Seeger version)

Song lyrics	Conditions/improvements wanted
Chorus: *So lidarity forever, solidarity forever, solidarity forever,* *For the union makes us strong!* When the union's inspiration through the worker's blood shall run, There can be no power greater anywhere beneath the sun Yet what force on earth is weaker than the feeble strength of one . . . But the Union makes us strong! *Chorus* They have taken untold millions that they never toiled to earn, But without our brain and muscle not a single wheel could turn. We can break their haughty power—gain our freedom when we learn That the Union makes us strong! *Chorus* In our hands is placed a power greater than their hoarded gold, Greater than the might of armies magnified a hundred fold. We can bring to earth a new world from the ashes of the old, For the Union makes us strong!	

Questions

- *Who is "they" in "They have taken untold millions that they never toiled to earn"?*
- *What is meant by "But without our brain and muscle not a single wheel could turn"?*
- *How does this song help workers to understand the importance of unions?*

Applying the Concepts

For students to understand and appreciate the role that unions can play in effecting change, we engage students in a labor negotiation simulation around classroom rules and practices. When we do this activity, we invite labor organizers to class, but you can conduct the simulation with the help of two colleagues or friends.

In the simulation, your students are labor, and you are management.

1. A single student comes up and tries to negotiate with you individually (for example, for less homework). You deny his or her request.

2. One of the "labor organizers" (an actual labor organizer or your colleague/friend) then works with the students (with you out of the room) to compile their list of collective demands (e.g., condition of chairs and desks, supplies, amount and type of homework, etc.). At the same time, you work with the other "organizer" to compile your own list of demands as the teacher (e.g., preparedness of students, amount and type of homework, etc.).

3. Students create songs (to the tune of one of the labor songs or a song they know) and posters that detail their demands.

4. You return to the room, and the "labor organizers" mediate a discussion between the two sides to work toward a settlement on as many issues as possible.

Questions following the simulation may include:

- *How did individual negotiation (when one of you came up on your own to try to get what you wanted) compare with collective bargaining (when you stood together) in terms of effectiveness?*

- *How do you account for the differences?*

- *How did developing songs and posters help your cause?*

- *What types of issues do you think labor unions find to be the most important?*

Extending the concepts in your class . . .

Enlist the music and art teachers to help with the creation of songs and posters.

If any of your children's parents are union members, have them share their experiences with your class.

Invite the president of the teachers' union in to discuss issues and tactics.

Set up a roundtable with secretaries and custodians to talk about their working conditions and negotiation issues.

Dolores Sanchez, labor organizer, says: "Even if we can't vote, we walk the streets to help elect representatives who can pass laws beneficial to workers." Invite a politician in to talk with your class about the extent to which the needs of working people have influenced her or him in formulating legislation.

Bloomers by Rhoda Blumberg

In the Newbery Honor book *Bloomers,* Rhoda Blumberg tells the story of women in the mid-1800s who fought for women's rights in a variety of ways. Although many people know about the struggle for suffrage, this story centers on the adoption of a new style of dress, bloomers, that would grant women more freedom of movement.

This book is often read during Women's History Month when teachers focus on how women won the right to vote. *Bloomers* can help students understand that suffragists had to make choices about which tactics would be most effective in gaining support for their message. While the bloomer costume granted women physical freedom, it also distracted from their central message of equal rights; thus, women's rights activists ultimately abandoned the style.

Social Studies Concepts and Discussion Questions

Social studies concepts	Questions to ask based on the text
Culture	Describe the clothing styles for women in the 1850s.
	How did the clothing style affect women?
	What is meant by the sentence, "Libby had freed herself from the female's 'cage' during her honeymoon in Europe?"
	Why did Elizabeth Cady Stanton like wearing the new pants style called bloomers?
Gender roles	Why did Libby feel that she needed her husband's approval when she decided to wear the pants costume on her honeymoon?
	How did Elizabeth Cady Stanton's family react to her wearing "black satin pants and dress that barely reached her knees?" Why did they react that way?
Justice and rights	For what rights were Amelia Bloomer, Elizabeth Cady Stanton, and Susan B. Anthony fighting?
	Why did some women work for both antislavery and women's rights?
	Why was Elizabeth Cady Stanton called a "radical revolutionary"?
Change	What was "temperance," and why did Amelia Bloomer promote it?
	How did Amelia Bloomer, Elizabeth Cady Stanton, and Susan B. Anthony get their message across?
	How did audiences respond to the women's ideas and their bloomer costumes?
	Why do you think women stopped wearing bloomers?

Activity

Many teachers use *Bloomers* to explore the evolution of women's clothing styles. The book also provides a terrific launching point for an analysis of women's lives and the tactics they employed in the struggle for equal rights. Because there is a rich array of primary source documents that are accessible to elementary age children, we engage students in a "History Mystery" to uncover what women's lives were really like in the mid-1800s. In a History Mystery, students do the work of historians as they read and analyze documents to draw conclusions about a time period. Although not all students will grow up to be historians, they will all grow up to be citizens who need to develop the skills of analysis so that they can draw conclusions and make informed judgments. The History Mystery in the following handout asks students to assess the lives of women by analyzing cartoons, speeches, letters, pictures, and artifacts. All of the documents are cut up and put in envelopes so that students can pick each one up individually and then categorize the documents to help them grapple with the History Mystery question.

Before the students begin their History Mystery, we demonstrate one aspect of the lives of women at that time with clothing artifacts—a floor-length skirt and a simulated corset (an ace bandage wrapped very tightly around the waist and diaphragm of one of the students)—so that students can see and experience how nineteenth-century fashion (prior to the advent of bloomers) affected women's everyday lives. When a volunteer is "dressed," we ask students to take a note to the teacher upstairs, but we remind her that she needs to take her baby (a doll) and her candle with her. Invariably, students find that they cannot hold up the dress while simultaneously protecting the baby from the candle. This demonstration reveals to students the lack of mobility women experienced due to their traditional garments. We then record this information in the chart that accompanies the History Mystery. The students are now ready to continue their analysis with their own set of documents.

Name _____ Date _____

Student Handout: History Mystery

Directions: You have all become historians. Historians are really detectives who find clues and put together puzzle pieces until a more complete picture emerges.

1. With your group, read through the documents in the packet.

2. As you read, record evidence you discover in the chart. Be sure to record the source of each piece of evidence.

Question to Investigate: Were Women's Lives That Bad in the Mid-1800s?

Evidence that women's lives were pretty bad	Evidence that women's lives were basically fine

Political cartoon, "Election Day" (The Library of Congress American Memory).

- -

"Nothing was more detrimental to health and beauty than the system of tight lacing [of the corset]."

> —Excerpt from a letter to the editor of *The Magnolia*

"excessive heat induced by an inordinate amount of clothing" led to "spinal affections" and excessive pressure caused "torpidity of the liver and portal circulation accompanied by constipation."

> —Excerpt from a letter to the editor of *The Lily*

> *Seneca Falls and the Origins of the Women's Rights Movement*

- -

A corset worn by women in the mid-1800s (drawing by Anne Herlihy).

- -

"It has been [stated] that 'chemistry enough to keep the pot boiling, and geography enough to know the location of the different rooms in the house, is learning . . . enough for a woman.' I have myself heard men, who knew for themselves the value of intellectual culture, say they cared very little for a wife who could not make a pudding, and [showed disgust] at the . . . thirst for knowledge exhibited by some women.

"[This behavior is just like] the policy of the slaveholder, who says that men will be better slaves, if they are not permitted to learn to read."

—Excerpt from a letter from Sarah Grimke to her sister, Angelina, 1838

"At marriage, she loses her entire identity. . . . But it will be said that the husband provides for the wife, or in other words, he feeds, clothes, and shelters her! Yes! He *keeps* her, and so he does a favorite horse; by law they are both considered his property. Both may, when cruelty of the owner [forces] them to run away, be brought back by the strong arm of the law . . . this is humiliating indeed, but nevertheless true."

—Excerpt from Ernestine Rose's speech at the Women's Rights Convention, Worcester, Massachusetts, October 15, 1851

"[A]ll of my sex are, by your honor's verdict, doomed to an inferior position under this so-called democratic government.

"Your denial of my citizen's right to vote is the denial of my right consent [agreement] as one of the governed, the denial of my right of representation as one of the taxed . . . [is a denial of] my sacred rights to life, liberty and property.

"[Yes, I have been tried according to law,] but by forms of law all made by men, interpreted by men, administered by men, in favor of men, and against women."

—Excerpt from Susan B. Anthony's speech in court when brought to trial for illegally voting in Rochester, New York, 1872

History Mystery (Possible Student Answers)

Question to Investigate: Were Women's Lives That Bad in Mid-1800s?

Evidence that women's lives were pretty bad	Evidence that women's lives were basically fine
• Long skirts were hard to walk in, especially up the stairs (artifact). • Corsets were so tight that women could barely breathe (artifact). • Tight dresses caused women lots of health problems (letter to Lily editor). • Women were not allowed to get the same education as men; they only needed to know how to cook and keep house (Grimke letter). • Women were kind of like slaves really (Grimke letter). • Women were "kept" by men . . . kind of like the way a man kept his horse (Ernestine Rose). • Husbands got control of the children and all of the property (Lucy Stone and Henry Blackwell). • Women couldn't vote (Anthony speech). • Men made the laws (Anthony speech).	• Husbands provided for their wives (Ernestine Rose). • There was a natural order of things with women caring for children and men going out to vote and work. Voting could upset all that (antisuffrage cartoon).

Discussion Questions

- *How bad were women's lives?*

- *What was the greatest problem facing nineteenth-century women?*

- *Was the United States truly a democracy?*

- *What options did women have to deal with the problems they faced? How might people who don't have the power to vote effect change?*

Applying the Concepts

After students have analyzed the situation of nineteenth-century women, they are ready to write a speech, poem, or song to protest the conditions and advocate for change or maintain the status quo for women. The substance of their speech, poem, or song is rooted in the History Mystery documents, as well as in the *Bloomers* book. In an effort to model this genre for students, we examine the song on the next page, an actual suffrage protest song that was performed on street corners to convince citizens of the need for women's suffrage.

Student Handout: Suffrage Song

Directions: As you read and listen to the song, circle the phrases that give arguments FOR and AGAINST women's suffrage.

"Winning the Vote" by Mrs. A. B. Smith 1912

http://creativefolk.com/suffrage.pdf
http://media.smithsonianfolkways.org/liner_notes/folkways/FW05281.pdf

BOYS:
I've been down to Madison
To see the folks and sights;
You'll laugh, I'm sure, to hear them talk
About the women's rights,
Now 'tis just as plain as my old hat,
That's plain as plain can be
That if the women want the vote,
They'll get no help from me.

Not from Joe, not from Joe;
If he knows it, not from Joseph;
No, no, no, not from Joe;
Not from me, I tell you no!

GIRLS:
Say, friend Joseph, why not we
Should vote as well as you?
Are there no problems in the State
That need our wisdom too?
We must pay our taxes same as you;
As citizens be true.
And if some wicked thing we do,
To jail we're sent by you.

Yes we are, same as you;
And you know it, don't you Joseph?
Yes you do, yet you boast;
You'll not help us win the vote.

BOYS:
But dear woman, can't you see,
Your home is your true sphere?
Just think of going to the polls
Perhaps two times a year.
You are wasting time you ought to use
In sewing and at work,
Your home neglected all those hours;
Would you such duty shirk?

Help from Joe? Help from Joe?
If he knows it, not from Joseph;
No, no, no, not from Joe;
Not from me, I tell you no!

GIRLS:
Joseph, tell us something new;
We're tired of that old song;
We'll sew the seams and cook the meals,
To vote won't take us long.
We will help clean house, the one too large,
For man to clean alone,
The State and Nation, don't you see,
When we the vote have won.

Yes we will, and you'll help,
For you'll need our help. Friend Joseph;
Yes you will, when we're in,
So you'd better help us win.

BOYS:
You're just right, how blind I've been,
I ne'er have seen it thus;
'Tis true that taxes you must pay
Without a word of fuss;
You are subject to the laws men made,
And yet no word or note,
Can you sing out where it will count.
I'll HELP YOU WIN THE VOTE!

Yes I will. [Girls] Thank you, Joe.
[All] We'll together soon be voters;
Yes we will, if you'll all
Vote "Yes" at the polls next fall.

Student Handout: Suffrage Song (continued)

Questions

1. *What arguments against suffrage do the boys present in the song?*

2. *How do the girls counter those arguments?*

3. *Why do the girls make reference to "taxation without representation" in their arguments for suffrage? How are their lives parallel to the lives of the colonists who argued for independence from Great Britain?*

Directions for Speech, Song, or Poem

Create your own speech, song, or poem arguing for or against women's suffrage. In your work, be sure to

- present at least three supporting arguments for the position you have selected (feel free to quote from relevant suffrage and antisuffrage documents, as well as from any relevant documents from the American Revolution).

- address the arguments of your opponents.

- make your arguments with passion.

Extending the concepts in your class . . .

Play and sing other protest songs with your students.

If any of your children's parents have participated in a protest movement, invite them in to speak.

Engage students in a discussion of whether there are any groups in America today that do not enjoy equal rights and, if so, what actions they have taken to try to remedy their situation. Ask students what sorts of actions they would recommend.

Examine anti-tax protestors today. Discuss whether their concerns are the same as those of women who had no vote.

We the Kids by David Catrow

This wacky take on the Preamble of the U.S. Constitution illustrates each line of the document as seen through the eyes of children on a camping trip. For example, the children's dog "provides for the common defense" of the children inside the tent.

Frequently used on Constitution Day, September 17, this book can provide the foundation for an ongoing analysis of U.S. government and the extent to which it lives up to the goals outlined in the Preamble. The goals serve as the criteria by which students can evaluate the performance of U.S. government at different points in history and today. We conduct the activity below prior to reading the book to students.

Activity

In many ways, the scenario of children going off on a camping trip in the story mirrors the state of nature that John Locke described. The chaos and disorder found in a state of nature where there is no organized government is the best argument for establishing a government. The activity below allows students to experience a state of nature and derive the need for government.

Scenario

All of the students in our school have been transported to an island. There are no other human beings on the island; indeed, no human beings have ever lived there. Some of the students in your group are nervous and are beginning to argue about what they should do to survive.

Task: Your job is to figure out how to make decisions about the best way to survive; it is NOT to answer basic survival questions.

Discuss the following questions:

- *Do you need a government? If so, how will you select the leader(s)?*
- *Who should be allowed to participate in the decision-making process (the kindergartners, second graders, sixth graders, etc.)?*
- *How will you prevent the strong from bossing around the weak?*
- *What should the weak do if the strong take over?*
- *Are all of the people on the island entitled to certain rights? Why or why not?*
- *To what rights are people entitled? How will you guarantee those rights?*
- *What will you do if people violate the rights of others?*

After students discuss the scenario, we generate a list of the problems they faced and their conclusions about the purposes of government and the challenges that face governments.

Island Problems and Solutions (Possible Answers)		
Problems in a state of nature		**Solutions government can provide**
People argue about how the leader should be selected.	→	Democracy (vs. dictatorship) People who understand the issues can vote (only fifth and sixth graders?).
People need to decide what the leader's job is.	→	Protect the people. Help the people get what they need.
The strong people bully the weak people.	→	Laws are passed to establish order and punish those who don't keep the peace
People take other people's stuff.	→	Laws are passed to protect property, with punishment outlined.
The weaker people work together to gang up on one of the stronger people and take all of his stuff.	→	No one should be more powerful than anyone else. All people are created equal.
People fight about what they are allowed to do/have.	→	People discuss what the basics are that everyone needs, and then everyone makes sure they have them.
People who disagree with the leaders are silenced.	→	Everyone is entitled to freedom of speech, even if it's against the leader.

After this activity is completed, we read the book aloud and pose the following concept questions. We then ask students to draw parallels between the language in the Preamble and the list of solutions that government can provide that they generated.

Social Studies Concepts and Discussion Questions

Social studies concepts	Questions to ask based on the text
Power	To whom does "We the people" (or "We the kids") refer? According the Preamble, where does government derive its power?
Government	What form of government does "We the people . . . do ordain and establish this Constitution of the United States of America" imply? What are the characteristics of "a more perfect union"?
Justice	Explain the concepts of "justice" and "injustice." Give examples. How can a government help ensure justice for all of its citizens?
Peace	What is meant by "domestic tranquility"? What is meant by "the common defense"? How are they similar or different?
Liberty	What are some of "the blessings of liberty" that Americans enjoy? What is meant by "posterity"?

Applying the Concepts

Students' analysis of the Preamble provides them with criteria to evaluate the U.S. government at different points in history or today. In the following handout, we have included a report card template, as well as a model of how to complete the template for a particular era.

Name _____ Date _____

Student Handout:
U.S. Government Report Card for the _____

Directions: Identify the time period you have been assigned. Use the template below to evaluate how well the government lived up to each of the goals in the Preamble to the U.S. Constitution.

Preamble goals	Grade	Comments
We the people….		
Form a more perfect union		
Establish justice		
Insure the domestic tranquility		
Provide for the common defense		
Promote the general welfare		
Secure the blessings of liberty to ourselves and our posterity		

From *Every Book Is a Social Studies Book: How to Meet Standards with Picture Books, K–6* by Andrea S. Libresco, Jeannette Balantic, and Jonie C. Kipling. Santa Barbara, CA: Libraries Unlimited. Copyright © 2011.

U.S. Government Report Card for the <u>New Deal Era</u>
(Sample Student Responses)

Preamble Goals	Grade	Comments
We the people . . .	B	*Not everyone could vote—African Americans in the South could not.*
Form a more perfect union	A	*The country felt united in its fight against the Depression. Everyone tried to do her or his part.*
Establish justice	B	*Not everyone got all the benefits of the New Deal—some of the poor people didn't.*
Insure the domestic tranquility	B+	*Even though one in four people were out of work, there were no major riots, although some workers went on strike. FDR won in a landslide in 1936, so he must have been liked by a lot of people.*
Provide for the common defense	A-	*In FDR's third term, the United States was attacked by the Japanese at Pearl Harbor, but we fought back and won in World War II.*
Promote the general welfare	A-	*New Deal programs were all about the people's welfare—relief for those out of work included programs like the CCC that paid people to clean up trails and help in the national parks. The programs didn't get us completely out of the Depression, but they were part of a massive effort to try.*
Secure the blessings of liberty to ourselves and our posterity	A-	*Many New Deal programs were established to help future generations have freedom from hunger and poverty. For example, the FDIC protected people's money in banks, so they wouldn't lose it all in a bank failure, and Social Security provided money when people got old, so that they wouldn't starve. But some people didn't like programs like Social Security because they didn't want the government taking money out of their paychecks for the future.*

Extending the concepts in your class...

Have students select aspects of the Preamble that should be adopted for your classroom Constitution.

Have students discuss the extent to which the goals of the Preamble are reflected in the way your school runs and to identify which goals need to be addressed more effectively.

Have students discuss the extent to which the goals of the Preamble are reflected in the way other countries run today and to identify which goals need to be addressed more effectively.

Recommended Books

For a list of related books of individuals who used their power to gain rights, please see "Biographies" on the Recommended Books list at the end of Chapter 5, "Individual Development and Identity." In addition, to access books about the struggle for civil rights, see Chapter 6, "Individuals, Groups, and Institutions."

Empowerment

Blumberg, R. *Bloomers.* New York: Aladdin, 1996. (Women's rights activists in the 1850s give up their corsets and long skirts for the new bloomer costume, which gives them freedom of movement.) *To what extent can clothing be a symbol of empowerment?*

Brown, A. *Piggybook.* New York: Alfred A. Knopf, 1986. (In this moralistic fable, the overworked and underappreciated Mrs. Piggott leaves her swinish husband and two sons to fend for themselves, and they literally turn into pigs.) *How can those with little power have a say in their homes?*

Bunting, E. *Rudi's Pond.* New York: Clarion Books, 1999. (When a sick boy dies, his friends and classmates remember him by building a schoolyard pond in his memory.) *How can those with seemingly little power have a say in society?*

Bunting, E. *Sunshine Home.* New York: Clarion Books, 2005. (When he and his parents visit his grandmother in the nursing home where she is recovering from a broken hip, everyone pretends to be happy until Tim helps them express their true feelings.) *How can one person find the power to help others?*

Cohn, D. *¡Sí, Se Puede! Yes We Can! Janitor Strike in L.A.* El Paso, TX: Cinco Puntos Press, 2005. (Bilingual story of the L.A. janitors' strike in 2000 seen through the eyes of a Mexican immigrant child, whose widowed mother cleans offices nights and weekends but still can't manage to support her family.) *How much power do workers have?*

Fine, E. H., and Josephson, J. P. *Armando and the Blue Tarp School.* New York: Lee & Low Books, 2007. (Armando and his father are trash-lickers in Mexico, but when a "school" comes—a blue tarp set down near the garbage dump—Armando's father decides that Armando must attend classes and learn. Based on a true story.) *How much power does one person have to make a difference?*

Golenbock, P. *Teammates.* New York: Harcourt, 1990. (PeeWee Reese's public act of acceptance and friendship of his teammate Jackie Robinson quiets the racial taunting that Robinson experienced as the first African American in Major League Baseball.) *How much power does one person have to make a difference?*

Hoose, P. *Hey Little Ant*. Berkeley, CA: Tricycle Press, 1998. (An ant pleads with a kid who is tempted to squish it.) *How much power should people have, and how can they use it justly?*

Munsch, R. *The Paper Bag Princess*. Toronto: Annick Press, 1980. (A princess saves her fiancé prince with her wits, but then he claims she isn't feminine enough. She decides not to marry him after all.) *How does courage empower people?*

Responsibility and Action

Bunting, E. *Fly Away Home*. New York: Clarion Books, 1991. (A homeless boy who lives in an airport with his father, moving from terminal to terminal and trying not to be noticed, is given hope when he sees a trapped bird find its freedom.) *What responsibility does government have to its citizens?*

Karr, K. *Mama Went to Jail for the Vote*. New York: Hyperion Books for Children, 2005. (A daughter comes to appreciate her suffragist mother's commitment to women's rights.) *How important is suffrage? How important is the right to protest for rights?*

McCully, E. *The Bobbin Girl*. New York: Dial Books for Young Readers, 1996. (Rebecca, a ten year old, helps support her family's meager income by working as a "bobbin girl" in 1830s New England.) *What responsibility does the government have to its citizens' well-being?*

Merriam, E. *Daddies at Work*. New York: Simon and Schuster Books for Young Readers, 1989. (The author examines different jobs performed by working fathers.) *What responsibility do citizens have to their families and communities?*

Merriam, E. *Mommies at Work*. New York: Alfred A. Knopf, 1961. (The author examines different jobs performed by working mothers.) *What responsibility do citizens have to their families and communities?*

Pinkney, A. D. *Sit-In: How Four Friends Stood Up by Sitting Down*. New York: Little, Brown Books for Young Readers, 2010. (A celebration of the fiftieth anniversary of the Woolworth's lunch counter sit-in, when four college students staged a peaceful protest that became a defining moment in the struggle for racial equality.) *What options do citizens have if government becomes unresponsive to their needs?*

Rappaport, D. *The School Is Not White! A True Story of the Civil Rights Movement*. New York: Hyperion Books for Children, 2005. (An African American family in Mississippi in 1965 pursues equal education for their children.) *What options do citizens have if government becomes unresponsive to their needs?*

Weatherford, C. B. *Freedom on the Menu: The Greensboro Sit-Ins*. New York: Puffin Books, 2007. (Weatherford describes the 1960 lunch-counter sit-ins.) *What options do citizens have if government becomes unresponsive to their needs?*

Governance

Catrow, D. *We the Kids: The Preamble to the Constitution of the United States*. New York: Puffin Books, 2005. (This text features the Preamble to the Constitution with wacky illustrations designed to make it comprehensible to kids.) *What are the most important ideas in the Preamble?*

Fink, S. *The Declaration of Independence: The Words That Made America*. New York: Scholastic, 2002. (This version of the Declaration of Independence that explains the meaning, line by line, through rich illustrations.) *What are the most important ideas of the Declaration of Independence?*

Fritz, J. *Shh! We're Writing the Constitution.* New York: G. P. Putnam's Sons, 1987. (A quirky behind the scenes look at the Constitutional Convention.) *How effectively were conflicting issues resolved in the Constitution?*

Kennedy, E. M. *My Senator and Me: A Dog's Eye View of Washington.* New York: Scholastic Press, 2006. (The author takes readers through a typical day in Washington for a senator from the perspective of the senator's dog.) *How important is the job of a senator to our democracy?*

Larsen, K. *Tara Pays Up!* New York: Kane Press, 2006. (When Tara pays for her new arts and crafts kit, she learns where the sales tax she pays goes and what it pays for.) *How important is government's power to tax to the community?*

Levy, E. *If You Were There When They Signed the Constitution.* New York: Scholastic, 1992. (Q & A about events leading up to and the discussions and compromises that resulted in the Constitution.) *Was it inevitable that we would end up with the form of government detailed in the Constitution?*

Maestro, B. *A More Perfect Union: The Story of Our Constitution.* New York: Lothrop, Lee & Shepard, 1990. (The story of the birth of our Constitution and the adoption of the Bill of Rights.) *What are the most important principles of the Constitution?*

The National Book and Literary Alliance, ed. *Our White House: Looking In, Looking Out.* Cambridge, MA: Candlewick Press, 2008. (More than one hundred renowned authors and illustrators contributed essay, stories, illustrations, and poems about the White House.) *How is the White House at the center of our democracy?*

Smith, L. *Madam President.* New York: Hyperion Books for Children, 2008. (A young girl fantasizes about being president and how she would fulfill the president's responsibilities.) *How does one govern effectively?*

Winters, K., and Brunkus, D. *My Teacher for President.* New York: Puffin Books, 2008. (A second grader who has been learning about the president's job thinks that his teacher would be the perfect candidate, given her qualifications.) *Is the president's job more similar to or different from being a teacher?*

References

About.com: Women's History. "Marriage Protest of Lucy Stone and Henry Blackwell—1855." http://womenshistory.about.com/library/etext/bl_marriage_stone_blackwell.htm (cited October 22, 2009).

The Elizabeth Cady Stanton & Susan B. Anthony Papers Project. "Remarks by Susan B. Anthony in the Circuit Court of the United States for the Northern District of New York (19 June 1873)." http://ecssba.rutgers.edu/docs/sbatrial.html (cited October 22, 2009).

The Library of Congress American Memory. "By Popular Demand, Votes for Women Suffrage Pictures, 1850–1920, Election Day!" http://memory.loc.gov/pnp/cph/3a50000/3a51000/3a51800/3a51845r.jpg (cited October 22, 2009).

McMillen, S. G. *Seneca Falls and the Origins of the Women's Rights Movement.* New York: Oxford University Press, 2008, 129.

Rise Up Singing Project. "Go to Work on Monday by Si Kahn." http://riseupsingingproject.blogspot.com/2009/10/go-to-work-on-monday.html (cited September 22, 2009).

Smithsonian Folkways Records and Service Corporation. "Winning the Vote, 1912." http://media.smithsonianfolkways.org/liner_notes/folkways/FW05281.pdf (cited October 22, 2009).

Songs for Teaching—Using Music to Promote Learning. "Drill Ye Tarriers." http://www.songsforteaching. com/folk/drillyetarriersdrill.htm (cited September 22, 2009).

Sunshine for Women. "Letters on the Equality of the Sexes Addressed to Mary S. Parker, President of the Female Anti-Slavery Society by Sarah Grimké—1837, Letter X: Intellect of Woman, Brookline, 8th Mo., 1837 Sarah K. Grimké." http://www.pinn.net/~sunshine/book-sum/grimke3.html (cited October 22, 2009).

Women's Rights from Past to Present—Primary Sources. "Ernestine Rose's speech at the Women's Rights Convention, Worcester, Massachusetts on October 15, 1851." http://www.womeninworldhistory.com/ WR-09.html (cited October 22, 2009).

Union Songs. "Look for the Union Label by Paula Green." http://unionsong.com/u103.html (cited September 22, 2009).

Union Songs. "Solidarity Forever by Ralph Chaplin." http://unionsong.com/u025.html (cited September 22, 2009).

YouTube, "Drill, Ye Tarriers Drill." http://www.youtube.com/watch?v=jmQtqW4G28g (cited September 22, 2009).

YouTube, "Look for the Union Label 1981 classic ad." http://www.youtube.com/watch?v=QO7VUklDlQw (cited September 22, 2009).

YouTube, "Si Kahn—Gonna Go to Work on Monday One More Time." http://www.youtube.com/ watch?v=TA85SmHrMT4 (cited September 22, 2009).

YouTube, "Solidarity Forever (Pete Seeger)." http://www.youtube.com/watch?v=kYiKdJoSsb8 (Pete Seeger version) (cited September 22, 2009).

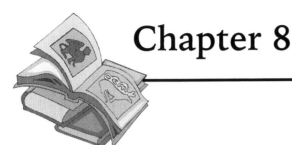

Chapter 8

Production, Distribution, and Consumption

In a second-grade classroom, students on the rug giggle as their teacher holds up the cover of Doreen Cronin's recent classic, *Click Clack Moo: Cows That Type*. When the teacher asks the students for predictions about the book, the picture of three cows, a hen, and a duck gathered around a typewriter prompts them to offer that this will be a silly story. After the story is read, the teacher asks students to list the characters and describe the setting, retell the story in order, explain the problem and its resolution, and then list all of the surprising things that happened (the cows discovering an old typewriter, learning to type, etc.). She introduces the word "communication," asks for a definition, and then asks students to list the different forms of communication in the story. She concludes the discussion by asking students to talk to a classmate about what the story says about the importance of language and communication. As a final activity, students write notes to each other that convey important messages (an invitation to play, a thank you for a gift, etc.).

This lesson reinforces language arts reading skills and highlights the power of language in the process of communication. Although these literacy skills and concepts are important, *Click Clack Moo* provides an excellent opportunity to discuss social studies concepts. Teachers can use the book to explore basic economic concepts such as wants (a diving board for the ducks in the pond), needs (electric blankets for the cows for warmth), goods (milk and eggs), and the negotiation of goods for wants and needs. In fact, this book may easily be viewed as a primer on negotiation and collective bargaining in which labor (the farm animals) uses its powerful weapon (strike) against management (Farmer Brown) to help precipitate an agreement, although resolution still requires the intervention of a third party, the labor arbitrator (Duck).

Our students love this lesson, especially when they can play the role of the duck; participating in decision making is empowering. This lesson helps students understand that economics is not simply about numbers and graphs; it's about decision making and real-life issues.

The three picture books highlighted in this chapter are *Chicken Sunday* by Patricia Polacco, *Uncle Jed's Barbershop* by Margaree King Mitchell, and *Fly Away Home* by Eve Bunting. The books enable students to grapple with essential questions that are rooted in economics concepts.

Essential Questions

How do individuals or societies deal with scarcity? How *should* they?

What is our economic responsibility to our neighbors in need? What is a community's economic responsibility to its neediest citizens?

How can individuals and societies make good economic decisions?

How important is economic justice? What are we, as individuals and a society, willing to do to achieve it?

Chicken Sunday by Patricia Polacco

Chicken Sunday is the story of children who want to purchase an expensive Easter hat for their grandmother. When they are falsely accused of throwing eggs at the hat owner's shop, they must find a way to prove their innocence and earn enough money for the hat at the same time.

Patricia Polacco's beautifully written books are often the focus of author studies in many classrooms. Teachers frequently use her books to examine word choice, style, voice, and the structure of personal narratives, all components of the study of language arts. Teachers may also use the books to address prominent social studies themes of friendship, community, family, tolerance and religious and cultural diversity. In addition to emphasizing these worthwhile themes, Polacco's book provides us an excellent opportunity to focus on economic concepts. We use the book to help students identify different types of resources needed to acquire a desired item. Ultimately, students identify a class goal and a strategic plan (which includes a list of the resources needed) to accomplish their goal.

Social Studies Concepts and Discussion Questions

Social studies concepts	Questions to ask based on the text
Tradition and change	Describe the Easter traditions in the Walker family.
	Describe the Easter traditions of the young girl's family.
	How does the coming of the freeway at the close of the book change the economic and community dynamics of the town?
	How do the children keep their traditions alive despite the changes in their community?
Identity	How do the children feel when Mr. Kodinski accuses them of throwing eggs at the back door of his shop?
	How do they respond to his accusation?
Wants and needs	Does the grandmother, Miss Eula, need the hat?
	What if she doesn't get it; would she still be OK?
	When confronted with their lack of monetary resources, what do the children do to accumulate them?

Social studies concepts	Questions to ask based on the text
Supply and demand	How could the children have earned more money? Would there have been a demand for these eggs in August?
Citizenship	Why doesn't the shop owner, Mr. Kadinski, take the children's money? How important is the money to him? What should the children do with the money they raised?
Community	How does the relationship that develops between the children and Mr. Kadinski reflect the importance of community?

Activity

After the first reading of *Chicken Sunday,* we introduce the three types of resources (natural, human, and capital) needed to create a product. We define terms and ask students to think of examples of each kind of resource. As we reread *Chicken Sunday,* students record on a chart the resources necessary to produce Pysanky eggs.

Resources Needed for Production

	Natural resources	Human resources	Capital resources
Definition	Found in or on the earth	People's labor and skill level	The tools used to create a product
Real-life example **Goal:** Produce T-shirts	*Cotton*	*Picking cotton, sewing the fabric*	*Factory, needles, thread, sewing machines, etc.*
Text example **Goal:** Produce Pysanky eggs (Teachers elicit student responses)	*The eggs*	*Painting the eggs*	*Brushes, beeswax, candle, small funnel with a wooden handle, packets of yellow, red, and black dye, etc.*

Applying the Concepts

As an application of the newly learned economic concepts, students come to consensus about a class goal and brainstorm a list of projects that they can design to accomplish the goal. One of the goals identified by our students was to get hermit crabs for our classroom. Students then worked collaboratively to design projects to raise money to purchase the pets and the supplies needed. Each group identified the resources it would need to complete its projects successfully. The following handout reflects the varied projects students conceived to fulfill our class goal. This activity required students to apply the economic concepts of entrepreneurship and resources introduced via the Polacco book.

Name _____ Date _____

Student Handout: Goals, Products, and Resources

Directions: Use the chart below to identify product ideas to raise money to achieve your class goal. Then identify the resources needed to complete your product ideas.

Our Class Goal: _____

Student product ideas	Natural resources needed	Human resources needed	Capital resource needed

Goals, Products, and Resources (Sample Student Responses)

Our Class Goal: *Buy hermit crabs*

Student product ideas	Natural resources needed	Human resources needed	Capital resource needed
Vegetable stand	• Home-grown vegetables: cucumbers, tomatoes, string beans, zucchini, peppers	• Planting • Weeding • Watering • Harvesting	• Seeds • Mulch • Fertilizer • Stakes • Baskets for storage • Table • Advertising/signs • Chairs
Sea glass jewelry	• Sea glass from local beaches	• Collect the glass • Polish the glass • Design jewelry	• Jewelry wire and clasps • Wire cutters • Table • Advertising/signs • Chairs
Pinecone fire-starters	• Pinecones fallen from local trees	• Collecting the pinecones	• Bags to bundle the pinecones • Table • Advertising/signs • Chairs

This activity enables us to raise interesting, upper-level questions, such as: What natural resources do we have available in our community? How does the availability of items affect their pricing? How do you go about pricing items? How do you identify a potential client base?

As an extension of this activity, students used this model to design and pursue individual service projects. For example, one student wanted to clean up the temple to which his family belonged. His chart focused on the human resources (labor of picking up trash, cleaning, and painting) and capital resources (cleaning supplies, paint, brushes, etc.) needed to accomplish his goal. A group of three girls wanted to beautify certain areas of the school by planting flowers that would attract butterflies. Their project was to raise money to purchase these plants by making and selling bird feeders. Their chart included natural (pinecones), human (assembling the bird feeders), and capital (peanut butter, seeds, string) resources. For these extended projects, the planning piece was critical in helping students envision and accomplish their tasks.

Extending the concepts in your class . . .

Create a class goal to pursue throughout the marking period, analyze whether the goal represents a want or a need, and devise a class plan to raise money for that goal.

Discuss goals that children have in their families and as individuals, identifying the wants and needs and the resources required to achieve those goals.

Have students examine the newspaper to identify successfully completed community projects. Discuss how the projects came to fruition, including the resources required.

Uncle Jed's Barbershop by Margaree King Mitchell

Jed, an African American barber, living in the Depression-era South, dreams of one day owning his own barbershop. Because Uncle Jed loses his money in a failed bank and uses his money to help his family and those in need in his community, this dream is deferred until very late in his life. The author's use of declarative sentences conveys the impact of segregation on the lives of African Americans without emotionality.

A favorite book of teachers, *Uncle Jed's Barbershop* is told through the voice of Uncle Jed's niece, Sarah Jean, and is often used to teach about poverty, discrimination, community, and sacrifice. Mitchell's book is also excellent for helping children understand the concept of opportunity cost and the process of decision making, because Jed has life-altering decisions to make. By the end of the lesson, students engage in an economic decision-making activity of their own.

Social Studies Concepts and Discussion Questions

Social studies concepts	Questions to ask based on the text
History	In what time period is the story set? Where is the story set? Describe the life of African Americans in this time period and place. What is a sharecropper? How did the Depression affect Uncle Jed's dream? How did the failure of the bank affect the community as a whole?
Family	Describe the relationship of Uncle Jed and his niece. How did Uncle Jed help his family in its time of need?
Prejudice and discrimination	Why did Sarah Jean have to wait in the "colored" waiting room? Describe her treatment. How else were African Americans segregated during this time period?
Community	How did members of the community help each other during the Depression? What kinds of sacrifices did Uncle Jed make for his community?
Savings, investing, and interest	What was Uncle Jed's expectation about putting his hard-earned money in a bank? Why do people put money in banks today, and how are banks safer?
Opportunity cost	What was the cost to Uncle Jed of helping his niece and his neighbors? What would have been the cost to Uncle Jed of not helping them?
Economic justice	Should people be denied surgery if they do not have enough money? How would the existence of health insurance have changed both Sarah Jean's and Uncle Jed's experiences? What insights does this story give us about the impact of race and class on daily life?

Activity

When making a decision, the most valuable alternative that you *don't* choose is your opportunity cost. To help students understand the concept of opportunity cost, we provide them with the following example.

> If a child has five dollars and wants to buy candy but also wants to purchase a present for her mother's birthday, the **opportunity cost** of buying only the candy will be feeling guilty about having no present for Mom. Or, conversely, choosing to buy the present for Mom would have an **opportunity cost** of not getting any candy.

Focusing on opportunity cost enables us to teach students the process of decision-making in a methodical way, including the importance of weighing the pros and cons of the alternatives. After discussing the definition and some examples of the concept, we ask students to identify Uncle Jed's opportunity cost throughout the story.

Dilemma: How should Uncle Jed spend his life savings?

Uncle Jed's options	Pros	Cons = opportunity costs
Use his money to pay the $300 needed for his niece's operation	• *Makes it easier for his family to pay for his niece's medical needs* • *Gets her better, faster care, thus saving her life*	• *Delays the purchase and opening of his barbershop* • *Defers his dream*
Continue to save his money for the barbershop (don't pay for the operation)	• *Fulfill his dream* • *Open the barber shop sooner*	• *His niece will have to suffer as she waits for the money for treatment* • *His niece may die*

Through interactive questioning, students supply the information recorded in the chart. Once the chart is complete, we ask students what recommendations they would make to Uncle Jed regarding how he should spend his money. Ultimately, students evaluate Uncle Jed's choice to defer his dream of opening his own barbershop.

Applying the Concepts

As an application of the newly learned concepts of opportunity cost and economic decision making, students work to resolve a classroom dilemma. In one of our classrooms, students raised money for Heifer International's Read to Feed program, in which students solicit sponsors who pledge a dollar amount for each book that they read. After raising thousands of dollars, students needed to decide how best to allocate their money. The following chart reflects the decision-making process of the students.

Name _____ Date _____

Student Handout:
Considering Opportunity Costs for Class Fundraiser

Directions: Use the chart below to brainstorm options for how to spend the money we raised. Consider the pros and opportunity costs for each spending option.

Dilemma: How do we spend the money we have raised for_____
_____?

Class Options	Pros	Cons = Opportunity Cost

Decision:

Opportunity costs:

Considering Opportunity Costs for Class Fundraiser

Dilemma: How do we spend the money we have raised for Heifer International?

Class options	Pros	Cons = opportunity cost
Each student can use the money she or he raised to purchase animals of his or her own choosing	• Individuals get more choice • We can benefit a lot of different communities in a small way	• Not everyone will raise enough money to purchase an animal • Students might compete, not cooperate, with one another in terms of raising money • The impact of one animal in a community may not be as great as one community receiving lots of animals
Students pool their money as a class and make a decision as a class as to what animals to purchase	• Students work together to accomplish a goal—cooperation vs. competition • Students who raise a small amount of money are still a part of the big project • Opportunity to purchase the more costly Ark (two of each animal for a single community), resulting in a larger impact on one community	• Each student gets less individual choice • Only one community will get animals • It isn't fair that students who raise more money get the same amount of say as kids who raised little money

Decision: Pool our money as a class and make a decision as a class about which animals to purchase.

Opportunity costs: We didn't all get to choose the animals each of us wanted; we will help one community, not a lot of communities.

This activity enables us to raise questions such as: What are some decisions you have made recently? What were the opportunity costs of those decisions? To what extent are you satisfied with your decisions and your decision-making process?

In addition to exploring students' individual choices and their opportunity costs, it is a natural extension, given the community emphasis in *Uncle Jed's Barbershop* and in our Heifer project, to explore opportunity costs of community choices. Decision making can be examined in the book with respect to the hospital's decision not to provide a service to Uncle Jed's family until they paid for the care. The opportunity cost of this decision is clearly the ill health of poorer citizens like Sarah Jean. Another, less obvious cost may be the diminished productivity of her entire family as they worry about her health. Although the issue of health care may seem to be beyond the grasp of second graders, it is likely that there are children in our classes who have already been affected in some way by a health care system that does not provide equally for all citizens. Sadly, some students may be far too familiar with the opportunity costs of such a system.

A discussion of the opportunity costs of not treating all members of society can lead to questions such as these: How is money spent in our community? Who makes those decisions? What are the individual and societal opportunity costs of some of those decisions?

Teaching students a process that enables them to represent visually the pros and cons and opportunity costs of their decisions leads to more thoughtful decisions. This skill has broad application in studying history, in analyzing literature, and in students' own lives as individuals and citizens of a community.

Extending the concepts in your class . . .

Students can analyze the opportunity costs of decisions about how money is spent in their homes, schools, and communities.

When your family decided to purchase_____, what was the opportunity cost of that decision for your family?

> (For example, if a child's family decided to buy a car, the opportunity cost might have been that they could not go on vacation that year.)

When your school decided to purchase_____, what was the opportunity cost of that decision for your school?

> (For example, if your school decided to buy new playground equipment, the opportunity cost might have been that they could not buy new computers.)

When your community decided to _____, what was the opportunity cost of that decision for your community?

> (For example, if your town decided to fix the basketball courts, the opportunity cost might have been that no one could play on the courts for three months.)

Fly Away Home by Eve Bunting

In *Fly Away Home,* a young boy tells his poignant tale of living in an airport with his father after his mother dies. He and his father move around the airport, trying to avoid detection. Even in this desperate situation, the boy finds a community of people who care for him as he learns to hope for a better future.

Eve Bunting often tackles topics that raise students' awareness about social issues. *Fly Away Home* is no exception; this extraordinary book deals with the difficult issue of homelessness. Friendship and community are the themes around which social studies lessons are often taught. We also use the book to teach about economic justice and engage students in a simulation about the realities of the cost of living.

Social Studies Concepts and Discussion Questions

Social studies concepts	Questions to ask based on the text
Wants and needs	What basic needs do the boy and his father have? How do they take care of their basic needs in the airport?
Community	What are the norms of public behavior in an airport? How are people treated when they violate those norms? How should they be treated?
Freedom	Why is the bird in the story significant? To what extent do the boy and his dad enjoy freedom?
Goods and services	What goods and services are offered at the airport? How do people in the story, especially the boy, try to earn money?
Resources and economic justice	Why do the boy and his father have such limited resources? Why isn't the father able to work full time?

Activity

We use *Fly Away Home* to emphasize economic justice; students explore issues of fairness in economic affairs and the idea that laws and government should treat people equitably, regardless of their level of wealth.

In an effort to delve beyond the distressing existence of homelessness and poverty in our society, we help students look at some of the key causes of these problems. We do so through both research and discussion. We have found that one of the best sources of research on these issues for our students is information provided by guest speakers who run soup kitchens or homeless shelters. In our county, representatives from Long Island Cares and the Interfaith Nutrition Network have provided our students with both the numbers and the stories behind the numbers to spark further questions and research from our students. Some of the questions arise from vocabulary used by the speakers; others from the vocabulary in *Fly Away Home*.

Poverty

- What is it?
- What is "the poverty line"?

Living wage versus minimum wage

- What is the minimum wage in our area?
- Why do some jobs pay more than others?

Working poor

- The father in this story has a part-time job; why doesn't he work full time?

Homelessness

- How long must one be without a home to be called "homeless"?

- What other options did the father in this book have?

- What causes homelessness?

- What are the connections among homelessness and low-paying jobs, unemployment, lack of affordable housing, lack of education, and too few services for people with substance abuse and mental illness issues?

Applying the Concepts

To help students understand the expenses of modern life and how hard it might be to cover those costs, we have found it valuable to engage students in a simulation in which they draw slips of paper from a hat with a job description, monthly salary, and family profile. Students then try to provide for their needs—housing, food, health care, child care, transportation, phone, utilities, education, clothing, and entertainment. They research how to meet these needs by looking in the newspaper for apartments, examining grocery store flyers to buy food, asking their parents about their monthly costs, and so on. After their analysis, students explore the realities of the costs of living and how quickly families can fall behind through questions such as those on the following handout.

Name _____ Date _____

Student Handout: Monthly Budget Worksheet

Directions: After consulting a variety of sources (such as newspaper housing ads, supermarket flyers, your parents), record costs of living in the chart below. Then calculate the difference between your monthly income and expenses. Your goal is to spend less than your income, based on your job description, monthly salary, and family profile.

Expenses	Monthly cost	Source of information
Housing (Mortgage or rent, property taxes, furniture, etc.)		
Food		
Clothing		
Health care		
Communication (Phone, Internet)		
Utilities		
Child care		
Transportation		
Education (Tuition, college savings, supplies)		
Entertainment (Dinner out or ordered in, movies, sporting events, gifts, vacations, electronic gadgets and equipment, dance classes, music lessons, camp, theatre, etc.)		
Total expenses		

Your monthly income (after taxes) $_____

minus

Your total monthly expenses $_____

=

$_____

Questions

- *Do you have enough money to cover your monthly expenses? If not, what can you eliminate from your monthly budget?*
- *On what did you spend the greatest percentage of your salary?*
- *Are any items in your budget expendable?*
- *If you have excess money, what will you do with it?*
- *Did the amounts in any of the expense categories surprise you?*

Average Annual Salary 2007

Fast Food Worker $16,700 Two children *After taxes:* $14,331 *Monthly wage:*	Lawyer $118,280 Legal Secretary $40,550 Two children *After taxes:* $114,358 *Monthly wage:*
Hair Salon Shampooer $17,480 School Bus Driver $26,190 Two children *After taxes:* $37,128 *Monthly wage:*	Teller $23,620 Two children *After taxes:* $20,077 *Monthly wage:*
Movie Theatre Ticket Taker $17,860 *After taxes:* $15,198 *Monthly wage:*	Carpenter $41,260 One child *After taxes:* $30,945 *Monthly wage:*
Supermarket Cashier $18,380 One child *After taxes:* $15,623 *Monthly wage:*	Police Officer $50,670 Registered Nurse $62,480 Three children *After taxes:* $84,683 *Monthly wage:*
Home Health Care Aide $18,940 Telemarketer $24,430 Two children *After taxes:* $38,488 *Monthly wage:*	Registered Nurse $62,480 One child *After taxes:* $46,860 *Monthly wage:*
House Cleaner $19,550 One child *After taxes:* $16,618 *Monthly wage:*	Computer Analyst $75,890 One child, one adult *After taxes:* $56,918 *Monthly wage:*
Short Order Cook $19,880 Manicurist $22,020 One child *After taxes:* $35,360 *Monthly wage:*	Psychologist $83,610 Judge $99,270 Two children *After taxes:* $131,674 *Monthly wage:*
Sewing Machine Operator $21,080 One child *After taxes:* $17,918 *Monthly wage:*	Pharmacist $98,660 Three children, one adult *After taxes:* $71,251 *Monthly wage:*
Vet Assistant $22,180 One child *After taxes:* $18,853 *Monthly wage:*	Optometrist $101,840 Pediatrician $145,210 Two children *After taxes:* $165,524 *Monthly wage:*
Taxi Driver $22,740 Janitor $22,710 Two children *After taxes:* $38,633 *Monthly wage:*	Airline Pilot $148,810 Two children, one adult *After taxes:* $107,143 *Monthly wage:*
Teacher Assistant $22,820 Teacher $52,450 Three children *After taxes:* $56,453 *Monthly wage:*	Orthodontist $185,340 Three children, one adult *After taxes:* $122,324 *Monthly wage:*

Source: www.money-zine.com/download/Average-Annual-Salaries.xls.

From *Every Book Is a Social Studies Book: How to Meet Standards with Picture Books, K–6* by Andrea S. Libresco, Jeannette Balantic, and Jonie C. Kipling. Santa Barbara, CA: Libraries Unlimited. Copyright © 2011.

Discussion Questions

- *Why do different jobs command different salaries?*

- *Are these differences fair?*

- *Is it possible for all people to stay within a budget?*

- *If you could not stay within a budget in real life, what consequences could you expect?*

After the simulation, students can compare their findings with statistical data on homelessness in America and in their community. Students are often surprised to discover how low the poverty line is for a family of four ($26,500 in 2008) and how difficult it would be to live with that level of income (or even double that amount).

As we discuss the issue of homelessness with our students, we move from the characters in the book to real people living on the streets. In *Fly Away Home,* when any of the homeless people living in the airport became "noticeable," the authorities took that person away. We ask students why this was so and whether it was wrong for the airport to do this. The documentary *Homeless in America* (Redford & Wiseau, 2004) provides real-life stories of people, many with jobs, who lost their homes and describes how society reacted to them. In the film, many New Yorkers were grateful for Mayor Rudy Giuliani's "quality of life" statutes against panhandling, sleeping on benches, and so on. We ask students why New Yorkers would be grateful and whether they agree that when homeless people are visible, it diminishes the quality of life for others. Finally, we want students to consider whether they find it justifiable to arrest people for panhandling and sleeping on benches.

Extending the concepts in your class . . .

Contact local organizations to speak to your students about the conditions, causes, and solutions for homelessness and poverty.

Research the most current statistics on the poverty line in the United States, as well as the percentage of people living below it in your community.

After doing your research, discuss the best way to address the problem of poverty and homelessness with the expert speakers and decide on a plan of action (e.g., working directly at a local shelter, conducting a clothing or food drive, writing a letter to your state assemblyperson or congressperson about the amount of money allocated for poverty programs in your community).

Recommended Books

Distribution of Resources, Economic Justice, and Scarcity

Bartone, E. *Pepe the Lamplighter*. New York: HarperCollins, 1997. (A young immigrant boy's father is angry that his son has taken a job lighting gas street lamps to support the family.) *What is the tension between work and education for children in families with little wealth?*

Baylor, B. *The Best Town in the World*. New York: Harcourt, 1995. (Children talk about their father's hometown, the best town in the world, where food tastes better and everything is superior.) *In a "good" town, are activities available to all, regardless of income?*

Baylor, B. *The Table Where Rich People Sit.* New York: Aladdin Paperbacks, 1998. (A girl discovers that her impoverished family is rich in things that matter in life, especially being outdoors and experiencing nature.) *How important is having money?*

Bunting, E. *A Day's Work.* New York: Clarion Books, 2004. (An older immigrant and his grandson try to earn money as day laborers in America.) *What is life like for a day laborer?*

Bunting, E. *Fly Away Home.* New York: Clarion Books, 1991. (A homeless boy who lives in an airport with his father, moving from terminal to terminal and trying not to be noticed, is given hope when he sees a trapped bird find its freedom.) *To what extent should society ensure that all families have homes?*

Cohn, D. *¡Si, Se Puede! Yes We Can! Janitor Strike in L.A.* El Paso, TX: Cinco Puntos Press, 2002. (A young boy's mother becomes leader of a strike, and he finds a way to help her.) *How important are unions in the struggle for economic justice?*

Demi. *One Grain of Rice.* New York: Scholastic Press, 1997. (Mathematical folktale in which a girl teaches a raja a lesson about fairness.) *What are the responsibilities of those in power to provide for equitable distribution of resources?*

Freedman, R. *Kids at Work: Lewis Hine and the Crusade Against Child Labor.* New York: Clarion Books, 1994. (This book provides photographic documentation of turn-of-the-century exploitation of children working in factories.) *Is it ever appropriate for children to work in factories?*

Guthrie, W. *This Land Is Your Land.* New York: Little, Brown Books for Young Readers, 2002. (The folk song, including the verses about the Depression, is illustrated in this book.) *What do the lyrics of the song tell us about the time period in which it was written, the Great Depression?*

Hazen, B. S. *Tight Times.* New York: Puffin Books, 1983. (A young child who is not allowed to have a dog because times are tight finds a starving kitten in a trash can on the same day his father loses his job.) *Why do some families find it hard to afford what other families would consider necessities?*

Hopkinson, D. *Saving Strawberry Farm.* New York: Greenwillow Books (HarperCollins), 2005. (Hopkinson tells the story of saving a struggling strawberry farm in a Midwestern town during the Great Depression.) *What economic responsibility do we owe our neighbors?*

Howard, G. *A Basket of Bangles: How a Business Begins.* Brookfield, CT: The Millbrook Press, 2002. (This book describes how the Grameen Bank and a microloan helped a woman in Bangladesh start her own business.) *How can micro lending be a positive force for change?*

Leonni, L. *Its Mine!* New York: Alfred A. Knopf, 1996. (Through frogs that argue over who owns which worm and fly, this tale explores the concept of private ownership versus sharing resources.) *Should individual people be able to own or control public resources?*

Lied, K. *Potato: A Tale from the Great Depression.* Washington, DC: National Geographic Children's Books, 2002. (Written by an eight-year-old girl in Kansas, this is the story of the girl's grandparents and how hard their life was during the Great Depression.) *How hard was life during the Great Depression? Whose responsibility is it to ensure that people have enough food during difficult economic times?*

McBrier, P. *Beatrice's Goat.* New York: Aladdin, 2004. (In Uganda, a young girl receives a goat that will help her family earn money to support themselves.) *How can individuals and governments best help families to support themselves?*

McCully, E. A. *The Bobbin Girl.* New York: Dial Books for Young Readers, 1996. (This is the story of a girl working and striking in an 1830s mill in Lowell, Massachusetts.) *What kinds of conditions are appropriate for workers?*

Menzel, P. *Material World: A Global Family Portrait.* San Francisco: Sierra Club Books, 1995. (Menzel provides a photo portrait of a statistically average family in every corner of the world.) *To what extent can all families in the world provide for their needs?*

Miller, W. *Rent Party Jazz*. New York: Lee & Low Books, 2008. (When a boy's mother loses her job during the Depression, a musician tells him how to organize a rent party to raise the money they need.) *What should the role of the community be in addressing individual economic problems?*

Mills, L. A. *The Rag Coat*. New York: Little, Brown Books for Young Readers, 1991. (A girl whose family can't afford to buy her a coat receives a coat made of squares from her classmates' old clothing.) *What is the responsibility of the community to those with fewer resources?*

Milway, K. S. *One Hen: How One Small Loan Made a Big Difference*. Tonawanda, NY: Kids Can Press, 2008. (How a small loan to a boy in Ghana made a big difference to his family, his education, and his community.) *How do loans fuel the economy?*

Polacco, P. *I Can Hear the Sun*. New York: Puffin Books, 1999. (A young boy living in a shelter for children learns to care for wild birds.) *Why are some children homeless?*

Polacco, P. *The Keeping Quilt*. New York: Aladdin Paperbacks, 2001. (Made by an immigrant great-grandmother and her friends, a beautiful quilt is composed of scraps of fabric from little girls' dresses, the aprons of aunts, and so on. It serves as a quilt, a tent, a huppah at a wedding, a tablecloth, and so on.) *How can you use the resources at hand (as opposed to monetary resources) to create something new that you and future generations can use and value?*

Ringgold, F. *Tar Beach*. New York: Crown, 1996. (A young girl dreams of flying free above her Harlem apartment during the Depression.) *What evidence of social and economic injustice does the book provide?*

Rosen, M. J. *Home: A Collaboration of Thirty Distinguished Authors and Illustrators of Children's Books to Aid the Homeless*. New York: HarperCollins Children's Books, 1992. (Thirteen authors and seventeen illustrators celebrate the things that make up a home.) *To what extent should society ensure that all families have homes?*

Rylant, C. *An Angel for Solomon Singer*. New York: Orchard Paperbacks (Scholastic), 1996. (A man deals with hopelessness as he lives alone in a hotel for men.) *How can we make a difference, individually and as a community, in addressing poverty?*

Rylant, C. *The Relatives Came*. New York: Aladdin Paperbacks, 2005. (The memorable experience of a large group of relatives visiting their family one summer.) *To what extent can families have fun together without a lot of money?*

Smith, D. J. *If the World Were a Village*. Tonawanda, NY: Kids Can Press, 2002. (Statistical look at standard of living in the world.) *What responsibility do we have to make sure that everyone in the world has access to clean water, education, and health care?*

Smothers, E. F. *The Hard-Times Jar*. New York: Farrar, Straus & Giroux, 2003. (A migrant family uses a jar to save for emergencies.) *How important are savings to a family's well-being?*

Steig, W. *When Everybody Wore a Hat*. New York: HarperCollins Children's Books, 2005. (This is a memoir of immigrant childhood in the Bronx nearly a hundred years ago.) *What evidence do authors give about the economic level of the families they write about (in this case, the author's own family)?*

Wilder, L. I. *Christmas in the Big Woods: My First Little House Book*. New York: HarperCollins Children's Books, 1995. (A young pioneer girl and her family celebrate Christmas in their cabin in the Wisconsin woods, focusing on the nonmaterial aspects of the holiday.) *How can presents be made from available resources when money is scarce?*

Wyeth, S. D. *Something Beautiful*. New York: Dragonfly Books, 2002. (A young girl finds beauty in her city neighborhood.) *What role should individuals and government (through taxes) have in maintaining a neighborhood?*

Zemach, M. *It Could Always Be Worse*. New York: Farrar, Straus & Giroux, 1990. (A rabbi's clever advice leads a husband and wife, who feel poor, to appreciate what they have.) *How much do people need?*

Goods, Services, and Economic Systems

Andersen, W. *Once upon a Company: A True Story*. New York: Orchard Books, 1998. (Andersen chronicles the first six years of the College Fund Wreath Company started by seven-year-old Joel and his two sisters. The text includes a glossary that explains business and economic terms.) *To what extent can you help produce goods or services to help your family's budget?*

Barber, B. E. *Saturday at the New You*. New York: Lee & Low Books, 1996. (A young African American girl wishes she could do more to help Momma with her customers at her beauty salon, then gets a chance to do so.) *To what extent can you help with any family member's work to produce goods or services?*

Carle, E. *Pancakes, Pancakes*. New York: Aladdin Paperbacks, 1998. (By cutting and grinding wheat for flour, a boy starts from scratch to make pancakes.) *Where does our food come from?*

Cronin, D. *Click Clack Moo: Cows That Type*. New York: Simon and Schuster, 2000. (When Farmer Brown's cows find a typewriter, they start making demands and go on strike until they get what they want.) *How much power do those who provide goods have?*

Davies, J. *The Lemonade War*. New York: Houghton Mifflin, 2007. (A business-savvy sister and a social butterfly brother compete with rival lemonade stands.) *How important is making money?*

Hall, D. *The Ox-Cart Man*. New York: The Penguin Group, 1983. (A nineteenth-century New Englander fills his cart with surplus harvest and handmade items to sell at a market, a ten-day journey away, then goes shopping for manufactured goods to bring home.) *How does a farmer participate in economic systems?*

Hartland, J. *Night Shift*. New York: Bloomsbury USA Children's Books, 2007. (Late at night, after children have gone to bed, people who work the night shift, like street sweepers, window dressers, newspaper printers, road workers, and donut bakers, are doing their jobs.) *How important are the goods and services that night shift workers provide?*

Hautzig, D. *At the Supermarket*. New York: Orchard Books, 1994. (Twenty-four hours, hour-by-hour, of what goes on in a supermarket is described.) *What are the hidden services, hour-by-hour, in other places of work (including delivery, inventory, organization, customers, workers, advertising, presentation, etc.)?*

Krull, K. *Supermarket*. New York: Holiday House, 2001. (Explains modern supermarkets and how they work, discussing how they organize, display, and keep track of the items they sell.) How does the organization of supermarkets reflect and address people's wants and needs?

Pilkey, D. *The Paperboy*. New York: Orchard Books, 1996. (A chronicle of the early-morning work of a paperboy.) How difficult is it for the newspaper to end up at your door every morning?

Polacco, P. *Chicken Sunday*. New York: Putnam, 1999. (To thank old Eula for her wonderful chicken dinners, the children decorate and sell eggs and buy her an Easter hat.) *To what extent are children capable of providing goods and services?*

Rotner, S., and Kreisler, K. *Everybody Works*. Brookfield, CT: The Millbrook Press, 2003. (A look at different types of work in rural and urban settings.) *How important are the goods and services that workers provide?*

Schwartz, D. *If You Made a Million*. New York: HarperCollins Children's Books, 1994. (Marvellisimo the Mathematical Magician and his children followers team up in various enterprises to make a million dollars and figure out along the way what that much money looks like and what it could be used for, especially if they have to pay back their loans.) *To what extent does making money mean making choices?*

Sis, P. *Madlenka*. New York: Farrar, Straus & Giroux, 2000. (A little girl's trip around her ethnically diverse neighborhood to tell about her loose tooth is like a trip around the world.) *To what extent are immigrants an economic force in your community?*

Opportunity Cost

Adler, D. *The Babe and I*. Orlando, FL: Voyager Books, 2004. (During the Depression, a boy finds a way to earn money to help his family.) *How can a child whose parent has lost a job contribute to the family?*

Kennedy, F. *The Pickle Patch Bathtub*. Berkeley, CA: Tricycle Press, 2004. (This warm story teaches children about the value of a dollar and how people can work together to achieve a goal.) *How does a family with little money decide what is truly important?*

Mitchell, M. K. *Uncle Jed's Barbershop*. New York: Aladdin Picture Books, 1998. (After facing a lifetime of obstacles, including the Great Depression and segregation, Uncle Jed, at the age of seventy-nine, finally achieves his dream of opening up his own barbershop.) *What is the opportunity cost of helping others to one's own business plans?*

Viorst, J. *Alexander, Who Used to Be Rich Last Sunday*. New York: Athenuem Books for Young Readers, 2009. (A young boy realizes all of the things he could have done with his money.) *How do you decide how to spend your money with respect to wants and needs?*

Williams, V. B. *A Chair for My Mother*. New York: Greenwillow Books, 1984. (A family loses everything they own in a fire and must make decisions about what they can afford to replace.) *How does a family with little money decide what is truly important?*

Resources—Local, National, and Global

Gibbons, G. *How a House Is Built*. New York: Holiday House Books, 1996. (The author provides a step-by-step guide for building a house.) *What human, capital, and natural resources go into building a house?*

Guthrie, W. *This Land Is Your Land*. New York: Little, Brown Books for Young Readers, 2008. (This book features an illustrated version of the folk song.) *What resources do different parts of the country have?*

Priceman, M. *How to Make an Apple Pie and See the World*. New York: Alfred A. Knopf, 1996. (Kids travel the world in search of the ingredients necessary to bake an apple pie, recognizing the global connection to food in their own homes.) *Is it either possible or desirable to be self-sufficient in today's world?*

Seuss, Dr. *The Lorax*. New York: Random House Books for Young Readers, 1971. (The Lorax warns against mindless progress and the danger it poses to the earth's natural beauty.) *How do we conserve resources and balance economic and environmental concerns?*

References

Heifer International. "Read to Feed." http://www.readtofeed.org/ (cited August 20, 2009).

Redford, Kaya, and Tommy Wiseau. *Homeless in America* [documentary]. Wiseau Films, 2004.

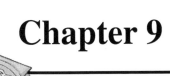

Chapter 9

Science, Technology, and Society

Students enter their first-grade classroom to find their teacher sitting beside a rather large cardboard box. Curious, they gather around on the rug. The teacher asks her students, "What is this?" They reply, "A box!" "Is it?" the teacher queries. She then reads *Not a Box* by Antoinette Portis. In the book, a rabbit is seen sitting in a box. When asked why, he explains that it is not a box; it's a roadster, a rocket ship, a boat, and so on. Children delight in the rabbit's playful explanations of his imaginative cardboard creations before being asked, once again, about the box in front of them, "What is this?" At this point, students are invited to come up and demonstrate for the class the various ways that they "see" the box.

Although this engaging lesson helps students develop their imaginations, the book can also be used to introduce students to the importance of imagination in innovation. Scientists and inventors are highly creative and inventive people who see beyond and think "outside the box." We ask students to draw pictures of scientists, which we then hang around the room. Most depict a man in a white lab coat with test tubes. We ask students to brainstorm what scientists do. The list generally includes mix chemicals, test drugs on animals, look at planets, use microscopes, help doctors, and so on. We then pose the question, "Is the rabbit a scientist?" A lively discussion ensues as we generate a list of characteristics of scientists and inventors.

Students begin to see the importance of creativity and imagination when it comes to seeing their world in new ways, looking for solutions to problems, and developing inventions that may make people's lives better. This lesson provides a foundation for deeper exploration of how science and technology are deeply intertwined with society.

Starry Messenger: Galileo Galilei by Peter Sis, *Dotty Inventions: And Some Real Ones Too* by Roger McGough, and *Letting Swift River Go* by Jane Yolen enable students to explore issues of scientific and technological advancement and the unintended consequences that result from them in our society.

Essential Questions

Does technological advancement always bring progress to all people?

How do we gather accurate information?

To what extent does technology expand our thinking?

How have intended and unintended consequences resulted from technological innovations?

Who should have the power to make decisions about the uses of technology?

Starry Messenger: Galileo Galilei by Peter Sis

This book tells the story of the famous astronomer who "looked at the sky and wondered, 'What if things are not as everyone believes them to be?'" Peter Sis chronicles the life of Galileo from birth to death, highlighting his discoveries, particularly the heliocentric universe and the dramatic reactions they engendered from the powerful Catholic Church.

Galileo Galilei might be used to study the genre of biography, but it can also be used to examine the relationship between science and society and discoveries that challenge accepted truths. In science class, students often learn about the kinds of advances in astronomy described in this book; it is rare that they discuss in depth the strong responses that such advances provoked when the status quo was challenged. For example, when the majority of scientists decided that Pluto was not a planet after all, there was widespread discussion among both the scientific community and the public as to whether they could accept this new conception of the solar system. In fact, we often begin our study of Galileo by examining this change in thinking about Pluto. Ultimately, students come to understand that scientists are people who do research in particular social and historical contexts that shape the way in which their discoveries are received.

Social Studies Concepts and Discussion Questions

Social studies concepts	Questions to ask based on the text
Power	Why did the Church perceive Galileo's popularity as a threat to its power?
	How did the Church exercise its power against Galileo?
Tradition and change	In the world into which Galileo was born, what did people think was at the center of the universe?
	When is it good to hold on to traditions, and when is it good to let them go?
	Why is changing what we believe so difficult?
Belief vs. knowledge	What information did Galileo use to challenge accepted beliefs about the universe? How were Copernicus's theories important to the development of Galileo's inquiries?
	What happens when "truths" are in conflict?
	How do we gather accurate information? How do we find "the truth"?
	What's the difference between belief and knowledge, faith and reason?
Technology	How did technology expand Galileo's thinking about the universe?
	How has technology today expanded our thinking about the universe?

Activity

In this activity, we have students diagram what happened when Galileo's new scientific discovery challenged the accepted beliefs of the time. Ultimately, students will apply their understanding of this case study to another situation in which science challenged accepted beliefs.

In pairs, students complete the diagram on the following page, detailing the clash of science and belief and its effects. We discuss and compile their responses on a class chart.

Name _____   Date _____

Student Handout: The Case of Galileo

What Happens When New Scientific Discoveries Challenge an Accepted Belief?

Directions: Use the graphic organizer below to identify the two different views of the universe and the effects of those conflicting views.

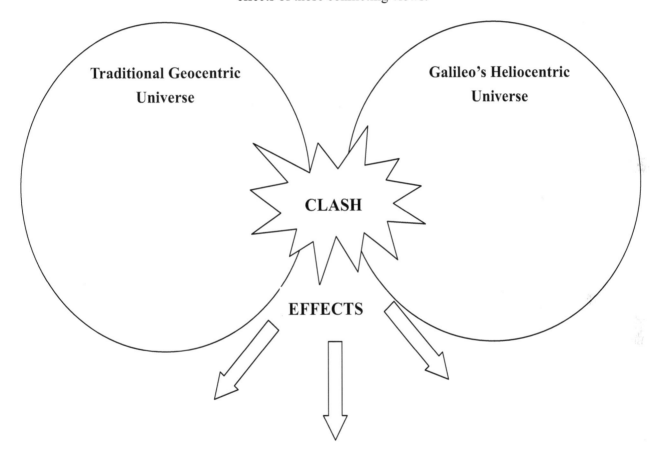

Student Handout: The Case of Galileo

What Happens When New Scientific Discoveries Challenge an Accepted Belief?

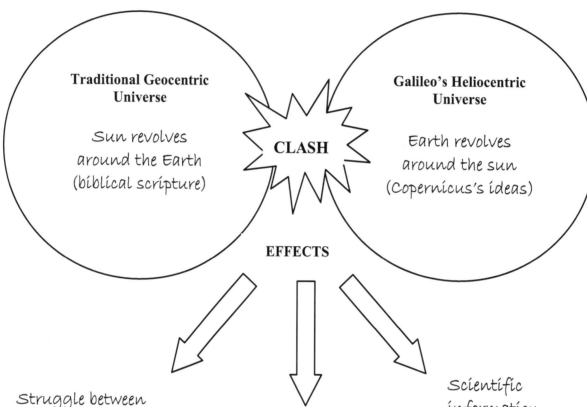

Traditional Geocentric Universe

Sun revolves around the Earth (biblical scripture)

CLASH

Galileo's Heliocentric Universe

Earth revolves around the sun (Copernicus's ideas)

EFFECTS

Struggle between the Catholic Church (established power) and Galileo (the scientific community)

People look to Galileo for answers rather than the Church (or priest) "No one could keep him from passing his ideas along to others until the day he died."

Scientific information challenges belief-based system; beginning of scientific revolution

Applying the Concepts

Students use the same template from the Galileo lesson to research another scientist who challenged conventional wisdom: Charles Darwin. They use books about Darwin (see Recommended Books at the end of the chapter) for their investigation.

Student Handout: The Case of Charles Darwin

Directions: Using the books you have read about Darwin, identify the traditional and Darwinian views of the origins of species and the effects of those conflicting views.

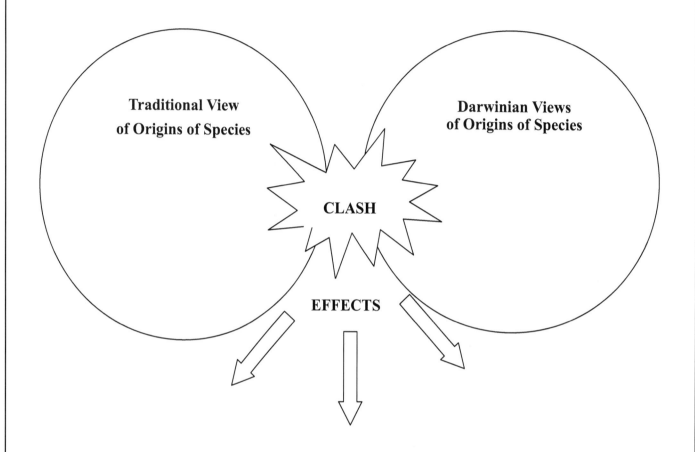

Discussion Questions

- *How did Darwin's scientific discoveries clash with accepted beliefs of the time?*

- *To what extent does Darwinian science continue to clash with beliefs in 2010?*

- *What were the long-term effects of Darwin's teachings?*

- *To what extent do Darwin's struggles compare with Galileo's?*

- *Is it possible to be a person of both faith and reason? (Clearly, this question is designed for abstract thinkers in upper grades.)*

Extending the concepts in your class...

Invite scientists in your community to speak with your students about the process and consequences of new discoveries.

Research other scientists whose work challenged the status quo and resulted in strong reaction from those in power.

Research others who presented social science research that challenged the status quo and resulted in strong reaction from those in power (e.g., Ralph Nader's data on car crashes that were preventable if car companies would employ proper safety design, detailed in *Unsafe at Any Speed*, was challenged by General Motors, and the company also tried to discredit him personally).

Dotty Inventions: And Some Real Ones Too by Roger McGough

Dotty Dabble is off to the National Science Museum to present her new invention. She realizes that many of the items she uses along the way (ballpoint pen, windshield wipers, etc.) were once new inventions, too. Graphics illustrate the genesis of the idea for and progression of each invention, including the trials and errors in its development.

It is often the case that the topic of "inventions" is taught as part of a science unit. However, inventions are a natural fit for social studies, because inventions are created in response to societal needs and wants, and they change people's lives in intended and unintended ways.

Social Studies Concepts and Discussion Questions

Social studies concepts	Questions to ask based on the text
Wants and Needs	What societal needs and wants led to the development of each invention (wipers, Velcro, frisbee, etc.) in the book?
Change	What intended and unintended consequences resulted from the invention? (For example, Velcro on shoes allows young children to fasten their own shoes. However, it is also the case that third graders today may not be able to tie their own shoes.) How did the use of the invention grow from its initial development?
Geography	How do geography and climate help determine where an invention is created (e.g., Velcro being invented by a Swiss mountaineer who comes across burrs on his jaunts in the country)? How have ideas and inventions spread from one place to another?
Values	What values drove the creation of each invention (e.g., parachute—safety, preservation of life; Velcro—safety, efficiency, independence)

Activity

To move students to thoughtful research about how and why inventions emerge and the changes they engender, we spotlight one invention, the windshield wiper, from the book. *Dotty Inventions: And Some Real Ones Too* prompts many questions that we explore with our students:

- There used to be a handle inside the car to run windshield wipers manually. How did electric wipers come to be?

- Who was involved in the development of modern-day windshield wipers?

- Where can we go to find a complete timeline of this invention?

We model how to complete a flow chart for an example illustrated in the book—for example, windshield wipers. Some of the information about each invention is right in the book; some of it is obtained through a simple Google search (The Great Idea Finder, "Windshield Wipers," no date).

The Invention and Evolution of the Modern-Day Windshield Wiper (Sample Student Responses)

Problem, Time, Place:

In an American city in the early 1900s, trolley drivers had to open their windows and use their hands to wipe the rain and snow off of the windshields to see to drive.

People's ideas to address the problems—early invention:

Mary Anderson invented the first windshield wiper, which had a rubber blade connected to a handle inside the car.

[Anderson was awarded a patent in 1903 for a window cleaning device; she tried to interest companies into producing the device, but no one was interested and the patent expired.

http://www.ideafinder.com/history/inventions/windwiper.htm]

The evolution of the invention:

In 1921, Fred and William Folberth invented automatic windshield wipers powered by an "air engine," powered by the car's motor.

In 1926, Bosch invented the electric windshield wiper.

In 1967, Robert Kearns patented the intermittent powered wipers found on all new cars today. Ford and Chrysler used his idea; Kearns spent years in litigation to gain recognition and compensation for his invention. He eventually won a multimillion-dollar judgment.

Impact of the invention on society:

Cars could travel in all kinds of weather.

Transportation safety was improved.

The wiper led to other inventions, such as windshield washer fluid and the spritzer device.

Questions

- *What surprised you in our research?*

- *In your opinion, who invented the windshield wiper? Who should get the credit?*

- *What is a patent, and what role does ite play in the development of an invention?*

- *How did the invention of the windshield wiper affect society?*

- *Were there any unintended consequences of the development and use of the windshield wiper in the auto industry?*

Applying the Concepts

Once we, as a class, have traced the development of the windshield wiper, students apply the research skills that they have acquired to an invention of their own choosing or one of those mentioned in the book (e.g., parachute, ballpoint pen, Velcro) with the ultimate goal being the creation of an illustrated page to be added to *Dotty Inventions: And Some Real Ones Too*.

Students can use the flowchart on the student handout as a template for their research.

Name _____ Date _____

Student Handout: Invention Research Guide

Directions: Select an invention to research. Use the flowchart below to record your findings.

Invention: _____

Problem, time, place:

People's ideas to address the problems – early invention:

The evolution of the invention:

Impact of the invention on society:

Students illustrate the invention they researched showing what it looked like at various stages of development and they draft the text that will accompany their illustrations.

Extending the concepts in your class . . .

Invite local inventors in your community to speak with your students.

Students research inventions that could use updating or improving.

Brainstorm local, national, and/or global problems that could be addressed with an invention.

Letting Swift River Go by Jane Yolen

Letting Swift River Go is a beautifully written prose poem that chronicles a young girl's treasured memories of growing up along the Swift River. From the opening line of the book, "When I was six years old/the world seemed a very safe place," we get the feeling that change is going to happen and that it may not be all good. Change comes in the form of Quabbin Reservoir, which ultimately destroys the town and displaces the people to satisfy the water needs of the larger city of Boston nearby.

This book is often used to introduce students to the concept and genre of memoir. The book serves as a model for children to find and write about moments in their lives that are significant. It also provides teachers with the opportunity to examine with students the double-edged sword of progress.

Social Studies Concepts and Discussion Questions

Social studies concepts	Questions to ask based on the text
Location	How does the location of a river town affect people's lives?
Resources	How did the people along the Swift River use their environment to meet their needs?
Community	What are the elements of the community that Sally Jane remembers?
Wants and needs	How do the needs of one group of citizens (in Sally Jane's town) conflict with the needs of another group of citizens (in Boston)?
Continuity and change	Describe how Sally Jane remembered her childhood along the Swift River. How do you think Sally Jane's life compared to her mother's and grandmother's? Why do you think that? How did the town change with the construction of the reservoir?
Technological development	What is a reservoir, and what is its purpose? How is a reservoir constructed? Is this technological development an example of "progress"?

Citizenship and society	Whose quality of life is more important, the larger number of people in the city or the smaller number in the small towns?
	What is the individual's responsibility in promoting the common good?
Democracy	How was the decision to build the reservoir made?
	What role did the people in the town play in making the decision? What role do you think they should have played?
Perspective	From whose perspective is this (his)tory told?
	How would the (his)story be different if it were told from the perspective of the residents of Boston? Of the governor? Of the people in the towns where the displaced were relocated?

Activity

In addition to the discussion generated by the foregoing questions, we focus on the implications of scientific and technological change on people in societies. We raise the issue of the double-edged sword of progress, the losses and gains related to the technological advancement. Prior to rereading the book, students are assigned the role of a citizen of either the small town or Boston. As we reread *Letting Swift River Go*, each student records how her or his town or city is affected by the construction of the reservoir. We use this information to create a class chart that helps students analyze the impact of the new reservoir and evaluate whether it should have been built.

Analyzing the Effects of Building the Reservoir

Citizens of the small town		Citizens of Boston	
Gains • *Helped the greater good* • *Room is warmer all winter long*	**Losses** • *Town destroyed (church, mill, trees, cemetery, etc.)* • *Loss of history* • *Relocated to different towns (without friends)*	**Gains** • *Accessible water*	**Losses** • *?*

Once we have compiled their responses, we ask students:

- *Who gains the most from the construction of the reservoir? Who loses the most?*

- *Which losses are the most significant?*

- *Is it fair to expect the townspeople to suffer for the benefit of the residents of Boston?*

- *Do some individuals in a community have to sacrifice for the greater good of the community as a whole?*

- *Should the reservoir have been built? Why or why not?*

Applying the Concepts

For students to see that the issue of technological development and "progress" is one that has confronted and continues to confront people across time and place, they research another time when this issue occurred or whether it is presently occurring. We provide students with a list of technological developments, past and present, and ask groups of students to research each project to identify the gains and losses for different groups. Our list of technological developments includes the Three Gorges Dam in China, the transcontinental railroad, a new highway, tunnels or bridge building projects in our local communities, and so on. To support students, we help them generate a list of questions to answer in their research. The list of questions is generated from what happened in the book. Questions some of our students have written include:

- *Where is the proposed project?*

- *Why is the project being proposed?*

- *Who will the project help?*

- *Who will the project hurt?*

- *What gets ruined because of the project?*

- *How long will the project take to finish?*

- *How might people feel when the project is finished?*

In addition to the questions students generated, we require students to include a visual (either hand-drawn or a photograph) of the project they are researching. Students have a variety of options with regard to how they present their research. They can prepare a poster presentation, a PowerPoint presentation, a skit of the town meeting where the proposed project is debated, a radio or television talk show on which the different groups share their views of the proposed project, or create a website that addresses the issues surrounding the project.

Name _____ Date _____

Student Handout: The Effects of Technological Developments

Research Topic: _____

Directions: For the technological development you have been assigned, use the organizer below to record your research findings. You will use these notes to develop your class presentation.

Research questions	Information	Source of information
Where is (was) the project?		
Why is (was) the project proposed?		
Who will (did) the project help?		
Who will (did) the project hurt?		
What will be (was) ruined because of the project?		
How long will (did) the project take to finish?		
How might (did) people feel when the project is (was) finished?		

Extending the concepts in your class . . .

Investigate technological developments in your community/school.

Investigate any technological developments that affected your community in the past.

Invite a local developer, environmentalist, politician, etc. to talk to your students about technological issues your community faces.

Recommended Books

Understanding the World Around Us

Bang, M. *My Light*. New York: Blue Sky Press, 2004. (Narrated by the Sun, this story investigates various forms of energy on Earth, all developed in one way or another from the heat and light of this solar system's major star.) *How can understanding the world around us lead to new technology?*

Jackson, D. *Wildlife Detectives: How Forensic Scientists Fight Crimes Against Nature*. New York: Houghton Mifflin, 2000. (Charger, an elk in Yellowstone Park, was found dead, and the killer had taken his antlers. This book tells the true story of how forensic scientists track people who commit crimes against nature.) *How can technology help us protect the world around us?*

Katz, S. *Looking for Jaguar and Other Rain Forest Poems*. New York: Greenwillow Books, 2005. (Readers can take an imaginary journey through some of the world's most famous tropical rain forests in this book of poems about the animals and plants you would see on such a journey.) *How can knowing about the different parts of the world help us be better caretakers?*

Kudlinski, K. V. *Boy, Were We Wrong About the Solar System*. New York: Penguin, 2008. (From the first humans looking at the night sky to the demotion of Pluto from planet status, this book looks at the mistakes and creativity that are part of scientific discovery.) *How do we know what we know? What role do mistakes play in scientific discovery?*

Pitkin, L. *Journey Under the Sea*. New York: Oxford University Press, 2003. (An imaginary expedition under the sea helps readers see the wonder of the world under water and the dangers that exist for the wildlife and plants beneath the sea.) *How can knowing about the different parts of the world help us to be better caretakers?*

Scieszka, J. *Science Verse*. New York: Viking, 2004. (On Wednesday in science class, Mr. Newton tells his students that they can hear the poetry of science in everything if they just listen close enough.) *How can understanding the world around us help us see things differently?*

Waring, G. *Oscar and the Moth: A Book about Light and Dark*. Cambridge, MA: Candlewick, 2008. (When Oscar the kitten has questions about light and dark, Moth explains about different sources of light, how shadows are made, and why it gets dark at night.) *How can understanding the world around us help us see things differently?*

Winter, J. *Steel Town*. New York: Atheneum, 2008. (Rhythmic text and nocturnal, glowing illustrations bring to life the process through which steel is produced, as well as the people who live in the town where it is made.) *How does technology affect people's lives?*

Innovation

Casey, S. *Kids Inventing: A Handbook for Young Inventors.* Hoboken, NJ: John Wiley & Sons, 2005. (Inventions solve problems in daily life, and this nifty book solves the problems of how to go about inventing. From identifying a problem in your work to thinking about how to solve it, the information is broken down into small, solvable parts.) *How does technology solve problems?*

Cobb, V. *Fireworks.* Minneapolis, MN: Millbrook Press, 2006. (Using photographs, this book shows readers exactly what happens during the production of fireworks.) *What are the different ways that technology can be used?*

Geisert, A. *The Giant Ball of String.* New York: Houghton Mifflin, 2002. (The children of Rumpus Ridge, Wisconsin, are proud to have the biggest ball of string in the world, so when they lose their treasure to a nearby town they devise a clever plan to get it back.) *How can technology help solve problems?*

Geisert, A. *Hogwash.* New York: Houghton Mifflin, 2008. (Wordless illustrations show the enormous and complicated contraption that Mama Pig uses to get her little piglets clean.) *How can technology help solve problems?*

Geisert, A. *Lights Out.* Boston: Houghton Mifflin, 2005. (A young pig constructs a clever way to turn his light out right at 8 P.M.) *To what extent does technology expand our thinking?*

Geisert, A. *Oops!* New York: Houghton Mifflin, 2006. (Depicts, in wordless illustrations, how a little spilled milk led to the destruction of the pig family's house.) *How have intended and unintended consequences resulted from technological innovations?*

Harper, C. M. *Imaginative Inventions: The Who, What, Where, When, and Why of Roller Skates, Potato Chips, Marbles, and Pie.* New York: Little, Brown Books, 2001. (Explores the origins of everyday items such as piggy banks, doughnuts, eyeglasses, high-heeled shoes, and chewing gum.) *How does technology affect our daily lives?*

Kummer, P. *The Calendar: Inventions That Shaped the World.* New York: Children's Press, 2005. (Starting with the concepts of chronological time and calendars based on the sun and the moon, this book explores various historical artifacts relating to time keeping.) *To what extent does technology expand our thinking?*

Kummer, P. *Currency: Inventions That Shaped the World.* New York: Scholastic, 2004. (The author explores the history of currency around the world, how money is made, and its potential use in the future. Information about early barter systems and the role that currency plays in modern society are also included.) *How does technology help people meet their needs?*

McCall, B. *Marveltown.* New York: Farrar, Straus & Giroux, 2008. (A 1950s vision of a futuristic place that shows there are no limits to the imagination.) *What kinds of inventions would make our lives better today?*

McGough, R. *Dotty Inventions: And Some Real Ones Too.* London: Frances Lincoln Children's Books, 2004. (A witty story about Professor Dorothy Dabble's journey to a science competition in London where, along the way, she learns the stories and facts behind the origins of everyday simple and complex things.) *How do inventions affect our daily lives?*

Pelley, K. T. *Inventor McGregor.* New York: Farrar, Straus & Giroux, 2006. (Story about an unconventional inventor who gets his inspiration from everyday things.) *How does living a wide-awake life produce inventions?*

Portis, A. *Not a Box.* New York: HarperCollins, 2007. (This book is a tribute to imaginative play, as seen through the creativity of a rabbit with a box.) *How can we get ourselves to "think outside the box"?*

Shonberg, M. *I Is for Idea: An Inventions Alphabet.* Chelsea, MI: Sleeping Bear Press, 2007. (Shonberg explores the development of many common things we typically take for granted.) *How do inventions affect our daily lives?*

Reynolds, A. *Metal Man.* New York: Puffin Books, 2010. (A tribute to a real metal sculptor, Mitch Levin, who makes sculpture out of junk and helps a boy bring out his own idea in metal.) *How can technology be used in the service of the creation of art?*

Technology and Change

Barker, D. *Maybe Yes, Maybe No: A Guide for Young Skeptics.* New York: Amherst, 1993. (Encourages having an open mind and checking things out to find the truth, rather than blindly accepting everything we hear.) *To what extent does technology expand our thinking?*

Collard, S. *The Prairie Builders: Reconstruction America's Lost Grasslands.* New York: Houghton Mifflin, 2005. (After American pioneers and settlers had destroyed much of the tall grass prairie that once dominated the central part of our nation, scientists today are trying to bring back the prairie to how it was long ago.) *How can technology help us repair the world?*

Collins, S. *When Charlie McButton Lost Power.* New York: Puffin Books, 2007. (This clever rhyming story is good for a discussion about how dependent we are on technology and how it is only when the buzzing stops that we realize what is really important.) *How large a role should technology play in our lives?*

DePaola, T. *Strega Nona Meets Her Match.* New York: G.P. Putnam's Sons, 1993. (A rival uses new inventions to put Strega Nona out of her healing business.) *Does technological advancement always bring progress to all people?*

Earnhart, S. J. *Ludwig the Lift.* Mustang, OK: Tate Publishing & Enterprises, 2009. (Readers learn about a hydraulic chair lift on a school bus, a valuable piece of assistive technology.) *To what extent can technology change differently abled people's lives?*

Hanse, A. *Nuclear Energy: Amazing Atoms (Powering Our World).* New York: PowerKids Press, 2010. (This book provides a simple, age-appropriate explanation of nuclear energy, explores fission and fusion, and discusses the pros and cons of this important energy source.) *Does technological advancement always bring progress to all people?*

Lester, J. *John Henry.* New York: Puffin Books, 1994. (The legendary race between man and machine.) *What are some of the unintended consequences of technological change?*

Novak, M. *The Everything Machine.* New York: Roaring Brook Press, 2009. (A story about how machines and technology have made life so easy for the Quirkians that they do not even need to get out of bed anymore. When the machines break down, this fictional society learns that things are much more interesting when you do them yourself.) *How large a role should technology play in our lives?*

Novak, P. O. *Engineering the ABC's: How Engineers Shape Our World.* Northville, MI: Ferne Press, 2009. (Answers questions about how everyday things work and how engineering is part of a child's everyday life.) *How important are engineers to everyday life?*

Raum, E. *The History of the Computer* (Inventions That Changed the World). Portsmouth, NH: Heinemann, 2007. (Examines what life was like before and after the computer changed the world we live in.) *How important was the invention of the computer?*

Yates, V. *Communication* (Then & Now). Minneapolis, MN: Lerner Publications Company, 2003. (Children can learn about different modes of communication in use today including what they were like in the past and how they have changed.) *Have changes in communication over time been more positive or negative for society?*

Yolen, J. *Letting Swift River Go*. Boston: Little, Brown & Company, 1992. (Yolen describes the effects of the drowning of the towns along the Swift River in western Massachusetts to form the Quabbin Reservoir.) *To what extent does change bring progress for all?*

Biographies of People Who Created Change

Brown, D. *Odd Boy Out: Young Albert Einstein*. New York: Houghton Mifflin, 2004. (This is the story of Einstein as a boy and how his brilliant thoughts and ideas isolated him from his peers and made many people (including his teachers) misunderstand him.) *To what extent does society nurture or ostracize people with creative ideas?*

Carlson, L. *Thomas Edison for Kids: His Life and Ideas, 21 Activities*. Chicago: Chicago Review Press, 2006. (A lively biography of one of the most creative and inventive minds in history with twenty-one activity pages that students can use to replicate some of the simplest of Edison's experiments.) *How can the technology of the past inspire technology for the future?*

Delano, M. *Genius: A Photobiography of Albert Einstein*. Des Moines, IA: National Geographic, 2005. (This book follows the life experiences and influences that helped make Albert Einstein who he was.) *What inspires a person who influences the future of the world?*

Fradin, D. *Nicolaus Copernicus: The Earth Is a Planet*. New York: Mondo, 2004. (This biography of Copernicus introduces the man and his work on the heliocentric theory, for which he is best remembered. The author explains how Copernicus came to accept the notion that the planets revolve around the sun and why it was such a revolutionary and dangerous idea.) *Why would some people resist change?*

Herbert, J. *Leonardo da Vinci for Kids: His Life and Ideas, 21 Activities*. Chicago: Chicago Review Press, 1998. (This dynamic biography of the ultimate Renaissance man describes Leonardo's life while offering a good deal of background about art and historical data about Italy. Youngsters will also gain insight into Leonardo as a scientist, inventor, and humanist.) *How does technology of the past influence technology in the future?*

Lasky, K. *One Beetle Too Many: The Extraordinary Adventures of Charles Darwin*. Cambridge, MA: Candlewick, 2009. (Darwin's life, from his childhood as a poor but remarkably curious student to landing a spot as the naturalist on the *Beagle*. The fanciful watercolors and collage capture Darwin's fascination with the natural world.) *How important is curiosity in scientific discovery?*

McGinty, A. B. *Darwin: with Glimpses into His Private Journal and Letters*. New York: Houghton Mifflin Books for Children, 2009. (The interweaving of third-person text with Darwin's own words and quotes from his contemporaries leads to a broader understanding of the scientist and the discoveries that rocked his time). *How do scientists further understanding? To what extent are new ideas welcomed by society?*

Nez, J. *Cromwell Dixon's Sky Cycle*. New York: G.P. Putnam's Sons, 2009. (Fictionalized account of the true story of fourteen-year-old Cromwell Dixon who, following the Wright Brothers' historical flight, built a flying bicycle.) *How do inventions inspire other inventors?*

Panchyk, R. *Galileo for Kids: His Life and Ideas, 25 Activities*. Chicago: Chicago Review Press, 2005. (Galileo's scientific discoveries challenged the ideas held by the Catholic Church, and he was tried for heresy. Additional information discusses how individuals and events influenced Galileo's life.) *Who should have the power to make decisions about the uses of technology?*

Schanzer, R. *How Ben Franklin Stole the Lightning*. New York: HarperCollins, 2003. (A story that portrays Franklin as having a playful mind and suggests that it was this trait, along with his curiosity, that allowed him to capture lightning in a jar with the famous kite experiment.) *Where do inventors and scientists get their inspiration?*

Sis, P. *Starry Messenger: A Book Depicting the Life of a Famous Scientist, Mathematician, Astronomer, Philosopher, Physicist, Galileo Galilei.* New York: Farrar, Straus & Giroux, 1996. (Sis describes the life and work of the courageous man who changed the way people saw the galaxy by offering objective evidence that the earth was not the fixed center of the universe.) *How do we gather accurate information?*

Sis, P. *The Tree of Life: A Book Depicting the Life of Charles Darwin, Naturalist, Geologist, & Thinker.* New York: Farrar, Straus & Giroux, 2003. (This text portrays the life of the famous nineteenth-century naturalist using text from Darwin's writings and detailed drawings by Sis.) *How do we gather accurate information?*

Thimmesh, C. *Girls Think of Everything: Stories of Ingenious Inventions by Women.* New York: Houghton Mifflin, 2000. (A dozen women are profiled in this collection of short, anecdotal biographies demonstrating that necessity, ingenuity, and luck all play a part in successful inventions. The final section tells girls how to patent their inventions, and an informed bibliography will do just that.) *Who should have power to make decisions about the uses of technology?*

Reference

The Great Idea Finder. "Windshield Wipers." http://www.ideafinder.com/history/inventions/windwiper.htm (cited July 23, 2009).

Chapter 10

Global Connections

Teachers have favorite books that they use during the holidays to teach children about different celebrations. One such book is *The Trees of the Dancing Goats* by Patricia Polacco, the story of Christian and Jewish families who are neighbors and friends. When the Christian families are stricken with scarlet fever right before Christmas, the Jewish family steps in to deliver trees to each home, make wooden ornaments to decorate the trees, and prepare food to bring Christmas to their friends' homes. In turn, when the Christian neighbors recover, they make a menorah out of the ornaments they received and present it to their Jewish neighbors. A beautiful holiday story, this book is typically used to examine holiday customs of different religions.

Already a favorite, Polacco's book presents teachers with an opportunity to explore how people of different backgrounds develop understanding and appreciation of, as well as support for, each others' cultures. This understanding and support are the basis for peace in our local and global communities. We lead students in a discussion of the sacrifices the Jewish family makes to help their Christian neighbors. We help students recognize that the Jewish family goes beyond the usual charitable act of bringing meals to a sick household. They bring Christmas trees, helping their neighbors celebrate a holiday that they, themselves, do not believe in.

There are many wonderful picture books that explore differences among people and cultures. Many emphasize the importance of tolerance. We try to use these books to challenge students not simply to tolerate but to understand and support people who are different from themselves. We embrace opportunities to raise deep issues that will help promote a more peaceful global society.

Encounter by Jane Yolen, *If the World Were a Village*: *A Book About the World's People* by David J. Smith, and *Silent Music: A Story of Baghdad* by James Rumford enable students to explore issues of global community and how close we are to achieving peace and justice in the global village.

Essential Questions

How do our actions affect the world and how does the world affect our actions?

How interdependent is our world? How interdependent should our world be?

To what extent does diversity strengthen our global community?

To what extent does the collision of cultures result in progress for all?

How close are we to achieving peace and justice in the global village?

How can we promote peace and justice in the global village?

Encounter by Jane Yolen

Jane Yolen imagines the first meeting between Columbus and the indigenous people of San Salvador, the Taino, through the eyes of a young native boy. The boy is warned in a dream that the strangers may bring trouble; however, his fears are ignored. The Tainos greet the strangers warmly, only to be repaid with the abduction of several of their young people. Years later, the boy, now an old man, looks back at the destruction of his people. In an author's note, Yolen indicates that, given the lack of historical evidence on the Taino side, much of this encounter is imagined.

Teachers use this book in connection with Columbus Day to examine the perspective of those already living in the Americas. The discussion does not have to end with the holiday, however. *Encounter* can be a springboard to an exploration of the global exchange of resources, germs, cultural practices, and ideas that occur when different groups encounter each other.

Social Studies Concepts and Discussion Questions

Social studies concepts	Questions to ask based on the text
Perspective	From whose perspective is the story told?
	What do the birds in the boy's dream symbolize?
	What were the Tainos' first impressions of the "strange creatures," the "men but not men" who came ashore?
	Why did the chief believe the men came from the sky?
	How do you think the "strangers" felt about the Tainos? Why do you feel this way?
	What interested and impressed the strangers about the Tainos? How do you know?
Cultural traditions	What was the Native American custom for welcoming strangers?
	What is a the boy's *zemis*? What role does the *zemis* play in the boy's life?
Economics	What gifts were exchanged between the Tainos and the "strangers"?
	What items did the "strangers" withhold from the Tainos?
	How did the exchange of gifts make the boy feel about the strangers?
Historical evidence	How did the boy feel about being taken aboard "the great canoe"? Why did he jump overboard?
	To what extent did the boy's dream become reality?
	What was the long-term outcome of the Native American encounter with the "strangers"?
	What was lost as a result of the encounter between the strangers and the Tainos?
	How accurate is the story told in this book? What evidence do we have about this time period?
	How did the historical record influence the illustrator's drawings?

Activity

Pairing Yolen's book with a story about Christopher Columbus raises the important issue of how one acquires reliable information about a time period and what conclusions can be drawn from that information. In this activity, students examine a variety of sources to determine: What happens when cultures collide? Did the cultural contact between Europeans and Native Americans result in progress for all people?

Note to Teachers: We did not include a fifth document that you may wish to access. We have used the woodcut commissioned by Bartolome de las Casas with our students, but it is not for the faint of heart. It depicts Tainos who did not mine enough gold within a certain time period suffering the penalty of having their hands chopped off as a lesson to others. (See the URL for the Center for the Teaching of American History in the references at the end of the chapter.)

Name _____ Date _____

Student Handout: When Cultures Collide

Directions: As you read each document on the next page, complete the chart with information regarding what happened when the Europeans encountered the Native Americans. Evaluate whether the encounter resulted in positive or negative changes for those involved. Use the back of this sheet if you need more space.

Source of information	What happened when Europeans encountered the Native Americans?
Document 1: *Columbus's Diary*	
Document 2: *Journal Entry of Bartolome de las Casas*	
Document 3: *The Columbian Exchange*	
Document 4: *Population Decline and Growth*	

Did the cultural contact between Europeans and Native Americans result in progress for all people?

From *Every Book Is a Social Studies Book: How to Meet Standards with Picture Books, K–6* by Andrea S. Libresco, Jeannette Balantic, and Jonie C. Kipling. Santa Barbara, CA: Libraries Unlimited. Copyright © 2011.

Document 1: *Columbus's Diary*

Saturday, 13 October. [1492] At daybreak great multitudes of men came to the shore, all young and of fine shapes, very handsome; their hair not curled but straight and coarse like horse-hair, and all with foreheads and heads much broader than any people I had seen; They came loaded with balls of cotton, parrots, javelins, and other things too numerous to mention; these they exchanged for whatever we chose to give them.

Document 2: *Journal Entry of Bartolome de las Casas*

They [the Native Americans] do not have weapons, nor do they know about them because when we showed them a sword, they cut themselves from grabbing the [blade].

Document 3: *The Columbian Exchange*

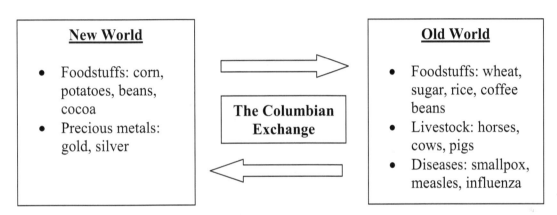

This diagram represents the movement of people and goods between Europe, the Americas, and Africa following Christopher Columbus's "discovery" of the "New" World.

Document 4: *Population Decline and Growth*

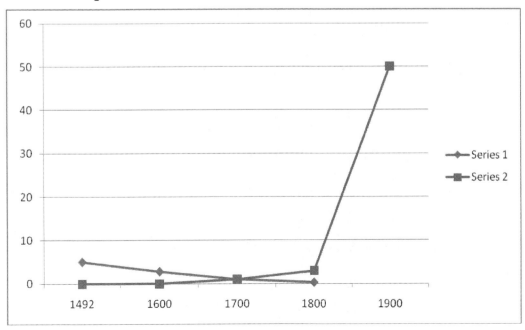

Student Handout: When Cultures Collide
(Sample Student Responses)

Source of information	What happened when Europeans encountered the Native Americans?
Document 1: *Columbus's Diary*	*Native peoples, who looked different from the explorers, came to greet Columbus and his crew with balls of cotton, parrots, javelins, etc.; they exchanged these items for whatever Columbus chose to give them.*
Document 2: *Journal Entry of Bartolome de las Casas*	*Native Americans did not have the same kinds of weapons as Europeans.*
Document 3: *The Columbian Exchange*	*Goods were exchanged:* *New World had corn, cocoa, gold, silver, potatoes, tobacco.* *Old World had horses, wheat, sugar, coffee beans, cows, diseases*
Document 4: *Population Decline and Growth*	*Big increase in non-Native population; big decrease in Native population*
(if this option is used) **Document 5:** *Woodcut Commissioned by B. de las Casas*	*Native people worked in gold mines for the Europeans. They were punished severely if they did not mine enough gold within a certain time period*

Did the cultural contact between Europeans and Native Americans result in progress for all people?

(Positives for Native Americans include the exchange of foods, animals, and other products. Negatives for Native Americans include diseases, poor working conditions, dramatic decrease in population, and torture. Positives for Europeans include exchange of foods, animals, and other products; gold; land; workers.)

Discussion Questions

- *What details in the sources are consistent with Yolen's story?*
- *How might things have turned out differently had Native Americans had the same kinds of weapons as Europeans?*
- *How did the world change because of the interaction between these two cultures?*

Applying the Concepts

As a result of activities like the one for this book, students come to realize that events can be viewed from a variety of perspectives. To reinforce this concept, we ask our students to compose a dialogue poem. Students work in pairs to write a poem that juxtaposes two perspectives on the same event, in this case, the encounter between Europeans and Native Americans. Each stanza contains two lines: one from the European perspective and one from the Native American perspective. The first stanza of the poem typically contains two identical lines as the two groups meet. Below is an excerpt from a student poem

Dialogue Poem on *Encounter*

Here come those funny-looking people.
Here come those funny-looking people.

They are dressed in feathers and have horse-like hair.
They are dressed in layers and layers of clothing and have such curly hair.

These people have only bows and arrows, we can make them do what we want.
These people have noisy sticks that put holes in people's hearts.

. . .
. . .

I have grown rich by being here.
I have lost everything since they came.

Name _____ Date _____

Student Handout: Dialogue Poem—*Encounter*

Directions: Work with your partner to write a dialogue poem from the paired perspectives of a European and a Native American. (It is easier if one of you writes the European lines throughout and the other writes the Native American lines throughout.) Be sure that your first stanza includes the same line for each person.

European: _____

Native American: _____

European: _____

Native American: _____

European: _____

Native American: _____

European: _____

Native American: _____

European: _____

Native American: _____

European: _____

Native American: _____

European: _____

Native American: _____

European: _____

Native American: _____

Extending the concepts in your class . . .

Students can research an explorer, plotting the course of each on a classroom map.

Utilize the dialogue poem to analyze different perspectives on a contemporary global issue.

Utilize the dialogue poem to analyze different perspectives in one's family (à la Judy Blume's *The Pain and the Great One*).

Place strings on a map of the world to illustrate the goods that were exchanged during this time period. Discuss the consequences of this exchange (e.g., the potato becomes a staple for Ireland, but, years later, Ireland is severely affected by the potato famine; the tomato, native to Peru, becomes a staple for Italy).

If the World Were a Village: A Book About the World's People by David J. Smith

To make the idea of a world of 6.2 billion people more comprehensible, David Smith suggests that children picture the population of the world as a village of just one hundred people, which then makes every statistic a percentage. Thus, one person in the "village" represents 62 million people in the real world. Surprising, sometimes appalling, statistics follow. For example, children in the United States take telephones for granted, but only fourteen people in the global village own one. Sixty people are always hungry, twenty-six are severely undernourished, sixteen go to bed hungry some of the time, and only twenty-four have enough to eat. Topics in the book include nationalities, food, language, religion, access to clean water, and more. As the author points out, the book is intended to give children a sense of "world-mindedness . . . the sense that our planet is actually a village and we share this small precious village with our neighbors. Knowing who our neighbors are, where they live and how they live will help us live in peace."

Many teachers have this book in their classrooms and leave it out as a reference for students. We have done that, but we also find that the book can help students begin to understand the world in which they live. It can become a catalyst for further research about standard of living and ways to address the inequities that exist in our world today.

Unlike the books we use in previous chapters, we do not read this entire book aloud to students. We read only page 7, "Welcome to the global village." We open our exploration of the book by asking the questions related to "Community" that follow. The subsequent concept questions are asked after the activity.

Social Studies Concepts and Discussion Questions

Social studies concepts	Questions to ask based on the text
Community	What makes a place a community? What makes the place in which you live a community? Can we consider the world to be a community? Why or why not?
Nation-state	Who are the people in the global village? Where do they come from? To what extent do people who identify with a particular nationality feel like members of a global village? What languages are spoken in the global village? To what extent do people's separate languages prevent them from feeling like a member of a global village?
Economics	How many people are under the age of twenty in the global village? What might be the economic impact of a country having a high percentage of young people? Is there enough food to feed people in the global village? What percentage of people in the global village do not have enough food to eat? If there is enough food for everyone, why do 76 percent of the people in the global village experience hunger? How much money do people in the global village have? How equitable is this? What might the political consequences be of this inequity?
Culture	How many religions are practiced in the global village? To what extent does religion divide or unite people in the global village?
Environment	Why is pollution a problem? How do people in the global village get water? What percentage of people in the global village live in an unhealthy environment?
Schooling and literacy	What percentage of school-age people in the global village attend school? What is the pupil–teacher ratio? How does that compare to the ratio in your own school? Why do you think more males than females are taught to read? What impact might illiteracy have on economic productivity?
Technology	How many people in the global village have electricity? How do the people use electricity? What are the consequences of not having electricity?
Change	How did the population of the global village change from 1900 to 2000? How is the global village expected to change in the next century? What are the implications of these changes? How should these anticipated changes govern our actions today?

Activity

There are eleven topics (nationalities, languages, ages, religions, food, air and water, schooling and literacy, money and possessions, electricity, the village of the past, and the village of the future) explored in the book through the prism of this hundred-person village. Because the world's population is represented as a village of one hundred people, there is a strong interdisciplinary connection to be made to percentages in mathematics. With this interdisciplinary goal in mind, we have pairs of students work together to create a pie chart that represents the data for their assigned topic. Some of the data is straightforward, and we assign that to our students who may struggle in math; some of the data requires extra mathematical operations. For example, in the category of Food, the book indicates that, "60 people are always hungry and 26 of these are severely undernourished." For our students to create the pie chart, they need to recognize that the severely undernourished are a subset of those who are always hungry and do the appropriate subtraction.

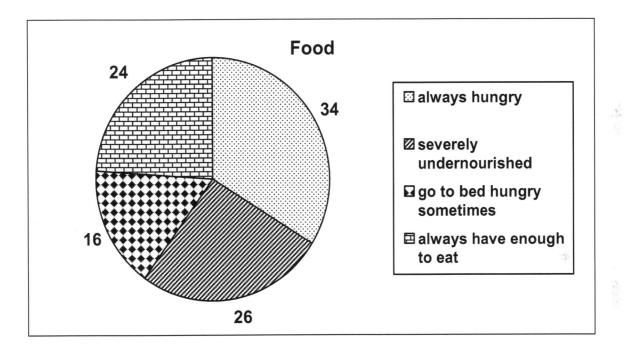

Students create their pie charts on large paper, share the information with the class in a short presentation, then hang them around the room for the class to analyze.

Name _____ Date _____

Student Handout:
If the World Were a Village Pie Chart

Directions: Create a pie chart that represents the data for your assigned topic. Be sure to create a key for your pie chart.

Topic: _____

Key:

☐
☐
☐
☐
☐

At this point, we return to the questions in the concept chart and the following discussion questions to guide our analysis.

Discussion Questions

- *What data surprised you?*

- *What data makes you feel concerned?*

- *What data made you want to acquire more information?*

- *What are the important geographic, political, economic, technological, and social-cultural issues affecting the world today?*

- *How well are these issues being addressed?*

Applying the Concepts

After introducing students to the concept of the global village, we engage them in an analysis of standard of living data across six specific nations. We use the United Nations cyberschoolbus website (http://cyberschoolbus. un.org/infonation3/menu/advanced.asp). The site is set up so that students can compare the data related to the population, economy, technology, health, and environment of up to six countries. Within those categories are five or six subcategories (e.g., infant mortality rate, access to clean water) that give students insight into standard of living. When students select the subcategory that they think is most valuable, the website then automatically generates a bar graph that represents the comparative data of the six nations selected.

In our classroom, we choose the six countries that groups of students will research and assign the aspect of standard of living on which each group will report. We choose countries from across the economic and geographic spectrum, as well as a country that has a higher standard of living than the United States to give students perspective. We also select at least one country in the news.

Each group of students researches a different aspect of standard of living: population, economy, technology, health, or environment. In consultation with us, the groups choose which statistics about standard of living to present to the class.

Discussion Questions

- *Which statistics surprised you?*

- *What countries have the lowest and highest standards of living?*

- *On what statistics do you base your judgment?*

- *What value is there in studying comparative standard of living data?*

- *What kinds of actions could raise the standard of living in the world?*

- *What responsibility do people have to their fellow citizens in the global community?*

After students have analyzed the standard of living of some of the countries in the world, they explore what they can do to make a difference. We share a list of websites with students, including UNICEF, Heifer International, Oxfam International, Free the Children, and Kiva (a micro-lending group). Students investigate the mission and programs of these organizations and then decide which projects to undertake. Groups of students design fund-raising projects for the organization that they think best addresses the standard of living issues they have researched. The project includes the creation of

- *easy-to-understand flyers with data about standard of living,*

- *handouts about the organization to which they are donating,*

- *fact sheets about how the money they raise will be spent, and*

- *a poster or PowerPoint presentation that illustrates the connection between raising money and raising standard of living.*

Extending the concepts in your class . . .

Students who wish to do further research may revisit the standard of living statistics, breaking them down and graphing them by gender. One resource is the GenderStats website.

Using the cyberschoolbus data, students can separate out the standard of living statistics that pertain particularly to children and compare this data to the relevant articles in the United Nations Convention on the Rights of the Child (or its summary) to see the extent to which children's rights are being protected or violated.

Students may elect to keep an e-mail list of those who donate and then continue to keep them apprised by sending updates of how the money they contributed was used and the difference it made.

Silent Music: A Story of Baghdad by James Rumford

A young boy who lives in Baghdad, faced with war all around him, tells of his love of soccer, music, and his greatest love, calligraphy. The story is intertwined with the tale of Yakut, a master calligrapher in ancient Baghdad. Yakut also lived during a time of war, and the young boy draws from Yakut's story to find peace in his own time.

Silent Music: A Story of Baghdad provides rich opportunities to explore simile and descriptive language with students. The illustrations beautifully incorporate Arabic calligraphy, which helps students to make connections among culture, language and the fine arts. The book also allows students to recognize the long history of war in the world, as well as the long history of people searching for peace amid war.

Before reading the book, we ask our students to draw their conception of "peace." Many of their drawings are limited to clichés like flowers, rainbows, and peace signs. We then read the book with our students and discuss the following questions.

Social Studies Concepts and Discussion Questions

Social studies concepts	Questions to ask based on the text
Geography	How do the colors of the illustrations reflect the geography of the setting?
Culture	What aspects of Ali's daily life are similar to or different from your own? What are Ali's favorite pastimes and why?
Cultural history	What do Yakut and Ali have in common? What does it tell you about Iraqi culture that Yakut is well known to children? Ali is preserving culture by practicing the ancient art of calligraphy. What aspect of American culture would you preserve if confronted by war in our country?
War and peace	What is meant when Ali tells us that Yakut "shut out the horror and wrote glistening letters of rhythm and grace"? How does Ali react to the bombing of his city? When Ali says that "the one war has become another," to what actual events in Iraq does he refer? What is significant about Ali noticing that writing "war" in calligraphy is much easier than writing "peace"?

Activity

After reading the story, we ask students to reflect on the idea of preserving culture as an aspect of peace, or, to approach it from the opposite direction, students think about what aspects of their everyday lives would be at risk in war. They complete a second drawing that reflects their expanded conception of peace. This time, their drawings contain things they care about, including family scenes, images from sports, their homes, musical instruments, song lyrics, favorite books and stories, and the Statue of Liberty.

Discussion Questions

- *How do your second drawings compare to your initial conceptions of peace?*
- *How might the elements of culture that you hold dear become an argument against going to war?*
- *How might the elements of culture that you hold dear become an argument for going to war?*

Applying the Concepts

We put the quotations on the next page about war and peace on sentence strips around the classroom. In groups, students walk around the room, discussing the meaning of each quotation. Then each student chooses a number out of a bag that correlates with one of the peace quotations and designs an illustration that captures its meaning.

Peace Quotations

(Adapted from *Peace Lessons Around the World*)

1. **You cannot simultaneously prevent and prepare for war**. —Albert Einstein (1879–1955), inventor, antiwar activist, winner of the 1922 Nobel Prize in Physics

- ✂ - -

2. **If you are neutral in situations of injustice, you have chosen the side of the oppressor**. —Bishop Desmond Tutu (1931–present), Bishop of Johannesburg, South Africa, founder of the Truth and Reconciliation Commission, winner of the 1984 Nobel Peace Prize

- ✂ - -

3. **The good we secure for ourselves is precarious and uncertain until it is secured for all of us and incorporated into our common life.** —Jane Addams (1860–1935), founder of the social settlement Hull House in Chicago in 1919, first president of the Women's International League for Peace and Freedom, winner of the 1931 Nobel Peace Prize

- ✂ - -

4. **There is no trust more sacred than the one the world holds with children. There is no duty more important than ensuring that their rights are respected, that their welfare is protected, that their lives are free from fear and want and that they grow up in peace.** —Kofi A. Annan (1938–present), former Secretary-General of the United Nations

- ✂ - -

5. **Peace begins when the hungry are fed.** —Anonymous

- ✂ - -

6. **In separateness lies the world's great misery; in compassion lies the world's true strength**. —The Buddha, founder of Buddhist religion and philosophy, born around 565 B.C. in present-day Nepal (Buddha means "enlightened one.")

- ✂ - -

7. **Wars make poor tools for carving out peaceful tomorrows**. —Martin Luther King Jr. (1929–1968), U.S. Christian minister and leader of the U.S. Civil Rights Movement, awarded the 1964 Nobel Peace Prize

- ✂ - -

8. **There is no way to peace. Peace is the way.** —Mohandas Gandhi (1869–1948), nonviolent Indian nationalist leader

- ✂ - -

9. **Peace is not only the absence of war but the presence of active justice.** —Reverend Allan Boesak (1945–present), South African anti-apartheid activist and president of Council of World Alliance of Reformed Churches

From *Every Book Is a Social Studies Book: How to Meet Standards with Picture Books, K–6* by Andrea S. Libresco, Jeannette Balantic, and Jonie C. Kipling. Santa Barbara, CA: Libraries Unlimited. Copyright © 2011.

The illustrations are displayed underneath their respective quotations. These pictures are students' third conception of peace; their first and second illustrations remain on display as well.

Discussion Questions

- *How do your first, second, and third conceptions of peace compare?*
- *Which conceptions of peace do you find most compelling?*
- *To what extent is peace the absence of war?*
- *How does inequality affect peaceful relations among people?*
- *How does the distribution of resources affect peace?*
- *Describe elements of a peaceful society.*

Extending the concepts in your class . . .

Read about the lives and work of leaders for peace. Discuss findings in literature circles.

Research Nobel Peace Prize winners' speeches and select excerpts to deliver to the class.

Research the conditions regarding the Iraq War(s) that you read about in the book.

Write a poem about a consequence of war that robs people of peace.

Write a Memorial Day speech that addresses the consequences of war and send it to your local newspaper.

Design a poster to raise awareness about children in a war-torn nation.

Research organizations that care for children in war-torn nations and decide to which you would most like to contribute.

Investigate conflict resolution strategies and decide whether they are appropriate for your classroom.

Recommended Books

For a list of books that explore issues of resources allocation and economic justice, please see *Distribution of Resources, Economic Justice, and Scarcity* on the Recommended Books list at the end of Chapter 8: "Production, Distribution, and Consumption."

Social Justice

Amnesty International. *We are all born free: The Universal Declaration of Human Rights.* London: Frances Lincoln Children's Books, 2008. (Each article of the Declaration is illustrated.) *What rights should all humans enjoy?*

Fridell, R. *Education for All: Floating Schools, Cave Classrooms, and Backpacking Teachers.* Brookfield, CT: Twenty-First Century Books/The Millbrook Press, 2003. (This book documents the condition of education throughout the world and suggests changes.) *What is the relation of education to higher standard of living?*

Kerley, B. *A Cool Drink of Water.* Washington, DC: National Geographic Children's Books, 2006. (Photos depict people around the world collecting, chilling, and drinking water.) *What responsibility do people in developing countries have for ensuring that everyone in the world who needs water has access to it?*

McBrier, P. *Beatrice's Goat.* New York: Aladdin, 2004. (In Uganda, a young girl receives a goat that will help her family earn money to support themselves.) *What responsibility do children in developed countries have to help children in developing countries?*

Menzel, P. *Material World: A Global Family Portrait.* San Francisco: Sierra Club Books, 1995. (Photo portrait of a statistically average family in every corner of the world.) *What responsibility should global citizens have for the standard of living in other countries?*

Shoveller, H. *Ryan and Jimmy and the Well in Africa That Brought Them Together.* Tonawanda, NY: Kids Can Press, 2008. (A young Canadian boy reaches out to a Ugandan village to build a well.) *What responsibility do children in developed countries to help children in developing countries?*

Smith, D. J. *If the World Were a Village.* Toronto, Canada: Kids Can Press, 2002. (The author provides stats about the world as if it were a village of one hundred people.) *What responsibility should global citizens have for the standard of living in other countries?*

Strauss, R. *One Well: The Story of Water on Earth.* Tonawanda, NY: Kids Can Press, 2007. (Data on the amount of, access to, and demands on the water supply on Earth, as well as how to conserve this precious resource.) *What responsibility do we have to protect the world's water supply and how can we do so?*

Whelan, G. *Waiting for the Owl's Call.* Farmington Hills, MI: Sleeping Bear Press, 2009. (A poignant story of an eight-year-old girl and her sister in Afghanistan who, instead of attending school, weave rugs until their fingers bleed and await the call of the owl that tells them their day of labor is over.) *To what extent do developed countries' demand for goods create issues of child labor in developing countries?*

Winter, J. *Nasreen's Secret School.* New York: Beach Lane Books, 2009. (Based on a true story, this book tells of a young Afghan girl who is drawn out of her shell of sadness through a secret school for girls.) *How important is education in societies around the world, and what can be done to promote it?*

Yolen, J. *Encounter.* New York: HarperCollins, 1996. (An alternative perspective on the Columbus story.) *To what extent can encounters between different peoples of the world result in unequal relations and conflict between them?*

Peace

Barclay, J. *Proud as a Peacock, Brave as a Lion.* Plattsburgh, NY: Tundra Books, 2009. (Through the stories of a young boy's grandfather, he learns about the different aspects of wartime that culminates in a somber, reflective ending about the hardships of war.) *Why is it important to know about the hardships of war?*

Blume, J. *The Pain and the Great One.* New York: Bantam Doubleday Dell Books for Young Readers, 1985. (Told from two different siblings' perspectives, this book tells how a six-year-old and his eight-year-old sister each see the other as troublemakers and the best-loved in the family.)

Bunting, E. *Gleam and Glow.* Orlando, FL: Harcourt Brace, 2005. (After his home is destroyed by war, a Bosnian child finds hope in the survival of two very special fish.) *How do children cope during times of conflict?*

Bunting, E. *Smoky Night.* Orlando, FL: Harcourt Brace, 1999. (In the violence and flames of the Los Angeles riots, neighbors of different ethnicities learn the value of bridging differences.) *To what extent does diversity strengthen a community?*

Cowley, J. *The Duck in the Gun.* Newtown, Australia: Walker Books, Australia, 2009. (A general has to delay war because a duck has built her nest in the cannon. While he and his soldiers wait for the eggs to hatch, they discover many reasons to wage peace instead of war.) *How can war be avoided?*

de la Garza, D. *The Great, Great Chicken War.* Austin, TX: Anchorage Press, 2007. (A story about a conflict begun by those who are too afraid, or chicken, to address why they are fighting in the first place. Good for starting a conversation about conflict.) *How can conflict be avoided?*

DePaola, T. *The Knight and the Dragon.* New York: The Putnam & Gosset Group, 1998. (A knight and a dragon ultimately turn competition into cooperation.) *How can conflict be avoided?*

Gilley, J. *Peace One Day: The Making of World Peace Day.* New York: The Penguin Group, 2005. (One person's work to get the United Nations to make September 21 a fixed date of global ceasefire and nonviolence.) *How can individuals work to bring peace into the world?*

Greenfield, E. *When the Horses Ride By: Children in the Times of War.* New York: Lee & Low Books, 2006. (Seventeen rhythmic poems and beautiful illustrations depict particular wars across time and place and also suggest the universal fears, dreams, and courage of children caught up in conflicts.) *How do children cope during times of conflict?*

Heide, F. P., and Gilliland, J. H. *Sami and the Time of the Troubles.* Orlando, FL: Harcourt Brace, 1995. (The authors describe a ten-year-old boy's life—much of which must be spent in the basement—in war-torn Beirut.) *How do children cope during times of conflict?*

Hollyer, B. *Wake Up, World!: A Day in the Life of Children Around the World.* New York: Henry Holt, 1999. (A look inside eight homes in eight countries shows where children sleep, what they eat, and how they learn and play.) *How can understanding our differences help us establish peace?*

Johnston, T. *Voices from Afar: Poems of Peace.* New York: Holiday House, 2008. (Selections focus on both peace and the devastation of war and its aftermath.) *How do images of war help us work for peace?*

Katz, K. *Can You Say Peace?* New York: Henry Holt, 2006. (On International Peace Day, children wish for peace in many languages.) *How can we promote peace and justice in the global village?*

Kerley, B. *A Little Peace.* Washington, DC: National Geographic Children's Books, 2007. (This beautiful photo-essay highlights simple actions, such as lending a hand, sharing a smile, and making friends, to demonstrate how each person can work to achieve peace.) *How can we promote peace and justice in the global village?*

Khan, R. *The Roses in My Carpets.* Markham, Canada: Fitzhenry & Whiteside, 2004. (Based on a true story of the author's foster child, the story tells of a young fatherless Afghan refugee boy caring for his mother and sister in a war-torn world.) *How do children cope during times of conflict?*

LaReau, K. *Rabbit and Squirrel: A Tale of War and Peas.* Orlando, FL: Harcourt Children's Books, 2008. (A humorous tale about the dangers of conflict escalation that arise because of simple misunderstandings.) *How can conflict be avoided?*

Lee-Tai, A. *A Place Where Sunflowers Grow.* San Francisco: Children's Book Press, 2006. (Based on the experiences of a girl's Japanese grandmother in an American internment camp during World War II, the story shows how creation can give one a sense and purpose of peace, especially during times of war that are characterized by destruction and hardship.) *How can art advance peace during wartime?*

Lionni, L. *The Alphabet Tree*. New York: Alfred A. Knopf, 2004. (A wordbug teaches letters on an alphabet tree to become stronger by banding together to form words. Then a caterpillar teaches the letters to become even stronger by forming sentences with a message of peace.) *How can we promote peace and justice in the global village?*

Lionni, L. *It's Mine!* New York: Alfred A. Knopf, 1996. (Three selfish frogs quarrel over who owns their pond and island until a storm lets them see the benefits of sharing.) *What are different causes of conflicts between people?*

Lobel, A. *Frog and Toad Are Friends*. New York: HarperCollins, 1979. (This tale of the delightful relationship of two friends is not a bad primer on techniques of conflict resolution.) *How can conflict be avoided?*

Lobel, A. *Potatoes, Potatoes*. New York: Greenwillow Books, 2004. (Two brothers are lured by the trappings of glory to become the commanders of opposing armies. After they lead their soldiers to war in their own mother's garden, they learn to value family and food more than fighting.) *What are different causes of conflicts between people?*

MacDonald, M. *Peace Tales*. Atlanta, GA: August House, 2005. (This collection of folktales from around the world reflects different aspects of war and peace.) *How can we promote peace and justice in the global village?*

McCutcheon, J. *Christmas in the Trenches*. Atlanta, GA: Peachtree, 2006. (This fictionalized account of the Christmas Truce of 1914 during World War I is told through the eyes of a grandfather.) *How can people bring about peace?*

Mochizuki, K. *Baseball Saved Us*. New York: Lee & Low Books, 1995. (A Japanese American boy learns to play baseball when he and his family are forced to live in an internment camp during World War II. His ability to play helps him when the war is over.) *How do children cope with war?*

Munson, D. *Enemy Pie*. San Francisco: Chronicle Books, 2000. (Hoping that the enemy pie that his father makes will help him get rid of his enemy, a little boy finds, instead, that it helps him make a new friend.) *How can people fighting bridge their differences and find their way to peace?*

Nye, N. S. *Sitti's Secrets*. New York: Aladdin Paperbacks, 1997. (A young girl describes a visit to see her grandmother on the West Bank and the difficult conditions she encounters there.) *How can understanding what it is like to live through conflict help bring peace to the world?*

Pin, I. *When I Grow Up, I Will Win the Nobel Peace Prize*. New York: Farrar, Straus & Giroux, 2006. (The author provides an introduction to the Nobel Peace Prize.) *How can people work for peace in the world?*

Polacco, P. *Pink and Say*. New York: Philomel Books, 1994. (Say Curtis describes his meeting with Pinkus Aylee, a black Civil War soldier, and their capture by Southern troops.) *How can friendship bring peace during times of war?*

Polacco, P. *The Trees of the Dancing Goats*. New York: Aladdin, 2000. (During a scarlet fever epidemic one winter in Michigan, a Jewish family helps make Christmas special for their sick neighbors.) *How can understanding others' customs help lead to peace?*

Popov, N. *Why?* New York: North South Books, 1998. (A wordless antiwar parable of an escalating battle between a frog and a mouse.) *What are different causes of conflicts between people?*

Preus, M. *The Peace Bell*. New York: Henry Holt, 2008. (Based on actual events during and after World War II in the United States and Japan, this story promotes peace and illustrates how war has an impact on individuals in a variety of ways.) *How can symbols of war become symbols of peace?*

Proimos, J. *Paulie Pastrami Achieves World Peace*. New York: Little, Brown Books for Young Readers, 2009. (This is the tale of a seven year old who works his way up to achieving world peace by starting small. Good for showing children that they, too, have agency to change the world.) *How can an average person work for peace?*

Radunsky, V. *What does peace feel like?* New York: Atheneum Books for Young Readers, 2003. (Simple text and illustrations depict what peace looks, smells, and feels like to children around the world.) *How can we promote peace and justice in the global village?*

Rubin, S. G. *The Yellow House: Van Gogh, Gauguin, and Nine Turbulent Weeks in Provence.* New York: Abrams, 2001. (The complicated dynamics of the arguments and relationship between the two artist friends.) *How can people who are very different learn to live together in peace?*

Rumsford, J. *Silent Music: A Story of Baghdad.* New York: Roaring Brook Press, 2008. (Rumsford tells of one boy's experience in a war-torn country to try to find peace through calligraphy.) *How do children cope with war?*

Scholes, K. *Peace Begins with You.* San Francisco: Sierra Club Books, 1994. (Scholes explains the concept of peace, why conflicts occur, how they might be resolved, and how to protect peace.) *What causes conflict and how can people avoid it?*

Seuss, Dr. *The Butter Battle Book.* New York: Random House Books, 1984. (The Yooks and the Zooks attempt to outdo each other with ever more sophisticated weaponry.) *How can wars be avoided?*

Thomas, S. M. *Somewhere Today: A Book of Peace.* Morton Grove, IL: Albert Whitman, 2002. (Gives examples of ways in which people bring about peace by doing things to help and care for one another and their world.) *How can individuals help bring peace into the world?*

Twinn, M. *War and Peace.* Auburn, ME: Child's Play International, 1996. (Compares minor family tiffs and family feuds to nations going to war.) *How can conflict be avoided?*

Uchida, Y. *The Bracelet.* New York: The Putnam & Gosset Group, 1996. (A Japanese-American girl is sent with her family to an internment camp; the loss of a bracelet that her best friend has given her proves that she does not need a physical reminder of their bond.) *How can people find peace during times of war?*

Udry, J. M. *Let's Be Enemies.* New York: Harper Trophy, 1988. (Two best friends break, then renew, their friendship.) *How can conflict be avoided?*

Vaugelade, A. *The War.* Minneapolis, MN: First Avenue Editions. (This antiwar parable about two fictional kingdoms locked in an eternal war is good for illustrating the futile aspect of wars.) *Is war ever justified?*

Walker, A. *Why War Is Never a Good Idea.* New York: HarperCollins, 2007. (This poem spread over the span of a picture book personifies the devastation and consequences of war through animals in the jungle and compels children to promote peace and think about the horrors or war.) *Is war ever justified?*

Williams, K. L. *Four Feet, Two Sandals.* Grand Rapids, MI: Eerdman's Books for Young Readers, 2007. (Two Afghan girls living in a refugee camp in Pakistan share a pair of sandals brought by relief workers.) *How can friends bring peace in times of conflict?*

Williams, M. *Brothers in Hope: The Story of the Lost Boys of Sudan.* New York: Lee & Low Books, 2005. (An eight-year-old boy, orphaned by the civil war in Sudan, finds the strength to lead other boys hundreds of miles to Ethiopia and then to the United States.) *How can one individual bring peace in times of conflict?*

Zolotow, C. *The Hating Book.* New York: HarperCollins Children's Books, 1989. (When a girl's friend ignores her completely, all the bad feelings get out of hand. The moral shows that communication is key.) *How can conflict be avoided?*

Zolotow, C. *The Quarreling Book.* New York: HarperCollins Children's Books, 1982. (Gruffness and anger is passed along from person to person until a little dog starts a chain of happiness that reverses the trend.) *How can conflict be avoided?*

Finding Peace After War

Bunting, E. *So Far from the Sea.* New York: Houghton Mifflin, 2009. (Story about the imprisonment of Japanese Americans during World War II, told from the point of view of a child who goes to visit one of the camps where her grandfather died, so far from the sea, where he had lived before his life was interrupted.) *How can individuals find peace after war?*

Bunting, E. *The Wall.* New York: Houghton Mifflin, 1992. (Bunting tells the poignant story of a young boy and his father's visit to the Vietnam Veterans Memorial in Washington, DC.) *How do people come to terms with loss after war is over?*

Cha, D. *Dia's Story Cloth.* New York: Lee & Low Books, 1998. (A story cloth chronicles the story of the author's family as Hmong people in their native Laos and as refugees following the war.) *How can families come to terms with loss after war?*

Coerr, E. *Sadako.* New York: G.P. Putnam's Sons, 1997. (Hospitalized with atom bomb disease—leukemia—a child in Hiroshima races against time to fold a thousand paper cranes to verify the legend that by doing so a sick person will become healthy.) *How can individuals find peace after war?*

Dalton, D. *Living in a Refugee Camp: Carbino's Story.* New York: Gareth Stevens, 2005. (A Sudanese boy, made a refugee at age eleven, recounts his story.) *How can remembering war bring peace into the world?*

Maruki, T. *Hiroshima No Pika.* New York: HarperCollins, 1982. (This book gives a child's perspective on the unprecedented nightmare that was the bombing of Hiroshima.) *How can remembering the horrors of war help to bring peace into the world?*

Myers, W. D. *Patrol: An American Soldier in Vietnam.* New York: HarperCollins, 2005. (A frightened American soldier faces combat in the jungles of Vietnam.) *How can remembering what war is like lead to peace?*

Tsuchiya, Y. *Faithful Elephants: A True Story of Animals, People and War.* New York: Houghton Mifflin, 1997. (The author recounts how three elephants were put to death in Tokyo because of the war, focusing on the pain of the elephants and the zookeepers who must starve them.) *How can remembering the horrors of war lead to peace?*

Volavkova, H. *I Never Saw Another Butterfly.* New York: Random House, 1994. (Children's poems and drawings from Terezin concentration camp in Czechoslovakia during World War II.) *How can remembering the horrors of war lead to peace?*

Peacemakers

Bunting, E. *Terrible Things: An Allegory of the Holocaust.* Philadelphia: The Jewish Publication Society, 1989. (An allegory that addresses the culpability of the ordinary citizens, "bystanders," who looked the other way when terrible things happened in Germany.) *How do our actions affect the world and how does the world affect our actions?*

Cutler, J. *The Cello of Mr. O.* New York: Puffin Picture Books, 2004. (A concert cellist plays for his neighbors in a war-besieged city.) *How can individuals promote peace?*

Demi. *Gandhi.* New York: Margaret K. McElderry Books, 2001. (This is a beautifully illustrated biography of the nonviolent activist for Indian independence.) *How can one person influence the world to bring peace?*

Innocenti, R. *Rose Blanche.* North Mankato, MN: Creative Editions, 1985. (World War II tale of a courageous German girl who discovers the horrors of a concentration camp.) *How do our actions affect the world and how does the world affect our actions?*

Judge, L. *One Thousand Tracings: Healing the Wounds of World War II.* New York: Hyperion Books for Children, 2007. (The story of the author's family in America who established contact with a family in postwar Germany and sent them, and hundreds of others in Europe, supplies, including shoes, based on the tracings sent to them.) *How do our actions affect the world and how does the world affect our actions?*

Leaf, M. *The Story of Ferdinand.* New York: The Penguin Group, 2007. (The story of a bull who loved to smell flowers, not fight as the other bulls do.) *How can being true to who we are as individuals promote peace in the world?*

Lewis, B. A. *The Kid's Guide to Social Action: How to Solve the Social Problems You Choose—And Turn Creative Thinking into Positive Action.* Minneapolis, MN: Free Spirit Publishing, 1998. (A practical manual for children who want to make a difference in the political process.) *How do our actions affect the world and how does the world affect our actions?*

Stamaty, M. A. *Alia's Mission: Saving the Books of Iraq.* New York: Dragonfly Books, 2010. (The heroic story, presented in comic book format, of an Iraqi librarian who rescued more than 30,000 volumes from her library in Basra.) *How can one person's actions bring peace into the world?*

Stevenson, J. *Don't You Know There's a War On?* New York: Greenwillow Books, 1992. (The author recalls his efforts during World War II, including collecting tin foil, looking for spies, and planting a victory garden.) *What can individuals do to support their nation in times of war?*

Winter, J. *The Librarian of Basra: A True Story from Iraq.* San Diego, CA: Harcourt, 2005. (In war-stricken Iraq, a librarian in Basra struggles to save her community's priceless collection of books.) *How can one person's actions bring peace into the world?*

Winter, J. *Wangari's Trees of Peace: A True Story from Africa.* Orlando, FL: Harcourt Books, 2008. (The story of the environmental and political activist in Kenya and winner of the 2004 Nobel Peace Prize.) *How can one person's actions bring peace into the world?*

Zalben, J. B. *Paths to Peace: People Who Changed the World.* New York: The Penguin Group, 2006. (One-page biographies profile sixteen world peacemakers, ranging from Emerson, Gandhi, and King to Daw Aung San Suu Kyi, a political prisoner in Myanmar, who was placed under house arrest intermittently for a total of fifteen years from 1989 through 2010, when she was finally released.) *How can one person's actions bring peace into the world?*

References

The Center for the Teaching of American History, Binghamton University, State University of New York. "The Columbian Exchange and Reaction: Cultural Contact and Adaptation in The Age of Exploration—Loss of Hand Because Gold Quota Not Met" and "The Columbian Exchange and Reaction: Cultural Contact and Adaptation in the Age of Exploration—Journal Entry of Bartolome de Las Casas." http://74.125.93.132/search?q=cache:qGT7BEgeVe8J:ctah.binghamton.edu/student/jaku/caseyprint.html+Bartolome+de+Las+Casas+do+not+have+weapons,+nor+do+they+know+about+them+because+when+we+showed+them+a+sword,+they+cut+themselves+from+grabbing&cd=1&hl=en&ct=clnk&gl=us (cited December 6, 2009).

Fordham University Center for Medieval Studies. "Medieval Sourcebook: Christopher Columbus: Extracts from Journal." http://www.fordham.edu/halsall/source/columbus1.html (cited December 6, 2009).

Heifer International home page. http://www.heifer.org/ (cited December 19, 2009).

Human Development Reports. "FAQ on HDR Statistics" (for standard of living statistics). http://hdr.undp.org/statistics/faq/#21 (cited December 19, 2009).

Kids Can Free the Children. http://www.freethechildren.org (cited December 19, 2009).

Kiva—Microloans that change lives. http://www.kiva.org/http://www.un.org/Pubs/CyberSchoolBus/infonation3/menu/advanced.asp (cited December 19, 2009).

Libresco, A., and J. Balantic, eds. *Peace Lessons Around the World*. New York: Hague Appeal for Peace, 2006, 14. http://www.haguepeace.org/resources/PEACE_LESSONS_FINAL.pdf (cited December 10, 2009).

Oxfam International home page. http://www.oxfam.org/eng (cited December 19, 2009).

UNICEF. "Information by Country." http://www.unicef.org/infobycountry/index.html (cited December 19, 2009).

United Nations Cyberschoolbus. "Infonation Global Teaching and Learning Project." http://cyberschoolbus.un.org/infonation3/menu/advanced.asp (cited December 19, 2009).

Chapter 11

Civic Ideals and Practices

Teachers often tell us that their favorite book for starting a unit on multiplication is Demi's *One Grain of Rice: A Mathematical Folktale*. In it, a little girl devises a clever plan to get the ruler of India to be more generous with his distribution of food. She asks the raja for one grain of rice to be doubled every day for thirty days. Through the power of doubling, one grain of rice grows into more than one billion grains of rice. As they read the story, teachers often ask the students to multiply or double the grains of rice brought in each day so that they can predict the amount that will be brought in the next day and, finally, to calculate the total. In addition, teachers draw students' attention to the ever larger animals in size and number needed to transport the increasing amounts of rice. As the raja learns a lesson about the importance of fairness, the students in third-grade classrooms generally learn about the power of multiplication.

Activities like those just described reinforce math skills such as computation and prediction. In addition, this activity can address the principle behind putting money in a savings account; that is, the higher the percentage that the bank pays on your money, the faster it will grow. Although these math skills and concepts are important, *One Grain of Rice* also provides an excellent opportunity to discuss social studies concepts. Teachers can use the book to explore civic values and ideals, focusing on concepts such as *justice and fairness* (a society in which people go hungry), *governance* (how decisions are made), *the power to make a difference* (out of concern for her fellow citizens, one girl takes action), *courage* (the girl chooses to act at possible risk to herself), and *problem solving* (finding creative solutions to make society a better place). In fact, this book can be used as an introduction to citizenship, whereby students read about a citizen who refuses to accept an unjust situation and devises an imaginative plan that changes one leader's mind and so changes a society. Although the story is a folktale, our students look to the little girl who had the courage to speak up as a role model. This focus allows students to recognize the power, not only of numbers, but also of people.

Yertle the Turtle by Dr. Seuss, *The Day Gogo Went to Vote* by Elinor Batezat Sisulu, *Aani and the Tree Huggers* by Jeannine Atkins, and *Planting the Trees of Kenya: The Story of Wangari Maathai* by Claire A. Nivola enable students to grapple with challenges that individuals in society face.

Essential Questions

What is a citizen's responsibility to her or his community?

How important is voting as a civic practice?

What are the most important characteristics of active citizens?

Is civil disobedience a civic practice? Is it ever OK to break the law?

How can we identify problems in society, and what are important steps in solving any societal problem?

Yertle the Turtle by Dr. Seuss

In *Yertle the Turtle*, the dictator, Yertle, attempts to build a bigger and bigger throne on the backs of his loyal subjects (literally). The turtles continue to join the ever-growing stack of turtles until the bottom turtle, "a plain little turtle whose name was just Mack," decides he's had enough.

Children and teachers alike relish the playful nature of Dr. Seuss, but there is also much substance to his picture books, especially with regard to citizenship. Many of his books (*The Lorax, The Sneetches, The Butter Battle Book,* to name a few) examine individuals' responsibility to their society, and *Yertle the Turtle* is no exception.

Activity

Because the book revolves around defining the behaviors of good citizens, it is logical to begin with that issue before even reading the book with second graders (thus, social studies concepts and discussion questions follow this opening activity). We read situations (see the handout that follows) with our students and discuss whether each is an example of good citizenship. As we do so, we develop a class list, "Behaviors of Good Citizens," that include items such as "keep their community beautiful," "help their community members without doing their work for them," "express their views in a variety of ways," "stand up for people's rights," "listen to others," "inform themselves," "vote," and so on.

Name _____   Date _____

Student Handout: What Is Good Citizenship?

Directions: Read each situation below. If you think it is an example of good citizenship, write **YES**. If you do not think it is an example of good citizenship, write **NO**.

	SITUATIONS	GOOD CITIZENSHIP: YES or NO?
1.	Picking up trash in the hall.	_____
2.	Helping another student understand the homework assignment.	_____
3.	Shoving to get on the bus first.	_____
4.	Writing a letter to the school newspaper to express your view.	_____
5.	Telling someone to stop teasing another person.	_____
6.	Turning off the water while you brush your teeth.	_____
7.	Running in the halls at school.	_____
8.	Listening to the principal's announcements.	_____
9.	Reading the school newspaper to find out what's going on in school.	_____
10.	Wearing a button that says, "Reduce. Reuse. Recycle."	_____
11.	Voting for a candidate for student government.	_____
12.	Volunteering to help clean up Jones Beach.	_____
13.	Presenting the principal with a petition, signed by lots of kids, that asks for an after-school sports club.	_____
14.	After noticing there was no recycling bin in your classroom, asking questions until a recycling bin is placed in the class.	_____
15.	After noticing that the local Denny's won't serve African American customers until all of the white people have been served first, you, your friends, and parents decide to do what you think Martin Luther King, Jr. would have done: you break the law by sitting-in at the lunch counter and refusing to move until they change their unfair rules.	_____

From *Every Book Is a Social Studies Book: How to Meet Standards with Picture Books, K–6* by Andrea S. Libresco, Jeannette Balantic, and Jonie C. Kipling. Santa Barbara, CA: Libraries Unlimited. Copyright © 2011.

We discuss in greater depth any conflicting information our students have about citizens; for example, the situations the students seem to have the most consternation about are numbers 13, 14, and 15 that deal with expressing one's point of view more forcefully and even, possibly, engaging in civil disobedience. We pose higher-level thinking questions that allow students to grapple with the relationship of citizenship to questioning authority.

Discussion Questions

- *Do good citizens sometimes raise issues that may be difficult to solve?*
- *May good citizens suggest new ideas to someone in power (like the principal)?*
- *Can it ever be a sign of good citizenship to break the law?*
- *Was Martin Luther King, Jr. a good citizen?*
- *Do good citizens always obey authority, or are there times when they may question authority?*

We then read Dr. Seuss's *Yertle the Turtle* aloud, identifying the civic concepts and posing questions that will enable students to engage in a book-based discussion about civic issues.

Social Studies Concepts and Discussion Questions

Social studies concepts	Questions to answer based on the texts
Dictatorship (one person makes decisions) vs. democracy (all people participate in decision making)	What kind of ruler is Yertle? What are the characteristics of a dictator versus a democratic ruler?
Freedom	Do the turtles have freedom? What are the characteristics of a free society?
Power	How do you think Yertle got his power? Is it possible to counteract the power of someone like Yertle who sets himself up as a dictator?
Bystanders	Are the turtles who get in the stack "innocent bystanders"? Is there such as thing as an innocent bystander?
Civil disobedience	To what extent is Mack's burp an act of civil disobedience? Is it appropriate?
Good citizenship	May good citizens suggest new ideas to or disobey someone in power? Is Mack a good citizen? Are the other turtles in the stack good citizens?

We ask students to look for good and bad citizens in the story and give reasons for their classifications. The students are quick to identify Yertle as a bad citizen and Mack as a good one; however, when asked to compare their assessments to their earlier definitions of good citizens, the students become less certain. Again, higher-level thinking questions allow students to assess the roles of authorities, activists and bystanders.

Discussion Questions

- *Is Mack being a good citizen when he talks back to and overthrows Yertle, who is in charge?*

- *Are the other turtles in the stack good citizens or not? (Interestingly, the students we have worked with notice that Mack uses the pronoun "we," and so they suggest that he is speaking on behalf of the other turtles; therefore, most students feel that the other turtles, too, are good citizens.)*

- *How "innocent" are bystanders?*

Applying the Concepts

Students refer back to the list of the characteristics of good citizens that they generated earlier in the lesson to nominate an individual for a Good Citizenship Award from our class. Students fill out a nomination form, and each person nominated is invited in to speak with our class during the month of April, which we designate as "Citizenship Recognition Month." The nominees come in for about twenty minutes, usually around snack time, and students who nominated them bring in special snacks for the class. Students are responsible for introducing their nominees to the class, explaining how they know them and why they were nominated. The nominees say a few words, and the class asks them questions (like the ones below) to find out more about the actions of each award winner.

Possible questions for students to ask nominees when they visit our class:

- What made you take this action [that you were nominated for]?

- Did you need any preparation to do it?

- What reaction did you get?

- How did it make you feel?

- Did you think of yourself as a good citizen before you were nominated for this award?

- What advice do you have to help others be good citizens?

- Is there anything you would like to ask us?

Name _____ Date _____

Student Handout: Nomination Form

Directions: Use the template below to nominate an individual for a good citizenship award.

Citizenship Award Nomination

I nominate _____ for a Good Citizenship Award. I know

_____ because he or she is _____

_____.

_____ deserves a Good Citizenship Award because she or he

_____

_____

_____

_____

_____

_____

_____

_____

_____

_____.

Signed,

_____

From *Every Book Is a Social Studies Book: How to Meet Standards with Picture Books, K–6* by Andrea S. Libresco, Jeannette Balantic, and Jonie C. Kipling. Santa Barbara, CA: Libraries Unlimited. Copyright © 2011.

At the end of the month, after all of our good citizens award winners have visited our class, we have a discussion about good citizenship.

Discussion Questions

- *What does a good citizen look like?*

- *Which actions did you most admire? Why?*

- *What do good citizens have in common?*

- *How did they prepare to be good citizens?*

- *In which activities that you heard about might you want to get involved?*

- *How can we all resolve to be better citizens?*

Extending the concepts in your class . . .

Have students nominate characters from literature for good citizenship awards.

Have students identify characters from literature who were bystanders and rewrite the story with those characters speaking out or taking action of some kind.

Brainstorm activities students can engage in for the betterment of their community.

The Day Gogo Went to Vote by Elinor Batezat Sisulu

In this multiple-award-winning book, a little girl accompanies her hundred-year-old great-grandmother, Gogo, to the polling place in the first election in which black South Africans are allowed to vote. Although housebound, the great-grandmother is determined to vote and does so with a little help from her community.

This child's-eye view of a milestone in South African history is often used around Election Day to show the importance of and enthusiasm for voting. This message can be enhanced through activities that contrast this enthusiasm in other countries with the lackluster voting statistics in the United States.

Activity

Before reading the book, we examine voting behavior in presidential elections in the United States. To do so, students read profiles of people and decide whether they would be likely to vote in the next presidential election. They work individually, then we tally their results on the board, recording all yes/no votes for each potential voter. Students give reasons for their decisions, and we compile a list of students' hypotheses about behavior of likely voters.

Name _____ Date _____

Student Handout: Who Votes?*

Directions: Read the following descriptions of potential voters and decide whether each one is likely to vote in a presidential election. Circle the answer that represents your decision.

YES   NO   1. Penny is 20 years old. She works as an electrician and lives in Mississippi. She has never been to college and is not planning to attend. She does not belong to a trade union.

YES   NO   2. Carlos is a lawyer, 54 years old. His family came from Mexico three generations ago. He is a family man and is interested in community affairs. He has three children and owns his own home.

YES   NO   3. Sally is an unemployed waitress who did not finish high school. She is 23 years old and lives at home with her mother.

YES   NO   4. Carl is 50 years old and is African American. He lives in Indiana, where he works as a carpenter and has held the same job for the past 25 years.

YES   NO   5. Sagar is a school teacher in California. He is 39 years old and is active in local PTA meetings. He is working on his master's degree in the evenings.

* activity adapted from Lynne O'Brien, Director of Academic Technology and Instructional Services for Perkins Library at Duke University.

To check the accuracy of their hypotheses, students work in pairs to analyze charts and graphs about voting percentages of different demographic groups (by age, race and ethnicity, gender, income, education, marital status, region, etc.) in the last election. These statistics can be accessed through the United States Census, the United States Election Project, and the Center for Information & Research on Civic Learning and Engagement. Students report back as to whether their hypotheses were accurate. Students then reexamine the profiles of potential voters and reevaluate their earlier decisions.

Discussion Questions

- *How accurate were the hypotheses you investigated?*
- *What evidence convinced you of your answers and why?*
- *Describe characteristics of someone who is likely to vote.*
- *Describe characteristics of someone who is unlikely to vote.*
- *How accurate were our original predictions?*

After this analysis of turnout, in which students discover the rather apathetic behavior of eligible voters in presidential elections in the United States, we read *The Day Gogo Went to Vote,* highlighting the following civic concepts.

Social Studies Concepts and Discussion Questions

Social studies concepts	Questions to answer based on the texts
Family	Describe the relationship between Gogo and her granddaughter.
	What does Gogo teach her granddaughter about her family's history? How does the family's history connect to the country's history?
History	Why is this the first time black people in South Africa were allowed to vote?
	Who is Nelson Mandela, and what is his significance?
Democracy	How did the people in South Africa decide when elections would be held? Why do they pick two days? Why were they made holidays?
	How did people prepare the morning of the election, and how did they feel?
	How did the government make sure that voting was done fairly?
	Why are ballots secret?
	If Thembi's uncles voted for different parties, is that a denial of or an example of democracy?
Civic participation	Why is it so important to Gogo to vote?
	Why were so many people willing to wait in long lines to vote?
	Why is voting necessary in a democracy?
Change	What political and social changes occurred during Gogo's lifetime? Were they positive?
	Why did people sing freedom songs after voting?

We can contrast what we know about voting statistics in the United States with what is presented about South Africa in the book. To make a text-to-world connection, we also share with our students a photo of the seven-hour lines in which black South Africans stood when they voted for the first time. This moving photo can be found at: http://images.google.com/images?hl=en&q=south+africa+voting+lines&gbv=2.

In this story, black people are allowed to vote for the first time in 1994. We use the story about South Africa as an opportunity to discuss voting rights in American history.

Discussion Questions

- *Which other groups were not allowed to vote in the past in the United States?*

- *What did members of these groups do to gain the right to vote?*

- *Are there any people who are not allowed to vote in our nation today, and is this fair?*

Applying the Activity

Our goal is for students to take the information they learned about voting patterns in America and the excitement for voting that they read about in *The Day Gogo Went to Vote* to develop a message aimed at boosting voter enthusiasm and participation in their own community. Students select from the menu of project options below to raise awareness about American voter apathy and encourage greater participation. Whichever medium they select, students need to use some of the data they acquired in their research about voter turnout in America.

- Poster

- T-shirt design

- 30-second public service announcement—TV or radio

- Flyer

Extending the concepts in your class . . .

Have students research when African Americans were granted the constitutional right to vote in the United States, as well as when they were *actually* able to exercise that right.

Analyze and then draw cartoons about voter apathy.

Discuss how we ensure that voting is done fairly.

Have students get involved in (or create) student council elections in your school.

Have students make buttons and bumper stickers for a get-out-the-vote effort.

Get involved in the Kids Voting project (www.kidsvotingusa.org), where children's votes are compiled nationally.

Planting the Trees of Kenya:
The Story of Wangari Maathai by Claire A. Nivola

The short biography of a Nobel Peace Prize winner, *Planting the Trees of Kenya: The Story of Wangari Maathai*, chronicles the work of the Kenyan activist who created a movement to reforest her country, restore the environment, and nourish the people of her community.

This book may be used as a resource for Earth Day near the end of April; indeed, it is an excellent reference for a study of the environment. However, it is also an important work for exploring the concepts of citizenship and civic responsibilities and demonstrating the possibilities for activism, even for the seemingly powerless.

Social Studies Concepts and Discussion Questions

Social studies concepts	Questions to answer based on the text
Environment	Describe Wangari Maathai's native land of Kenya when she was a young girl. Describe the changes she encountered in her native land upon her return to Kenya from America. Why are trees important to the environment? What happens to the soil when they are cut down?
Economics	What did the people of Wangari Maathai's community grow before and after her return? What was the economic impact of the changes in farming in her community?
Science and society	What evidence convinced Wangari Maathai that her community needed more trees? How does her observation of scientific phenomena help her decide how to improve the community? How are trees important for the health of the community and its citizens? How does access to water affect the health of a community and its citizens?
Citizenship	What did the government do to address the problems associated with deforestation? What role *should* the government have played in addressing the problem? In the absence of governmental responsiveness, what does Wangari Maathai do to address the problems associated with deforestation?
Community	How does the fact that trees were distributed to everyone (inmates, soldiers, etc.) strengthen the community as a whole? How was she able to get over 30 million trees planted?

Activity

Planting the Trees of Kenya raises the issue of who is responsible for the well-being of a community. Of course, different people in a community may have different ideas about what constitutes the well-being of a community. The role-play activity that follows requires students to balance the needs of different stakeholders in a community when dealing with an environmental dilemma. In the following scenario, students are assigned to one of the five stakeholder groups (lumber company, developer, citizens groups or environmentalists).

Stakeholders (Photocopy Role-Play Cards)

Lumber Companies—You want to maximize your profits in your business. Not only that, there are an awful lot of people who need houses built and you need a lot of trees to achieve that goal.

Developers—You believe the land has valuable use as a commercial use property (hotel, condo, mall, resorts, etc.). You want to clear the land and maximize your profits.

Concerned Citizens Group 1—You find trees provide special places of value, beautifying the community, providing hiking trails, habitats for animals and birds, as well as opportunities to gather fruits and berries from the natural growth.

Concerned Citizens Group 2—You are intrigued by the idea of having more commercial properties nearby because you want easier access to stores and more job opportunities.

Environmentalists—You know that the roots of trees prevent erosion and make the soil more productive. Without trees, there's no shade, and topsoil dries to dust. You are also concerned about losing the natural habitats for a variety of species.

Name _____ Date _____

Student Handout:
Environmental Dilemma—Role-Play

Directions: Read the scenario below. Assume the role you have been assigned and work with your group to develop your position on how the public land should be used. You should be ready to present your position to the other stakeholders (the class) and the mayor (your teacher).

> **Scenario:** A resolution has been put forth to take away 1,000 acres from the wooded preserve in your town in the Midwest. A tremendous debate has begun over how this public land should be used. The mayor has convened a town forum to discuss the issue.

<u>**Your Role:**</u> _____

Arguments for development	Arguments against development

Each group meets to develop its position on the issue; each group then presents its position to the other stakeholders (the class) and the mayor (the teacher). As the class listens to each position, the students record the information on a comparison chart. Different stakeholder groups discuss whether they could live with certain positions. (Introduce language to students to help them clarify their views and look for compromise: "As a ___, this doesn't work for me and here's why . . ." "I could live with _____, but not with _____.") Groups should also be able to articulate another group's point of view to help them come up with a workable solution. Each student ultimately makes a recommendation to the mayor as to which course of action should be pursued.

Student Handout:
To Develop or Not to Develop? Considering All Views....

Directions: During the class presentations, use the note-taking guide below to record the views of each stakeholder group regarding how to use the public land.

Stakeholders	Arguments for development	Arguments against development
Lumber Companies		
Developers		
Citizen Group 1		
Citizen Group 2		
Environmentalists		

Name _____ Date _____

Student Handout: Julia Butterfly Hill

Directions: Read about Julia Butterfly Hill below and answer the questions that follow.

Julia Butterfly Hill lived in the top of a 1,000-year-old redwood tree for 738 days—just over two years—to protest the destruction of ancient forests. The outcome of her civil disobedience was the protection of that tree and the creation of a three-acre buffer zone.

For more information on Ms. Hill and her act of protest, visit her website: http://www. juliabutterfly.com.

Do you think Julia Butterfly Hill did the right thing? Explain your answer: _____

_____

_____

_____

_____

_____

_____

_____

Can you imagine doing what she did? Why or why not: _____

_____

_____

_____

_____

_____

_____

_____

_____

From *Every Book Is a Social Studies Book: How to Meet Standards with Picture Books, K–6* by Andrea S. Libresco, Jeannette Balantic, and Jonie C. Kipling. Santa Barbara, CA: Libraries Unlimited. Copyright © 2011.

Applying the Concepts

After carefully weighing all of the arguments for this issue, students write a letter to the mayor recommending the course of action he or she should pursue using information from the chart to support their recommendation.

Although the above scenario demands a compromise, we also want students to consider times when compromise isn't an option because of deeply held ethical beliefs. We have students read the following selection to evaluate whether, on occasion, more drastic action, including civil disobedience, is justified.

Discussion Questions

- *Who owns public lands? How are decisions made about them?*

- *Are there any issues about which you feel so strongly that you would engage in civil disobedience?*

- *What if you believe that the right solution wasn't found? What would be your civic responsibility?*

- *In the role-play that we did, would any of the stakeholders have been justified in performing acts of civil disobedience?*

- *Are there some issues on which individuals should not compromise?*

- *How do you balance the needs of individuals with the needs of society?*

Extending the concepts in your class . . .

If there is any issue in your school or community (building a school playground, a large box store being built, a road through a national wilderness, whether dirt bikes can use any portion of a park or road, adding a third track to the railroad, etc.) that is being debated, have your students identify the stakeholders and their positions on the issue.

Have students look in newspapers and watch television news (local and national) to alert themselves to and be informed about issues in which they might have a stake.

Have students conduct local environmental research. Discuss the value of trees in your community. Where are the trees in your community? Create a bar graph on the age and size of trees on a particular block to see whether the town is attending to repopulation of neighborhood trees.

After students have researched an issue, they can take a stand on it, writing to the local newspaper or local officials; they can also work to raise awareness by creating informational handouts or posters.

Recommended Books

For a list of books that explore citizens who fought for rights, see *Civil Rights* on the Recommended Books list at the end of Chapter 6, "Individuals, Groups, and Institutions," and *Empowerment* at the end of Chapter 7, "Power, Authority, and Governance."

Citizenship Through Care for Our Fellow Humans

Brown, M. *Arthur's Halloween*. New York: Scholastic, 1999. (After gathering reliable information, Arthur and his friends discover that their neighbor is not a witch, and, together, they clean her yard.) *How can you be a good citizen in your neighborhood?*

Browne, A. *Piggybook*. New York: Alfred A. Knopf, 1990. (When Mom leaves, Dad and sons realize how much she did for them; they resolve to pull their weight and share jobs.) *How can you be a good citizen in your own family?*

Bunting, E. *A Day's Work*. New York: Clarion Books, 1997. (Francisco and his grandfather accidentally pull out the flowers instead of the weeds when they are hired for the day to garden, and his grandfather insists that they take responsibility for their mistake.) *What do good citizens do when they have made a mistake?*

Bunting, E. *Wednesday Surprise*. New York: Clarion Books, 1989. (A girl teaches her grandmother to read.) *How might learning to read change what one is able to do in society?*

Cooney, B. *Miss Rumphius*. New York: The Penguin Group, 1985. (A woman makes the world more beautiful by planting flowers.) *How can you help beautify your community?*

Cowen-Fletcher, J. *It Takes a Village*. New York: Scholastic Press, 1999. (The entire village watches out for a child.) *What is an individual's responsibility to her/his community?*

DiSalvo-Ryan, D. *Uncle Willie and the Soup Kitchen*. New York: Mulberry Books, 1997. (A young boy who is afraid of homeless people gains a new perspective when he works with his uncle at a soup kitchen.) *What responsibility do we have to our fellow citizens?*

Greenwood, M. *The Donkey of Gallipoli: A True Story of Courage in World War I*. Cambridge, MA: Candlewick Press, 2008. (Tribute to a World War I foot soldier, and the donkey he used to evacuate the wounded, doesn't shy away from representing the grimness of war.) *How can courage be displayed during wartime in ways other than fighting?*

Hewett, J. *Public Defender: Lawyer for the People*. New York: Lodestar Books/Dutton, 1991. (Hewett's photo-essay describing a public defender's work.) *How are public defenders community helpers?*

Houston, G. *My Great Aunt Arizona*. New York: HarperTrophy, 1997. (A woman has an exponential effect on a town by staying to teach rather than traveling around the world.) *Why are teachers important to a community?*

Javernicke, E. *What If Everybody Did That?* Tarrytown, NY: Pinwheel Books, 2010. (A view of what society would look like if everyone broke the rules.) *What is a citizen's responsibility to her or his community?*

Lionni, L. *Frederick*. New York: Alfred A. Knopf, 1987. (A mouse imagines beautiful images to help his friends get through the winter.) *How do artists benefit their communities?*

Mills, C. *Gus and Grandpa and the Christmas Cookies*. New York: Farrar, Straus & Giroux, 2000. (When baking with his grandfather, a young boy named Gus learns two ways of helping others.) *What responsibility does a citizen have to people in her or his community?*

Mitchell, M. K. *Uncle Jed's Barbershop*. New York: Aladdin Paperbacks, 1998. (A man uses hard-earned money to help others in trouble and delays his own dream of owning a barbershop.) *How can one balance individual needs with community responsibility?*

Moss, P. *Say Something*. Gardiner, ME: Tilbury House, 2008. (A girl who witnesses bullying ultimately decides that being a bystander is unacceptable.) *How much power do individuals have to be good citizens?*

Pearson, E. *Ordinary Mary's Extraordinary Deed*. Layton, UT: Gibbs Smith, 2002. (An ordinary girl who lives in an ordinary town does a small deed that starts a chain reaction around the world that multiplies exponentially.) *To what extent does civic responsibility benefit everyone?*

Pfister, M. *The Rainbow Fish*. Zurich: North South Books, 1995. (A beautiful fish ultimately shares his prized possessions.) *How can one balance individual wants with others' needs?*

Polacco, P. *Applemando's Dreams*. New York: Philomel Books, 1991. (A boy's dreams change the village and the people.) *How do artists benefit their communities?*

Polacco, P. (2000). *The Tree of the Dancing Goats*. New York: Aladdin Paperbacks, 2000. (Jewish and Christian neighbors reach out to each other.) *How can different people find common ground?*

Stover, J. A. *If Everybody Did*. Greenville, SC: Journeyforth, 1989. (A cautionary tale of what it would look like if everyone did what she or he wanted without worrying about consequences to the community.) *What responsibility does a citizen have to her/his community?*

Thurber, J. *The Great Quillow*. New York: HarperCollins, 1990. (A tiny toy maker defeats a giant and saves a town.) *How can one person make a difference in her or his community?*

Untermeyer, L. *One and One and One*. New York: Crowell-Collier, 1962. (Four animal friends build a home together.) *How can working together benefit one's family or community?*

Wallace, N. E. *The Kindness Quilt*. Tarrytown, NY: Marshall Cavendish, 2006. (The students in Mrs. Cooper's class are challenged to do acts of kindness and create an impressive quilt that depicts them doing so in their drawings.) *How can children make a difference in their communities?*

Consciousness and Political Action as Citizenship

Atkins, J. *Aani and the Tree Huggers*. New York: Lee & Low Books, 1995. (Based on real events in the 1970s, Aani and other women in her village defend their forest from developers.) *How much power do citizens have to make a difference?*

Bang, M. *Common Ground: The Water, Earth, and Air We Share*. New York: Blue Sky Press, 1997. (This book provides an introduction to environmental issues.) *How do we balance short-term needs and wants with long-term societal needs?*

Cone, M. *Come Back, Salmon: How a Group of Dedicated Kids Adopted Pigeon Creek and Brought It Back to Life*. San Francisco: Sierra Club, 2001. (Activist kids reclaim and restore their stream in Washington State.) *How can children make a difference in their communities?*

Demi. *One Grain of Rice: A Mathematical Folktale*. New York: Scholastic, 1997. (A reward of one grain of rice doubles day by day when a selfish raja is outwitted by a clever village girl.) *What responsibility do citizens and leaders have to their community?*

DiSalvo-Ryan, D. *City Green*. New York: Morrow Junior Books, 1994. (An urban community works together to turn an empty city lot that is now the city of a building that has been demolished into a beautiful community garden.) *What responsibility does a citizen have to her/his community?*

The Earth Works Group. *50 Simple Things You Can Do to Save the Earth*. Ashland, OR: Earthworks Press, 1995. (This book and video detail the actions that kids of all ages have taken to clean up the environment.) *What steps can you take to clean up your environment?*

Jacobs, F. *Follow That Trash! All About Recycling*. New York: Grosset & Dunlap, 1996. (Jacobs offers an introduction to the recycling process, beginning to end.) *How do individual actions and societal commitment better our communities?*

King, C., and Osborne, L. B. *Oh, Freedom! Kids Talk About the Civil Rights Movement with People Who Made It Happen.* New York: Alfred A. Knopf, 1999. (Kids interviews civil rights activists.) *What lessons do activists of previous generations have for us today?*

Knudsen, M. *Carl the Complainer.* Minneapolis, MN: The Kane Press, 2005. (Carl learns how to turn complaints into petitions and use personal involvement, action, and voice to become a more effective citizen.) *How much power do citizens have to make a difference?*

Lewis, B. *The Kid's Guide to Social Action: How to Solve the Social Problems You Choose—and Turn Creative Thinking into Positive Action.* Minneapolis, MN: Free Spirit Publishing, 1998. (This is a handbook for kids who want to change things.) *How can you go about making change in your community?*

Nivola, C. A. *Planting the Trees of Kenya: The Story of Wangari Maathai.* Farrar, Straus & Giroux, 2008. (Biography of Kenyan activist Wangari Maathai, who was awarded the Nobel Peace Prize in 2004 for her environmental and human rights achievements.) *How much power do citizens have to make a difference?*

Seuss, Dr. *Yertle the Turtle.* New York: Random House, Inc., 1958. (A turtle named Mack shows his fellow turtles that sometimes being a good citizen means that you must disobey authority.) *Is it ever an act of good citizenship to break the law?*

Van Allsburg, C. *Just a Dream.* New York: Houghton Mifflin, 1990. (After dreaming about a future that is created by his careless actions, a young boy named Walter decides to act responsibly.) *What responsibility does a citizen have to people in her or his community?*

Voting and Elections in Our Democracy

Christelow, E. *Vote!* New York: Clarion Books, 2008. (Introduction to voting through a mayoral election in which the mother of a young African American girl is one of the candidates, while two humorous dogs provide commentary on the action.) *To what extent are elections the essence of democracy?*

Cronin, D. *Click, Clack Moo: Cows That Type.* New York: Simon & Schuster Books for Young Readers, 2000. (When the literacy rate on Farmer Brown's farm goes up, the cows express their grievances to him the democratic way.) *How important is literacy to democracy?*

Davies, J. *Tricking the Tallyman: The Great Census Shenanigans of 1790.* New York: Alfred A. Knopf, 2009. (Skeptical residents of a small Vermont town try to trick the man who has been sent to count their population for the first United States Census.) *How important is the census to our democracy?*

DiPucchio, K. *Grace for President.* New York: Hyperion Books for Children, 2008. (A hardworking, independent girl runs for president in her elementary school.) *What qualities make for a good candidate and leader?*

Grodin, Elissa, and Jahasz, Vitor. *D Is for Democracy: A Citizen's Alphabet.* Chelsea, MI: Sleeping Bear Press, 2007. (This excellent, upper-level book emphasizes the importance of asking questions in a democracy, as well as the purpose of taxes, among other things.) *What are the most important elements of a democracy?*

Herold, M. R. *A Very Important Day.* New York: HarperCollins, 1995. (Over two hundred people from more than thirty countries make their way to downtown New York in a snowstorm to be sworn in as citizens of the United States.) *What is so meaningful about becoming an American citizen?*

Rappaport, D. *Lady Liberty.* Cambridge, MA: Candlewick Press, 2008. (The history of the Statue of Liberty told by the many people who played a role in its journey to America.) *How effective a symbol of America is the Statue of Liberty?*

Sisulu, E. B. *The Day Gogo Went to Vote*. New York: Little, Brown Books for Young Readers, 1999. (This is the story of the first election following the end of apartheid when the narrator's grandmother goes to vote.) *How important was the election of Nelson Mandela to the South African people?*

Stier, C. *If I Ran for President*. Morton Grove, IL: Albert Whitman & Co, 2008. (Six children take turns covering the election process in great detail as if they were running for president, discussing their decision to run, campaigning, primaries and conventions, debating, being interviewed, meeting the public, voting, and inauguration.) *How effective is our system of electing a president?*

Wells, R. *Otto Runs for President*. New York: Scholastic Press, 2008. (Two candidates for president of Barkadelphia School, who are rather sure of themselves, are challenged by a candidate who listens to the students.) *How much do/should issues matter in an election?*

White, L. A. *I Could Do That! Esther Morris Gets Women the Vote*. New York: Farrar, Straus & Giroux, 2005. (In 1869, a woman helps Wyoming become the first territory to allow women to vote, then becomes the first woman to hold public office in the United States.) *How important was getting women's suffrage for our democracy?*

References

Center for Information & Research on Civic Learning and Engagement. "Voter Turnout." http://www.civicyouth.org/?page_id=235 (cited November 2, 2009).

Google Images: South Africa Voting Lines. http://images.google.com/images?hl=en&q=south+africa+voting+lines&gbv=2 (cited November 2, 2009).

Julia Butterfly Hill. "About Julia" http://www.juliabutterfly.com (cited November 19, 2009).

Kids Voting USA. http://www.kidsvotingusa.org/index.cfm (cited November 2, 2009).

United States Census Bureau. "Voting and Registration in the Election of November 2008." http://www.census.gov/population/www/socdemo/voting/cps2008.html (cited November 2, 2009).

United States Election Project. "Voter Turnout." http://elections.gmu.edu/voter_turnout.htm (cited November 2, 2009).

Chapter 12

Conclusion

Essential Question

How can we find and teach social studies in every picture book we encounter?

The strategies and activities detailed in the preceding chapters are planned around *our* favorite picture books. You can, of course, implement them immediately in your classroom, but the strategies and activities detailed in this book have broader application than the specific topics for which they were written. We hope that you will transfer many of the ideas as you plan lessons for *your* favorite picture books. (For a template to help you connect the literature you already use to social studies concepts, see Appendix C.)

Following is a comprehensive list of the activities included in the chapters of this book that you can apply to other picture books.

- *History Mystery*—analyze primary source documents to investigate a historical question

- *Graphic organizers and charts*—visually represent information and ideas

- *Songs*—listen to and write lyrics about historical time periods

- *Role-play*—assume the role of an historical figure or literary character and maintain a diary or write a speech or letter to acquire perspective

- *Oral history*—write questions based on books they read and conduct interviews to acquire firsthand information about people's experiences

- *Monuments*—create a monument to people who made a difference

- *Children's books*—write and illustrate their own picture books

- *Local history*—engage in historical investigations in their schools and communities

- *Museum exhibit*—create a museum installation with informational "museum cards"

- *Mural*—design a mural to represent a real or imagined place

- *Illustrated timeline*—students use pictures and words to create a timeline of their life or an historical time period

- *Map it!*—draw a map of the location and place, real or imagined, described in any book

- *Family homework*—extend activities to include dialogue with families

- *Compare and contrast*—read a variety of picture books on the same topic or person and indentify the similarities and differences

- *Jigsaw*—read a variety of books on the same person or topic, then share information with other groups

- *X marks the spot*—identify where you would locate yourself in a country, in a town, in a school, in a classroom, in a house

- *Memory-keeper*—create and maintain a scrapbook, weblog, video diary, etc.

- *Guest speakers*—invite people into your classroom to share their experiences; teach students how to write questions and conduct interviews

- *Wide awake*—read local papers, and pay attention in your neighborhood to find ways to be a good citizen in your community

- *Bio-poem*—write a biographical poem about someone who made a difference

- *Journal writing*—write entries from the perspective of a person in history

- *Tuned in*—keep the community posted on what you're doing via letter to the editor, newspaper article, blog, poster, PSA, or other text

- *Archeologist*—use artifacts of long-ago times to understand more about life in a different time period or place

- *Report card*—grade the government or an individual on how they are doing

- *Draw it!*—illustrate key phrases or concepts from important documents

- *Gallery walk*—compile information on large post-it paper hung around the room

- *Service learning*—devise a project to benefit your neighbors, school, or community on those in need; have the class plan to create a product to sell

- *Dialogue poem*—create a poem from the paired perspective of two historical figures

- *Democracy*—use democratic decision making to solve classroom issues

---

Which of these activities can you transfer to other books that you already use?

All of these activities require rich historical and sociological data. The picture books are a starting point; students then supplement them with varied sources of information from the census, their families, interviews, photos, speeches, and other resources. (Although we tend to think of document analysis as a skill suited for only upper elementary students, it is worth noting that primary students are also capable of collecting and analyzing documents; they just need to use different kinds of documents. See Appendix D for an activity that introduces primary level students to document analysis.) Students collect, analyze, and use the data to make informed decisions, which is the most important work of citizens. They can then employ a variety of the strategies above to present their findings to their classmates and community and act on them.

Developing a Social Studies State of Mind in Ourselves and Our Students

Highlighting and discussing the social studies concepts in our favorite picture books leads students to discuss ideas such as democracy, justice, equality, and culture. Once students have an understanding of social studies concepts, they may apply them to every aspect of our classrooms, from how the rules are established to how conflicts are resolved to how we speak to one another. Ultimately, we hope our students carry this state of mind beyond the classroom walls, as they begin to think of everything as a social studies question and become active citizens in their class, school, and community.

Next Steps

Well, you have come to the end of a book filled with ideas about how to make connections and design activities that link picture books and social studies concepts. Now what?

Not surprisingly, the question of what to do next reminds us of a yet another favorite picture book. Jon Muth's *The Three Questions* retells Leo Tolstoy's story of a boy who searches for the answer to three questions: When is the best time to do things? Who is the most important one? What is the right thing to do? Through helping others, the boy learns the answers. The time is now. The most important one is the one you are with. The right thing to do is to help. The boy's guru concludes "This is why we are here."

The answers to these three questions are applicable to teachers who seek to implement some of the ideas in this book.

When is the best time to do things?

> The time is now—don't wait until next year to implement these ideas.

Who is the most important one?

> The most important one is the one you are with—your students in your class.

What is the right thing to do?

> The right thing to do is to help—help your students find social studies in every book, in every situation.

This is why we are here.

Planning your curriculum . . .

What books do you already use that have social studies concepts embedded in them?

What questions can you ask about them?

What skills do you want students to develop?

What teaching strategies can you employ to actively engage students?

What opportunities can you provide for your students to apply information?

How can you assess their understanding?

How can you link social studies and literature all year long? (See Appendix E for a unit planning template.)

Reference

Muth, J. *The Three Questions.* New York: Scholastic Press, 2002.

Appendix A

Templates for Creating a Book

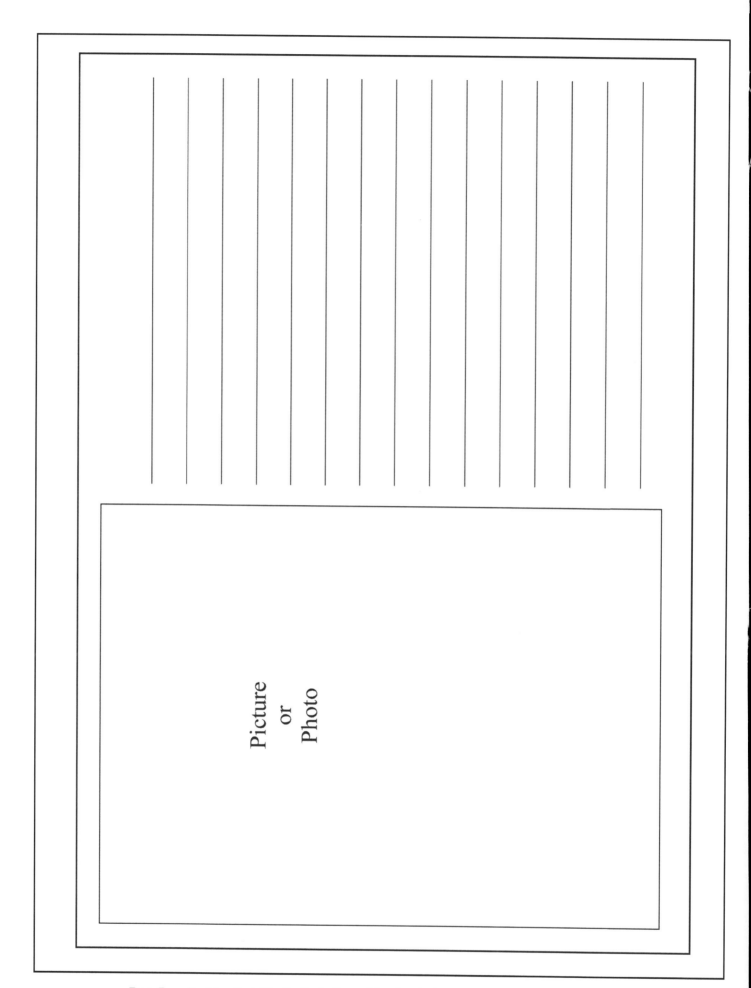

Picture
or
Photo

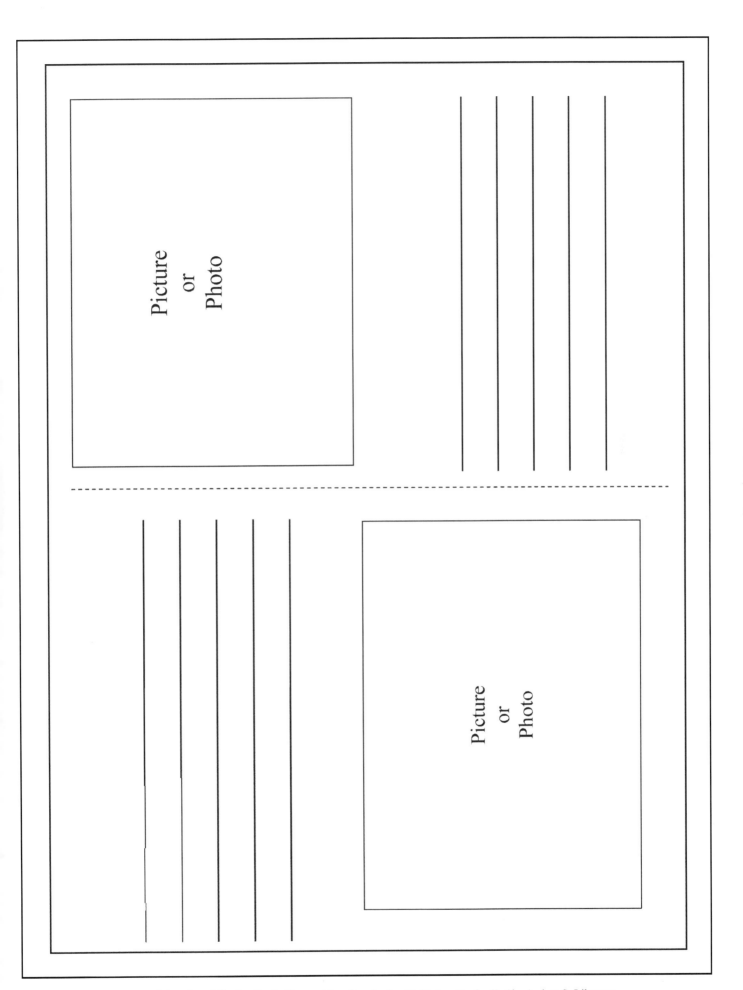

Picture
or
Photo

Picture
or
Photo

Appendix B

Cartoons

Name _____ Date _____

Student Handout: Analyzing Political Cartoons

Directions: To understand political cartoons, it is necessary to anticipate the issues and people who may appear in a cartoon. It is also helpful to think about how they might be drawn. Work with a partner to complete each of the four activities. An example is given in each activity to get you started.

1. What issues might appear in cartoons? Look through the newspaper and brainstorm issues that you think a cartoonist might focus on. The issues should be ones about which people might have strong opinions.

   1. War in _____   4. _____

   2. _____   5. _____

   3. _____   6. _____

2. Who are the people who might appear in cartoons? How might they be drawn?

People in the News	A picture of the person	Features the cartoonists might emphasize
Barack Obama		Big Ears

From *Every Book Is a Social Studies Book: How to Meet Standards with Picture Books, K–6* by Andrea S. Libresco, Jeannette Balantic, and Jonie C. Kipling. Santa Barbara, CA: Imprint Name. Copyright © 2011.

3. What kinds of symbols might appear in cartoons? How might they be drawn?

Draw a picture to represent each word in the boxes below.

America	*Peace*
Democracy	*Power*
Liberty	*Justice*
Greed	*Death*

4. Now you are ready to analyze a cartoon.

Go through the steps below for the cartoon you have been given.

1. What do you see? Identify setting, people, symbols, words, and action taking place.

2. What does it mean? Connect what you see to an issue in the news.

3. What is the cartoonist's message about the issue portrayed? Look for evidence in the cartoon of how the cartoonist feels about the issue.

4. What is your opinion? Do you agree or disagree with the cartoonist's position?

Name _____ Date _____

Student Handout: Drawing Political Cartoons

Now it is your turn . . . you don't have to be able to draw well—

you just have to have a point of view!

Directions: Select a topic or event about which you will draw a cartoon. Think about what your position or opinion is on that topic or event. As you begin to consider what you want to draw, think about other cartoons you have seen to help give you a few ideas. Ask yourself the following questions:

- What is your topic/issue (the president, war, the Supreme Court, Wal-Mart, immigration, the economy, the housing market, etc.)?

- What is your opinion or position on the topic or issue?

- Who are the people you want to portray?

- Where will the scene take place—does it have to be the real thing?

- What symbols can you use to represent the issues and/or people?

Symbols for:

The United States

The World

If you can't draw people, how will we know who is in your picture?

After you have answered the questions, sketch something. This will help you develop your idea. Try to fill the entire page with your cartoon (don't make the people, objects, or words too tiny), and feel free to add color to your cartoons.

You MUST get your message across to people—it can be hard to do, but it is the point of drawing a cartoon. You are not simply illustrating an event; you must convey a message (your opinion).

Go for it! Once your cartoon is completed, show it to someone to see if she or he "gets it"—is your opinion clearly represented?

Appendix C

Social Studies Concepts and Discussion Questions Chart

Social Studies Concepts and Discussion Questions

Social studies concepts	Questions to ask based on the text

Appendix D

Documents and Artifacts

Name _____ Date _____

Student Handout: Documents and Artifacts of Our Lives

What can we infer from the data around us?

Directions: Historians often look at documents and artifacts from the past to understand what life was like. We can find out about our own lives with documents and artifacts.

On the left side of the chart, list all of the documents and artifacts you can think of that are part of your lives. On the right side of the chart, record what we might infer from each document. As you can see from the example below, sometimes comparing two similar documents gives you very interesting information.

Documents/artifacts of my life	What we may infer
Story I wrote in Kindergarten (3 lines long, no vowels in some of the words), and a story I wrote in 2nd grade (2 pages, clear sentences, and it's funny).	• *Writing was a struggle when I was younger.* • *I learned a lot about writing between kindergarten and 2nd grade.* • *I had good teachers.*

From *Every Book Is a Social Studies Book: How to Meet Standards with Picture Books, K–6* by Andrea S. Libresco, Jeannette Balantic, and Jonie C. Kipling. Santa Barbara, CA: Imprint Name. Copyright © 2011.

Appendix E

Unit Planning Template

	September	October	November
Unit Title (est. Time)			
Major Content Points			
Essential Questions			
Writing Assignments Points			
Skills			

Grade Level _____

	December	January	February
Unit Title (est. Time)			
Major Content Points			
Essential Questions			
Writing Assignments Points			
Skills			

Grade Level _____

	March	April	May
Unit Title (est. Time)			
Major Content Points			
Essential Questions			
Writing Assignments Points			
Skills			

Grade Level _____

June		Major Content Points	Essential Questions	Writing Assignments Points	Skills
Unit Title (est. Time)					

Grade Level _____

Index

About the Authors

ANDREA S. LIBRESCO is an associate professor and the graduate director of elementary education in the Department of Teaching, Literacy and Leadership at Hofstra University, New York. Dr. Libresco, former social studies chair (grades 7–12) and lead teacher (grades K–6), has written extensively on teaching elementary social studies.

JEANNETTE BALANTIC is the social studies curriculum coordinator in the Garden City School District, New York. Ms. Balantic has also worked as a social studies methods instructor at Hofstra University and Teachers College, New York, a curriculum developer, and pedagogical adviser for the China Institute and Asia Society.

JONIE C. KIPLING teaches a multiage middle school class at the Keegan Academy in Temecula, California. She was an elementary and middle school teacher and served as president of the Long Island Council for the Social Studies in New York, as well as a social studies methods instructor at Hofstra University, New York.

Made in the USA
Lexington, KY
08 January 2012